New Political Economy

Edited by

Richard McIntyre
University of Rhode Island

A Routledge Series

NEW POLITICAL ECONOMY
RICHARD MCINTYRE, *General Editor*

MIRACLE FOR WHOM?
Chilean Workers under Free Trade

Janine Berg

Routledge
New York & London

Published in 2006 by
Routledge
Taylor & Francis Group
711 Third Avenue
New York, NY 10017

Published in Great Britain by
Routledge
Taylor & Francis Group
2 Park Square
Milton Park, Abingdon
Oxon OX14 4RN

First issued in paperback 2013

International Standard Book Number-10: 0-415-97633-2 (Hardcover)
International Standard Book Number-13: 978-0-415-97633-6 (Hardcover)
International Standard Book Number-13: 978-0-415-65559-0 (Paperback)
Library of Congress Card Number 2005021112

Library of Congress Cataloging-in-Publication Data

Berg, Janine.
    Miracle for whom? : Chilean workers under free trade / Janine Berg.
        p. cm. -- (New political economy)
    Includes bibliographical references and index.
    ISBN 0-415-97633-2
    1. Unskilled labor--Chile. 2. Chile--Foreign economic relations. 3. Wage differentials--Chile. 4. Free trade--Chile. 5. Cosmetics industry--Chile--Employees. 6. Agricultural processing industry workers--Chile. I. Title. II. Series.

HD8296.5.B475 2005
331.1'0983--dc22

2005021112

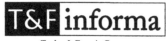

Taylor & Francis Group
is the Academic Division of T&F Informa plc.

Visit the Taylor & Francis Web site at
http://www.taylorandfrancis.com

and the Routledge Web site at
http://www.routledge-ny.com

Contents

vi   Contents

List of Tables

List of Figures

Preface

This book is about Chile and how its workers have fared under free trade. Initially, my interest in studying this topic was to learn how globalization had affected workers in developing countries, as so much of the debate among academics and policymakers had been centered on the U.S. and Europe. Yet in the 1990s, trade liberalization—along with other Washington Consensus policies such as financial liberalization, privatization and labor market deregulation—was being pursued throughout Latin America and much of the developing world. This was evident not just in the national lowering of trade barriers across the region, but also by the number of bilateral and multilateral trade agreements that came into effect and continue to be negotiated well into the 2000s. The Free Trade Agreement of the Americas, which looms in the distance, indicates the resilience of free trade in Latin America as well as the continued need to understand how workers are affected.

Because Chile was the first country in Latin America to open its goods and capital markets it has become a model for other developing countries pursuing free trade. Though the country endured 15 difficult years of adjustment after liberalizing in 1974, including two severe recessions in 1975 and 1982, its high economic growth rates in the 1990s and its success in exporting natural-resource-based products, have led many to label it an "economic miracle." But have its workers benefited from this miracle?

I felt that the best way to answer this question was through a firm-level analysis of how free trade affected Chilean firms' competitive strategies and in the process, their use of labor. I specifically chose to do a study of firms' and workers' experiences because I felt that the economics profession had too often favored quantifying the effects of free trade as opposed to understanding how these effects occur. Chile was also a good choice for a study of this type since by the 1990s and 2000s the macroeconomic environment was stable, making firm-level analysis much more feasible.

But a study of how workers were affected by free trade could not be properly answered without considering the political and institutional setting of the country. Thus in this study of Chile—as would be the case in a study of any other country—its unique national experience was fundamental to my analysis of how workers have fared. Indeed, without an understanding of a country's history, social institutions and legislation, it is not possible to accurately assess policy results or to know to what extent the advice can be applied to other countries. Institutions were therefore a fundamental methodological consideration and also proved to be a fundamental determinant of how Chilean workers have fared under free trade.

This study was financed by the Fulbright-Hays Doctoral Dissertation Research Abroad Fellowship Program, the Organization of American States Regional Training Program, as well as the Center for Economic Policy Analysis at the New School for Social Research. I am extremely grateful to William Milberg for his guidance throughout the project, to Jorge Katz, who kindly gave me an office space and access to CEPAL's excellent resources during my year-long stay in Chile, and to Diego Sánchez-Ancochea, Lance Taylor, Dante Contreras, Nelson Barbosa, Monique Morrisey and Mica Hall, for help with many parts of the study. Richard McIntyre, editor of the Routledge Series in New Political Economy, provided many valuable comments that I hope I have done justice to. I would also like to thank my sister, Carolyn Berg, for introducing me to Chile, and my parents, for their encouragement and support. My deepest gratitude, however, is to my husband, Joseph Pendergast, for accompanying me to Chile and for his continuous support of my work.

Chapter One
Introduction

INTRODUCTION

In the 1990s the countries of Latin America abandoned import-substitution industrialization (ISI) and embraced free trade. Two decades earlier, in 1974, Chile had made a similar decision. Disenchanted with the progress of ISI, and influenced by the free-market beliefs of Chicago-trained Chilean economists, Chile reduced its tariffs on consumer goods from an average of 105 percent in the early 1970s to 10 percent by 1979. But how the open economy would affect Chilean workers was left to speculation.

In part, the Chilean decision to liberalize its goods market was motivated by the belief in the Heckscher-Ohlin-Samuelson theory of international trade. The theory postulates that under free trade a country will shift production toward its relatively abundant factor of production. For developing countries, this factor is labor, as opposed to capital, and low-skilled labor as opposed to skilled labor. As a result, ISI was believed to have created a bias towards greater incorporation of capital goods into production that would be reversed under free trade, since, without tariff protection, industries would more readily use the available low-skilled labor. Thus it was expected that removing trade protections, including the preferential exchange rate on capital good imports, would favor job creation in Chile since labor would be favored over capital (Corbo and Meller, 1982). Increased demand for low-skilled labor under free trade would, in turn, increase the wages of these workers, resulting in a compression of the wage distribution and reduced inequality. However, precisely the opposite occurred: wage inequality increased under free trade.

Wage inequality can be considered an "output" of economic policies, while trade policy operates as an "input variable." A wide range of other economic policies, besides trade policy, can be considered inputs. Some of these inputs are internal to Chile, such as changes in labor laws, industrial promotion policies, or macroeconomic conditions, while other factors are external, such as foreign exchange rate and commodity price fluctuations, policies of multinational corporations, and technological change.

To analyze the causes of increased income inequality in Chile simply by identifying an outcome and then hypothesizing about its causes provides little understanding of the mechanisms by which trade liberalization alters demand for workers in developing countries. Unfortunately, this has so far been the typical approach. Most of the studies of rising wage inequality in Chile post-liberalization have been econometric studies documenting the occurrence, but only hypothesizing, with little or no evidence, as to the sources of wage dispersion.

The purpose of this study is to learn how industrial restructuring in Chile, in response to free trade, changed firms' competitive strategies and in the process, their use of labor. I do this based on case studies of two Chilean industries: cosmetics and agroindustry. My analysis considers the effects of changing strategies of multinational firms, increased competition, technological change, and a changed labor-relations environment, on the employment and pay of skilled and low-skilled workers. By studying the dynamic processes that cause openness to lead to increased relative wage dispersion, I present a more comprehensive picture of the causes for rising wage inequality under free trade. My analysis provides several insights into the applicability of the traditional view of trade and wages (HOS), versus alternative explanations, such as skill-biased technological change and labor market rigidity. In doing so, I illustrate the need to consider other changes in the economy besides just the price and use of certain labor.

RISING WAGE INEQUALITY

Despite the debate on the causes of rising wage inequality, there is consensus that inequality has indeed increased. Different measures of income and wage inequality lend support to the general pattern of increased earnings dispersion in Chile under free trade. Figure 1.1 shows the increase in returns to schooling for university-educated workers compared with other workers between 1958 and 1998 in the Greater Santiago area. During the late 1950s and early 1960s, when the economy was relatively closed, the returns to schooling for university and high-school educated workers was similar, it then increased in the late 1960s, only to compress again during the three years that the Popular Unity government was in power (1970–1973). After the coup d'etat of September 11, 1973, which ushered in the 17-year military dictatorship headed by General Augusto Pinochet,

Figure 1.1 *Returns to Schooling for University, High-School and Primary-School Educated Workers, Greater Santiago, 1958-1998*

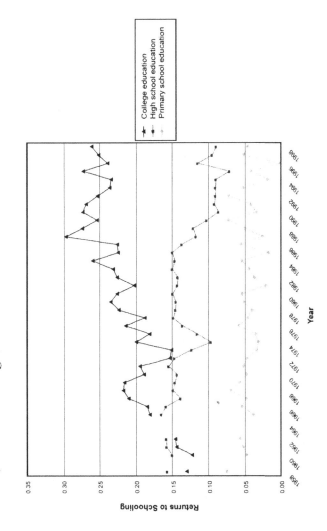

Source: Berg and Contreras (2004), based on University of Chile Employment Survey.

earnings of university-educated workers rose continuously, while that of high-school educated workers fell. By the early 1990s, the returns to high-school education had fallen from nearly fifteen percent to less than ten percent, just slightly above the earnings of workers with primary schooling. However, the returns to university-educated workers were substantial by this point, approaching a thirty percent wage premium, after controlling for other differences.

Other measures of inequality, using different data sources, reflect similar patterns. For example, the Gini coefficient for Greater Santiago increased from .506 in 1964–1969 to .586 in 1987–1990. Income inequality persisted during the 1990s as well. Based on the national household survey, CASEN, the Gini coefficient was .554 in 1990, .553 in 1996, and .559 in 2000 (CEPAL, 2002). Bravo et al. (1999) also find that during the 1990s, under democratic rule, income inequality did not improve, despite strong economic and real wage growth and increased social spending.

WHY CASE STUDIES?

I use a case study methodology to trace the restructuring of two Chilean industries in order to learn how industrial restructuring affected the relative demand for skilled and unskilled labor. By studying changes in corporate strategies and labor relations, I sought a better understanding for why wage inequality had increased in Chile in the years following the country's 1974 political-economic shift.

Case studies offered the most appropriate route for studying this phenomenon, because they ask "how" or "why" questions, which can be used to research "operational links that need to be traced over time, rather than mere frequencies or incidences" (Yin, 1994, p. 6). Furthermore, the case study methodology is a comprehensive research strategy that is able to consider many variables of interest and use a variety of information, both qualitative and quantitative, to establish patterns.

Yin (1994) explains that evidence for case studies may come from six sources: documents, archival records, interviews, direct observation, participant-observation and physical artifacts. The case studies undertaken in this book relied upon documents (such as collective bargaining agreements, newspaper and magazine articles, company annual reports), interviews (of firm managers, labor leaders and outside experts), and direct observation (factory tours). The studies also benefited from an annual survey of Chilean manufacturing firms, which provided important quantitative information of number of firms and workers, wages, equipment expenditures and revenues for each sector. The use of different sources of evidence is one of the strengths of case study research because it allows the researcher to triangulate. Triangulation enlists multiple sources of evidence to show convergence upon a line of inquiry, for example, when evidence from interviews, databases and direct observation all support the same finding. If the researcher's multiple sources of evidence corroborate one another, then the conclusions of the study are likely to be more convincing and accurate than if just one source of evidence is given.

Two industries were studied: the cosmetics industry, an import-competing industry, and agroindustry, an exporting industry. Each of the case studies included nine representative firms, as well as other firms and actors linked to the industry. In some respects, the study had cases within the cases, as firms within the same sector were quite heterogeneous. Because this is a case study of industries, it was important to ensure that sufficient information was gathered to establish representativeness *within* the case. I believe this was accomplished, as many of the firms that participated in the interviews had substantial market share. Other types of information—such as interviews with industry analysts, company documentation, business press articles and industry survey data—allowed me to corroborate information from the interviews and check that it was representative of the industry. This is not to imply, however, that the industry cases are representative of Chilean industry or Chile as a whole. Nor is this the intention. As Yin (1994) states, "case studies should not be used to assess the incidence of phenomenon." Continuing, he argues,

> Case studies, like experiments, are generalizable to theoretical propositions and not to populations or universes. The case study, like the experiment, does not represent a "sample" and the investigator's goal is to expand and generalize theories (analytic generalization) and not to enumerate frequencies (statistical generalization). (p. 10)

Thus, this approach differs from econometric work, which relies on databases that are representative of a population to quantify effects. Econometric analysis has the benefit of showing the extent to which one variable affects another for a given population, but, unlike case studies, it offers little understanding of how and why certain processes occur.

As the literature review given in Chapter 2 will show, there have been numerous econometric studies documenting rising wage inequality in Chile post trade liberalization, and much hypothesizing as to possible causes. Yet the multitude of studies documenting the rise in wage inequality has been matched with a dearth of studies explaining why. This book is an attempt to fill a void in our understanding. My analysis uses the neoclassical theory of international trade as a template to compare the empirical results of the case study. Certain findings match the predictions of the theory, while others do not. I then attempt to account for findings that did not conform to neoclassical trade theory, by identifying patterns, which I use to develop a theory about rent sharing. Though based on the findings from two industry case studies, the theory elucidates certain structures of international trade as well as managerial strategies and labor relations, allowing for further analyses of unequal wage distribution in Chile.

CHOICE OF CASES

This book analyzes the effects of industrial restructuring under free trade on the cosmetics and agro industries. The cosmetics industry is an import-competing industry, protected from imports during the period of import-substitution industrialization, and then exposed to the effects of free trade beginning in the mid-1970s, but particularly during the latter half of the 1980s and in the 1990s. Agroindustry is a successful exporting industry that emerged in the early 1980s, following the economic, financial and land ownership reforms of the second half of the 1970s and 1980s, giving way to dynamic growth in the 1980s and first half of the 1990s.

A variety of factors were taken into consideration when choosing these industries, including feasibility, but also whether the case offered an interesting study. For example, for my choice of an import-competing sector, I deliberately stayed away from dying industries, such as apparel and footwear, which have suffered tremendous and continual job loss since the 1970s. I felt that doing an analysis of a dying sector would reveal little new information; the cosmetics industry, on the other hand, offered an interesting case since employment in the manufacturing plants of that sector, which I broadly define to include all toiletry products, had expanded over the past several decades despite significant restructuring. In 1979, cosmetics firms with factories employed 4,359 workers growing to 6,239 by 1997, according to data from the annual manufacturing survey. Another important factor in my decision to study the cosmetics industry was its technological accessibility. Cosmetics products had been successfully produced in Chile for a century, thus their production did not pose a scientific hurdle for the country. Simple perusal of supermarket and pharmacy shelves also indicated that there was substantial domestic and foreign presence in the sector, offering the possibility for an analysis of foreign direct investment. The fall in trade barriers, transportation costs and more aggressive market-seeking by multinational cosmetics firms offered enough challenges to make its story worth telling.

Agroindustry offered an interesting case because it was a successful exporting sector that emerged under free trade, based on the comparative advantages of the abundant and high quality natural resources and low-skilled labor. Its story is similar to that of other successful natural-resource-based manufacturing industries such as fishmeal, canned fish, wood chips and cellulose. Like these other export-intensive industries, agroindustry shows the effects of Chile's relatively recent diversification into non-traditional export sectors, specifically the opportunities and limits inherent in these sectors. Moreover, studying agroindustry offered possible under-standing of the linkages to world markets. Agroindustry has had substantial job growth, nearly tripling its workforce from 5,700 workers in 1979 to 15,668 in 1997. For these reasons, I felt that its story would also be worth telling.

By studying both an import-competing sector and an exporting sector I was able to conduct a more comprehensive analysis of the effects of free trade on skilled and low-skilled workers, than if I had studied just one sector. Theoretical models in economics treat shifts in production differently depending on the sector's market, necessitating an analysis of both local and export market conditions. By having an industry from each sector I felt I could better analyze traditional international trade theory as well as consider alternatives.

Definition of Skilled and Low-Skilled Workers

Economists tend to use the terms skilled and low-skilled workers rather loosely, and unfortunately, this study is no exception. The adjectives are sometimes inappropriate as they presume that difficulty in work is associated with degree of decision-making and workforce hierarchy, without considering the degree of difficulty of the specific task, even if the difficulty is just physical. Essentially, I define skilled workers as workers with greater than secondary education, either with some years of university studies or completed university studies. Generally, skilled workers are non-production workers, although university-trained production workers such as food scientists that supervise laboratories or engineers that design machinery are also considered skilled. Low-skilled workers range from primary education to completed secondary education. The definition I use corresponds with the Chilean manufacturing survey's (ENIA) definition of skilled and low-skilled production workers. Because of the sectors studied, the low-skilled workers tend to be production workers hired to perform repetitive tasks that involve little training. They are thus easily replaceable. In the analysis I also distinguish between low-skilled and semi-skilled production workers, noting that the semi-skilled workers possess knowledge that makes them valuable to the firm, typically know-how about fixing a machine or mixing chemicals. The categories have a strong gender bias, with low-skilled positions dominated by women, semi-skilled positions dominated by men, and skilled jobs biased towards men.

OVERVIEW OF THE BOOK

The book is structured to provide the necessary theoretical and contextual background for the analysis of the case studies. The case studies, presented in Chapters 4 and 5, are then followed by an analytical discussion of the findings, and a summary and conclusion.

Chapter 2 reviews the contemporary literature on the causes of rising wage inequality in the industrialized and developing world, including Chile. Following a brief discussion of the neoclassical theory of the determination of wages under free trade, I review competing hypotheses such as skill-biased technological change and labor market rigidity. The empirical evidence in support of these hypotheses is limited, based at times on residuals in regression equations that are interpreted as technological change. I point out the limits to econometric work, offering examples from the industrial relations literature of promising alternative approaches to analyzing rising wage inequality.

The uniqueness of the Chilean experience is evident in Chapter 3. In this chapter, I review the major economic and political shifts that occurred in Chile, starting with the September 1973 coup d'etat that overthrew the Socialist government of Salvador Allende and ushered in the military dictatorship of General Augusto Pinochet for seventeen years. The Pinochet government unveiled a radical economic program centered on market liberalization, becoming the first country in Latin America to depart from import-substitution industrialization and embrace free trade. Market flexibility in goods was complemented with policies of financial flexibility, deregulation and labor market flexibility. Labor union leaders were persecuted and there was no recognized freedom of association until a new labor code took effect in 1979. Yet the new labor code severely limited the power of labor, weakening the movement. Labor in Chile continues to be weak, despite the more than ten years that have passed since the return to democracy.

In Chapter 4, I analyze the shifts in competitive strategies of the Chilean cosmetics industry. The changing strategies of multinationals have affected the competitive environment of the industry, as imports skyrocketed in the 1990s. Because of this, Chilean-owned cosmetics firms have developed competitive strategies based on technological upgrading to increase output and improve productivity. From the workers' perspective, the strategies have not been helpful, and in the case of multinational subsidiaries, quite harmful. Multinational companies have regionalized production to other Latin American countries, shutting Chilean-based factories built during import-substitution industrialization, and dismissing production staff. At the Chilean-owned firms, improvements in productivity have not been accompanied by wage increases for the low skilled, though skilled workers have benefited. Unionization is low in the sector, despite a history of union involvement that dates back to the 1940s. A main conclusion of the research is that Chilean-owned cosmetics firms have compensated for the decrease in rents that resulted from the sector's opening by squeezing the wages of their production staff.

Chapter 5 analyzes the birth and growth of agroindustry, a successful exporting sector, in light of the employment and earnings of its workforce. Agroindustry started in the early 1980s, spurred by the availability of discards from the fresh-fruit exporting sector and an ample supply of available labor. Since its modest beginnings, the industry has developed into a technologically sophisticated provider of high-quality supplies to Northern processed food manufacturers. Yet its position in the global value chain has restricted it to the production of low value-added intermediate goods. Firms interested in entering the high-rent activities of retail, marketing and distribution are limited to the domestic or Latin American market. The constraints imposed on this sector by the international trading environment have encouraged firms to hire workers on temporary contracts even if they are employed year-round. Because agroindustry workers can be hired for contracts that specify the processing of a particular crop, the contract can easily and legally be renewed continuously. Moreover, workers on temporary contracts do not have the right to bargain collectively, making labor rotation much more fluid, while at the same time keeping workers' wages down. The case studies show that regardless of a firm's competitive strategy, reliance on a temporary labor force, even when production is year-round, is a hallmark of the industry's human resource policy.

Based on the findings from the industry case studies, I develop, in Chapter 6, an alternative explanation for why wage inequality has increased in Chile under free trade. I hypothesize that there has been a hoarding of rents at three levels, with each level contributing to limit the pay of low-skilled Chilean workers. The first level of rent-hoarding occurs in the international trading regime, between Northern and Chilean capitalists. The second level occurs at the domestic level and concerns how firms divide rents into profits and wages. This level is influenced by macroeconomic as well as institutional conditions. Finally, I argue that there has been a division of rents between skilled and low-skilled workers, and that Chilean firm managers have used the weak institutional environment to constrain the wage growth of easily replaceable and poorly organized low-skilled workers.

Chapter 7 summarizes the major findings and themes of the book. I also consider its policy implications, in particular, the role that better labor relations could play in encouraging firms to pursue policies that emphasize training and worker commitment. I argue that in the long run more labor-friendly policies may prove more beneficial for Chile's development than the cost-based strategies that have been used since liberalization.

Chapter Two
Why has Inequality Increased Under Globalization?

INTRODUCTION

The increased integration of the world economy in the 1990s was coupled with rising wage inequality throughout most of the developed and developing world. Just as countries were embracing free trade, they were finding that their most vulnerable workers—the low-skilled—were suffering a decline in earnings. If increased wage dispersion were the result of international trade, would it be wise to pursue more free trade agreements and greater economic integration? The importance of this question at a time of falling trade barriers led to a wave of economics articles on the causes of rising wage inequality.

This chapter reviews some of the more important studies in the literature on rising wage inequality in the industrialized world, the developing world and in Chile. Though the research areas are different, many of the hypotheses given to explain increased wage dispersion are quite similar. Essentially, the analyses can be broken down into four causes: (1) international trade, (2) skill-biased technological change, (3) labor market impediments, and (4) changes to the institutional labor relations environment. In most cases, more than one explanation has played a role, for example, increased international trade is associated with increased use of communication technologies and is also associated with lessened union power as capital has become increasingly mobile, but workers are largely immobile.

THE DETERMINATION OF WAGES UNDER NEOCLASSICAL TRADE THEORY

The starting point for analyses of the effects of free trade on wages is the well-known neoclassical trade theory, Heckscher-Ohlin. The theory postulates that under conditions of free trade, countries will export goods that use intensively the factors of production with which they are relatively abundantly endowed, and import goods that use intensively factors of production that are relatively scarce. Originally the two factors conceived to explain the theory were land and labor or capital and labor. In the 1990s, the theory was used to predict the effect of trade on different types of workers, namely skilled and low-skilled labor. Thus, according to the theory, if the United States is relatively abundant in high-skilled labor and Chile is relatively abundant in low-skilled labor, then the goods they trade will reflect these endowments.

Two important corollaries, the Stolper-Samuelson theorem and the factor-price-equalization theorem are associated with the Heckscher-Ohlin theorem. The Stolper-Samuelson theory predicts the effect of trade on wages. Because of Samuelson's important contribution in extending the Heckscher-Ohlin model to consider the returns to the factors of production, the theory is often referred to as the Heckscher-Ohlin-Samuelson (HOS) theory. Under HOS, technology is assumed as given (everyone is operating under a similar production function), thus any change in price will cause a change in the value of the labor used to produce the item. Thus, if Chile and the United States liberalized trade and the United States, which is relatively scarce in low-skilled labor, imported a good from Chile produced with low-skilled labor, the price of the low-skilled-intensive good in the US would fall, as would the wages of low-skilled workers in the US. In other words, workers' wages will be affected, but whether the effect is positive or negative will depend on whether it is the relatively scarce or the relatively abundant factor.

Under the factor-price-equalization theorem, the returns to the factor endowments will equalize across nations. Thus, if the endowments are skilled and low-skilled labor, then trade will make low-skilled labor in developed countries and skilled labor in developing countries less scarce and will thus cause a reduction in these workers' wages. By contrast, trade will increase the production of goods made by skilled labor in developed countries and by low-skilled labor in developing countries, so that their wages will rise. Thus, the theory postulates that factor prices will be equalized throughout the world, such that a low-skilled worker in a developed country will receive the same pay as his counterpart in a developing country, and similarly for skilled workers (Freeman, 1995). An important prediction of HOS is that low-skilled workers in developing countries will benefit from the free trade since the country will shift production to low-skilled-intensive industries, as these countries are relatively abundant in low-skilled labor. The result will be an increase in the wages of low-skilled workers.

The HOS theorem gives powerful predictions for the effect of trade on the wages of workers of different trading countries. Nevertheless, its results are based on extremely strict assumptions, such as identical technology, perfect competition, constant returns to scale in production, international factor immobility, no factor-intensity reversals, full use of factors (no unemployment), and just two factors of production. Although these assumptions are very strict—prompting some debate in the profession on its usefulness—the influence of HOS theory in formulating economic policy, particularly world trade policy in the 1990s, makes the theory highly relevant, even if the real world can never fully match the theory's assumptions. Cline (1997) suggests interpreting the theorems "as meaningful long-run tendencies and, therefore, important grounds for formulating trade policy with key side measures to ensure equitable distribution from the gains from free trade" (p.36).

EVIDENCE FOR INDUSTRIALIZED COUNTRIES

The predictions offered by HOS have been at the center of the debate on the declining economic position of low-skilled workers in the United States and other industrialized countries. This debate focuses on the effects of trade versus technology. Are the declining wages of low-skilled American workers due to competition with cheap labor from abroad or is it because computers and other technological advances have revolutionized the workplace, lessening the demand for low-skilled labor?

Emphasizing a conventional supply and demand framework, most economists have argued that international trade or skill-biased technological change (SBTC) has shifted the demand curve for low-skilled labor in developed countries inward, while causing demand for skilled workers to shift outward. The demand shifts are presumed to have been large enough to mitigate the increased supply of university-educated workers, both in the United States and Europe. Moreover, labor market rigidities have been blamed for preventing movements in the labor market, leading to rising unemployment in Europe, while the more flexible American labor market has allowed low-skilled workers to retain their jobs, though at less pay.[1]

International Trade

One of the first and most vocal proponents of the negative effect of international trade on labor demand for low-skilled workers in the United States has been Adrian Wood. Wood (1995) estimates that international trade has reduced manufacturing employment in the United States by five percentage points, virtually all of which has been concentrated on low-skilled labor.

He estimates that the overall drop in labor demand for low-skilled workers has been 10 percent. As he explains, trade negatively affects low-skilled labor markets in developed countries through two principal effects: first, by depressing the prices of labor-intensive goods, and second, by forcing firms to find ways of using less low-skilled labor to stay competitive, often leading to the adoption of labor-saving technologies, which he describes as "defensive innovation."

Sachs and Shatz (1994) are also sympathetic to the viewpoint that trade has had a negative impact on labor demand for low-skilled workers, particularly in the U.S. apparel and footwear industries, though they argue that overall, workers have only been modestly affected. Using disaggregated data from 131 manufacturing sectors and 150 trading partners, they find that increased net imports between 1978 and 1990 led to a 7.2 percent fall in production jobs, while non-production jobs fell by a much smaller 2.1 percent. Though they conclude that increased international trade has contributed to rising wage inequality in the United States, they also suggest that technological change has also played an important role, independent of internationalization.

Slaughter (1997) tests whether international trade has increased the elasticity of demand for US labor in recent decades. His study moves away from price effect studies that analyze whether or not the prices in sectors that use extensively low-skilled labor have fallen greatly, instead concentrating on the pressure put on labor markets by international trade. He finds that labor demand for production workers has become more elastic over time, while demand for non-production workers has not.

Feenstra (1998) describes how production has disintegrated under integration of the global economy, explaining how trade makes certain occupations obsolete in "much in the same way as replacing these workers with automated production" (p.13). Furthermore, because of increased capital mobility, as a result of direct investment abroad and outsourcing, globalization has strengthened the bargaining position of capital, placing labor in an even weaker position. As with the equalization of factor prices between countries through traditional trading arrangements, Feenstra argues that outsourcing accelerates low-skilled and high-skilled wage equalization across countries.

Skill-Biased Technological Change (SBTC)

Labor economists studying rising wage inequality in the United States have put greater emphasis on skill-biased technological change in causing rising wage inequality, than on international trade. A principal influence for this point of view is the finding that most increased wage inequality has occurred within industries, rather than between them. According to international trade theory, shifting production to relatively more abundant factors means a movement across sectors rather than between.[2]

One of the first studies to review the causes of increased wage inequality in industrialized countries was a 1992 study by Bound and Johnson. The authors review a number of explanations for the increase in the skill premium since 1980 and conclude that much of the variation in the skill premium is attributed to a residual trend, which they interpret as skill-biased technological change (Bound and Johnson, 1992). Attempting to make better sense of the residual, Berman, Bound and Griliches (1994) investigate the shift away from low-skilled labor in US manufacturing in the 1980s. Rather than a reallocation of employment between industries, they find that the increased use of non-production workers is strongly correlated with investment in computers and research and development. Most of the shift to non-production employment occurred in non-import-competing manufacturing industries. The shift toward skilled (non-production) labor occurred despite an increase in the relative wages of skilled labor, contradicting supply and demand analysis, which would predict a preference for low-skilled (production) workers in the face of declining relative wages. Since they find that inputs, primarily of labor, grew less rapidly than output, they argue that this suggests labor-saving technological change, which is the result of increased expenditures on computers and R&D.

Howell (2002) criticizes the Berman, Bound and Griliches study, arguing "the entire increase took place between 1980 and 1982; between 1983 and the early 1990s the non-production share remained essentially unchanged" (p. 26). The difficulty with the timing of their study presents an obvious challenge, given that most of the investments in new technology occurred after the mid-1980s.

Most of the debate has been based on econometric studies. Econometrics is a useful tool for gauging whether a relationship exists between two variables and how significant the relationship is, but it cannot explain how or why it exists. Another drawback to econometric analysis is that correlations between variables can sometimes be spurious, especially if key determinants are missing from the equation. An alternative methodology is to use case studies. Case studies offer greater insight into how or why international trade or skill-biased technological change can affect a worker's earnings. Brown and Campbell (2001) studied the semiconductor industry in four countries between 1993 and 1996, analyzing how employment distribution, skill acquisition, work activities and compensation were affected by globalization and technological change. They find that technological change widened the skill gap between occupations favoring high-skilled workers, but that it did not lead to increased wage inequality. They conclude that the wage increases for more educated and experienced workers is not simply because of SBTC but rather "how technological change, globalization and other factors are changing firms' market power and rent-sharing with workers" (p.464).

Institutionalist Perspectives

A less popular, but highly plausible explanation of increased wage inequality in industrialized countries requires moving beyond the conventional supply-demand model, and acknowledging the central role of labor market institutions in wage determination. Fortin and Lemieux (1997) attribute one-third of the growth in inequality in the 1980s in the U.S. to the fall in the real value of the minimum wage, the decline in unionization rate and economic deregulation. Howell (2002) acknowledges the importance of this and other studies that analyze the effect of quantifiable institutional variables on wages, but also argues that these variables "reflect only the most easily measurable manifestations of the more fundamental sources of the wage collapse, which are at once ideological and structural" (p.36). As he explains,

> In the institutionalist and labor relations traditions, employers are recognized as capable of offering a variety of starting wages and one of many wage-tenure profiles, determined within a range set by demand and supply forces, social norms and legal constraints . . . Imperfect information about worker performance, the importance of teamwork in production, the degree of price-making behavior in product markets, the share of labor in total costs, the collective power of workers, managerial preference over competitive strategy, and government regulations will all influence wage-setting and contribute to different wage outcomes for similarly skilled workers in similarly attractive job establishments (p.36).

Thus, the wage structure can be altered independently of the skill structure. And as he points out, many of the determinants of wages cannot be quantified. Not only are they immeasurable and thus not included in the econometric models, neoclassical models of wage determination cannot account for them either.

Fortunately, the industrial relations literature has made great strides in showing how corporate strategies have altered labor relations and in doing so, have affected work life, including promotion ladders, job security, work tasks, and earnings. The studies reveal the complexity of wage setting, which encompasses far more considerations than merely the marginal productivity of a worker.

Locke et al. (1995) document how firms and industries in eleven industrialized countries have adapted their employment practices "to the new terms of international competition" (p.359). Although a new approach to employment relations has emerged in all countries, the particular forms it has taken differ both across and within nations depending on the historical conditions prevalent in the industries, firms and regions. The authors' findings stress the role of national institutional arrangements, particularly labor standards, in creating work practices that are either more or less labor friendly. Yet despite the different national institutional arrangements, Locke and his colleagues find that unions are experiencing major challenges in all countries as a result of restructuring, a more diverse workforce and smaller firms. As they put it, "everywhere unions are in decline and management is resurgent" (p.364). Even so, countries lacking strong national or sectoral bargaining agreements have seen the greatest increase in wage differentials.

Similarly, Katz and Darbshire (2000) analyze changing employment patterns in the automotive and telecommunications industries of seven industrialized countries. They identify four employment patterns common across industries and nations and show how, despite their differences, the employment strategies adopted by the industries are closely related to the decline of unions and growing income inequality. Although they find that there has been an increase in the variation of employment patterns within countries, their findings suggest that the nature and origins of these variations are similar in the seven countries.

Looking more closely at the effect of corporate decentralization strategies, Harrison (1997) argues that the search for flexibility, by managers of both big and small companies, has undermined employment security and reduced incomes, exacerbating inequality. As he explains, big firms have decentralized, subcontracting firm activities through networks and alliances with small firms. Yet decentralization has not reduced the economic power of the large firms. Instead it has meant greater labor market segmentation as low-wage, insecure employment has proliferated in the small, network firms. He refers to this as the "dark side of flexible production" (p.190).

EVIDENCE FOR DEVELOPING COUNTRIES

In the debate on the declining wages of low-skilled in the U.S., it is typically assumed that the position of low-skilled workers in developing countries is improving as jobs have migrated from the U.S. to these lower cost areas. It is thus rather surprising to learn that in many developing countries, there has also been a fall in the relative demand and wages of low-skilled workers since trade liberalization. This finding is true for maquiladora-intensive countries such as Mexico (Hanson and Harrison, 1995, Feenstra and Hanson, 1997; Ravenga, 1997) as well as natural-resource exporting countries such as Chile, Argentina and Colombia (Robbins, 1996).

The econometric studies on the causes for rising wage inequality in the developing world since trade liberalization have proposed many of the same explanations as the studies done on industrialized countries, though sometimes with a slight twist. Some authors have embraced HOS in theory, arguing that "labor market rigidities" have prevented the market from clearing and wage differentials from narrowing. Others, however, have proposed alternative causes for rising wage inequality. By far, the most popular explanation is what Robbins (1996) has dubbed "skill-enhancing trade," which is essentially skill-biased technological change adapted to developing countries. Other explanations concern foreign direct investment or increased international outsourcing. Most studies maintain the assumption, prevalent in the literature on industrialized countries, that wages are determined according to aggregate labor supply and demand, with little, if any, consideration of institutional influences.

Skill-Enhancing Trade

Robbins (1996), in a study of nine developing countries including Chile, argues that trade liberalization has been associated with increased relative wage dispersion in developing countries because of "skill-enhancing trade." As he explains, skill-enhancing trade is the result of increased physical capital and technology imports following trade liberalization and the associated demand for skilled workers to work with this technology:

> In LDCs emerging from Import-Substitution-Industrialization strategies that stifled adoption of foreign technologies, [trade liberalization] will lead to an initial large jump to more modern and skill-intensive industries. Subsequently, the liberalized LDC will continue on a skill-intensive biased trend similar to that being observed in the North. Relative wages would follow a similar path conditioned by supply changes (Robbins, 1996, p.40).

Figure 2.1 illustrates how increased machinery imports that result from trade liberalization can lead to increased wage inequality if the imports are skill-biased.

Figure 2.1: Skill-Biased Technological Change and Wage Inequality

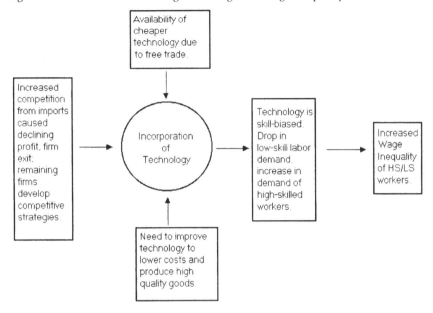

Source: Author's illustration.

Sharing Robbins's views, Hanson and Harrison (1995) find that liber-alization led to widening wage dispersion in Mexico. They explain simi-larly, "in developing countries trade and technology are complements, not substitutes, since trade is the vehicle through which new technologies enter most developing countries" (p.2). The studies essentially argue that free trade leads to the importation of capital machinery, which forces embodied technical change in the production process. A *capital-skill complementarity* exists between the imported machinery and skilled labor, meaning that the elasticity of substitution between capital equipment and low-skilled labor is higher than it is between capital equipment and skilled labor (Griliches, 1969). In other words, the machinery is labor-saving, which decreases the demand for low-skilled production workers and subsequently further reduces these workers wages. At the same time, the demand for skilled workers to operate the machinery increases.

As with industrialized countries, the skill-biased technological change or skill-enhancing trade hypothesis has won an increasing number of con-verts compared with HOS. For example, Berman and Machin (2000) argue that the declining wage bill of production compared with non-production workers in their sample of developing countries is the result of increased computer imports in the 1980s. Similarly, Behrman et al. (2000) argue that it is technological progress, rather than trade flows, that have caused increased wage differentials in Latin America in the post-reform period. Yet the work on developing countries shares the same flaw as the work on industrialized countries, namely the failure to explain the dynamic processes that lead to increased wage dispersion. As the studies are based on econometric work that measures statistical correlations, issues that cannot be easily proxied for, such as labor market deregulation, are ignored in the analyses. Consequently, the possibility remains that the results are spurious, with trade reforms, machinery imports, and wage inequality increasing simultaneously, but not necessarily as the direct result of one another.

Foreign Direct Investment and Wage Inequality

Under globalization, the relationship between trade and FDI has shifted markedly. During import-substitution industrialization, FDI acted as a substitute for trade, but since liberalization it has become associated with increased trade flows (Milberg, 1999). Although most FDI is between industrialized countries, the developing country share of world FDI has increased during the 1990s, and by 1997 represented 37 percent of flows. Some authors have argued that the increased FDI to developing countries has caused rising wage inequality.

Feenstra and Hanson (1997), studying Mexico, find that growth in FDI is positively correlated with the relative demand for skilled labor and accounts for a large portion of the skilled labor share of total wages. They find that in Mexican regions with heavy foreign investment, FDI's growth accounted for 52.4 percent of the increase in the non-production worker wage share. They reason that the flows of FDI from the North to the South lead to higher capital-output ratios in the South, which raises the relative demand for skilled workers because of the complementarity between capital and skill. Hanson and Harrison (1995) also find Mexican wage inequality to be positively and significantly associated with foreign ownership, greater capital intensity, larger plant sizes and export orientation. Industries with a high share of foreign plants were found to hire a significantly larger share of skilled workers. The same result was found for industries that imported raw materials, indicating that maquiladora production might have contributed to rising inequality.

Technology Imports and Efficiency Wages

Amadeo (1995) offers a contrasting explanation for the increase in the skill wage premium in his study of the manufacturing sector in São Paulo, Brazil. Amadeo turns to efficiency wage theory to explain the increase in wage differentials. He argues that since liberalization, manufacturing firms have modernized their production processes by importing advanced technology. As these more advanced methods increase the scope for negligence or sabotage, managers attempt to mitigate this risk by paying their workers a higher-than-market wage to discourage them from damaging the production process. Thus the introduction of innovative technologies via liberalization will cause a rise in these workers' wages for reasons of efficiency, not because of a scarcity in supply. Inequality in the labor market increases rather than decreases, and the situation of the low-skilled worker in these countries does not improve with the policy reforms.

Outsourcing

Another related effect of increased multinational activity under globalization is increased outsourcing. Outsourcing refers to the decision by firms to disperse operations, nationally or internationally, either within the firm (internalization) or by subcontracting other firms to perform the operation (externalization). Outsourcing by Northern multinationals has increased significantly since the liberalization of trade and financial markets, altering the composition of world trade.

The low-cost strategy of outsourcing production on the part of multinationals is well documented in Benería and Roldán's study (1987) on industrial homework in Mexico. Over 85 percent of the subcontracting firms they surveyed, were either multinationals or were under contract with multinationals. As production was outsourced, firm size decreased as did labor protections and wages. At the sweatshop level, workers received the minimum wage, yet without fringe benefits, while homeworkers earned an equivalent of one-third of the minimum wage. Though subcontracting boosted the competitive position of firms by lowering costs and mitigating risks associated with economic slumps, it also weakened the position of labor, contributing to an increase in wage inequality between skilled and low-skilled workers.

Outsourcing can also occur within the domestic economies of developing countries. In the more advanced sectors of an economy, outsourcing occurs because the lead firm recognizes that the subcontracting firm is more specialized in the task and can therefore perform it better. But outsourcing can also be a way to reduce costs and increase flexibility. Singer (1997) attributes the increase in informal employment in Brazil since the opening of its domestic market in 1990, to an attempt on the part of import-competing firms to lower costs. In this case, foreign competitors have gone informal or have informal suppliers and subcontractors in order to cut costs.

Hierarchical Pay and Rent-Sharing

In a study of rising wage inequality in Brazil during the 1960s, Bacha and Taylor (1978) review explanations of the causes of increased wage dispersion, much along the same lines as what has been emphasized in the recent literature (demand shifts, technological change). They dismiss these explanations, arguing instead that the fall in the minimum wage under the military government prevented Brazilian workers from getting their fair share of productivity gains. They suggest that the labor market is segmented into two non-competing groups, "managers" and "laborers," and that hierarchical position in the firm, rather than qualification or marginal productivity, determines a person's earnings. As managers share in the residual income left over after laborers are paid, they attempt to squeeze laborers' pay.

The Bacha and Taylor article illustrates an institutional approach to wage determination that considers the important role that bargaining plays in assigning rents within a firm. Supply and demand in the labor market is just one of many variables that determine wages; employers will also base their decision on a firm's market power, the collective strength of its workers, government regulations, enforcement and the socio-political climate. These and other considerations affect how a firm's profits are shared with its workers.

EVIDENCE FOR CHILE

As in many industrialized and developing countries, Chile has also seen an increase in wage inequality since 1974 when it liberalized trade and implemented other economic reforms. For example, the earnings ratio of workers with a university degree compared with those who did not complete secondary school nearly doubled from 3.9 in 1957–1963 to 6.7 in 1987–1990 (Larrañaga, 1999). In the manufacturing sector, between 1975 and 1992, the relative wage between skilled and low-skilled workers increased by 8.3 percent (Meller and Tokman, 1998). Most of the studies on Chile have focused on skill-enhancing trade or labor market rigidities to explain rising wage inequality. Little work has been done emphasizing institutional shifts in labor relations.

The Education Premium

One of the first important studies to document rising wage inequality in Chile was Robbins (1994).[3] In this study, Robbins decomposes changes in wages using data from the University of Chile's household employment survey. He shows that during 1974–1990, the premium associated with increased education caused the wage distribution (the variance of log wages) to increase by 0.15, whereas the counter-effect of increased educational supply decreased the distribution by half that amount (–0.073). Since the demand effects swamped the supply effect, he concludes that the economic reforms increased the demand for skilled workers.

Similarly, Bravo and Marinovic (1997) estimate a wage decomposition for the 1957–1996 period. They conclude that two-thirds of the changes in the wage distribution can be explained by variations in the quantities or prices of observable human capital, such as years of schooling, experience and occupation. They observe that the richest segments of the population drive inequality, as income distribution within the poorest groups shrank during the period. During 1957–1996, the demand for workers with less than 12 years of schooling increased by 9.3 percent, compared with the demand for university-educated workers, which increased by 111 percent.[4]

Skill-Enhancing Trade

Though the rise in wage inequality is well documented, there is little evidence on its causes. Robbins (1994, 1996) and Gindling and Robbins (2001) argue that increased wage inequality in Chile is consistent with skill-enhancing trade, meaning that competition from trade liberalization forced firms to import new technologies. To support their argument, they cite evidence of increased machinery imports following trade liberalization. Bravo and Marinovic (1997) likewise attribute the skilled-labor bias to an economic restructuring, brought about by free trade and increased technological adoption in the country. Morley (1999), however, finds little relationship between trends in capital intensity and the skill differential and suggests that capital imports are not necessarily associated with skill-biased demand. Rather, he argues that the recurrent recessions and the weakening of union power were important causes, along with trade liberalization, of rising wage inequality; yet it is difficult to discern the degree of importance of each.

One supporting source of evidence for skill-enhancing trade (or skill-biased technological change) is that only ten percent of job reallocation in Chile following trade liberalization (1979–1986) was between sectors, the rest was within sectors (Meller and Tokman, 1998; Levinsohn, 1999; Pavcnik, 2002). Since HOS would cause job reallocation between sectors, this finding supports capital deepening as the cause of increased inequality. However, Pavcnik (2002), using data from Chile's manufacturing census for 1979 to 1986, finds no evidence that capital deepening—defined as the use of imported materials, foreign technical assistance and patented technology—increased demand for skilled workers after controlling for unobserved plant characteristics. She concludes that the adoption of foreign technology is not associated with skill upgrading, and is unable to support Robbins's hypothesis that skill-biased technological change due to trade liberalization caused rising income inequality in Chile.

Arguing in support of both the HOS and skill-biased technological change hypotheses, Beyer et al. (1999) regress the wage differential from 1960 to 1996 on a proxy for openness, a relative price index of textile products and the proportion of the labor force with a college degree. Their analysis reveals a negative and significant coefficient for the price index of textiles, which they argue supports HOS and explains the increase in the wage distribution. The regression results also give a positive and significant coefficient for openness, indicating that increased openness has increased wage differentials. They interpret this finding as technological change that was biased against low-skilled labor in the 1980s and 1990s as well as a change in the productive structure of the economy towards natural resource exploitation. Nevertheless, their findings should be interpreted with caution, as there are structural problems with the model such as labor supply and labor demand in the same equation, and no correction for endogeneity.

The Labor Market: Rigid or Flexible?

Another line of research concerns the effect of labor market rigidities in causing unemployment and inequality.[5] For example, Cox-Edwards and Edwards (1997) argue that inflexibility in the Chilean labor market, due to the presence of a minimum wage, caused unemployment in the period after liberalization. Using the Ricardo-Viner model, they demonstrate theoretically how in the short-run, when labor is the only mobile factor, the presence of labor market rigidities (such as minimum wage laws or wage indexation) will prevent wages from falling as they should with tariff removal. Thus, the authors attribute the prolonged unemployment in Chile to the minimum wage and wage indexation, which prevented firms from adjusting more quickly to the new competitive environment, despite the sharp fall in minimum and average wages during the 1970s and 1980s. They argue that wages were not able to fall as much as they needed to and as a result, unemployment was high. Their analysis, however, is tautological, since the Ricardo-Viner model presupposes full employment; failure to have full unemployment is thus the result of wage rigidity. Also supporting the wage rigidity hypothesis, Pagés and Montenegro (1999) associate severance pay legislation with a substantial decline in the rate of employment among young workers in Chile.

The emphasis on labor market rigidity appears unfounded, however, given the substantial evidence of job turnover in Chile following liberalization. For the years 1979–1986, Levinsohn (1999) finds that in all years except 1985, about a quarter of all workers changed jobs, indicating an extremely high rate of job turnover. As he explains, "if one associates Japan with the notion of lifetime employment, Chile during liberalization is at the other end of the spectrum" (p.342). Moreover, Berg and Contreras (2004) find empirical support of labor market flexibility in the post-1973 period. They estimate a wage curve for the years 1957–1973, before the military government, compared with during and after the military government (1973–1996). They find a coefficient on unemployment of –0.08 for the second period, comparable to estimates of many industrialized countries with deregulated labor markets, such as the US and the UK. More flexible labor laws, especially concerning worker dismissal, meant that workers feared job loss during unemployment and more readily accepted lower wages.

Though studies have shown the Chilean labor market to be flexible, this does not imply that it operates strictly according to the principles of supply and demand. Like all labor markets, the Chilean labor market is a social institution (Solow, 1990). Because it is a social institution, empirical studies often find results that are not compatible with marginal productivity theory. For example, Romaguera (1991) documents the existence of inter-industry wage differentials in Chile using data from both the annual manufacturing survey and the University of Chile household employment survey. Her findings reveal a persistence of inter-industry wage differentials across time, occupation and firm size.

CONCLUSION

Many economists believe that today's international economy demands more skilled workers, either because of increased international trade or because of skill-biased technological change, or perhaps as a result of both. Authors holding this view believe that there has been an outward shift in the demand curve for skilled workers and a contraction in demand for low-skilled workers. Supply cannot meet demand, so skilled workers' earnings have risen, while falling demand for low-skilled workers has depressed these workers' pay. Greater wage inequality has thus ensued.

Despite the statistical evidence given to support the competing explanations, the debate remains largely unresolved, mainly because of the difficulty in separating causes. As many authors point out, trade and technology are not always mutually exclusive explanations, especially in developing countries. Adding to the difficulty of the analyses, trade is no longer the simple commodity exchange that David Ricardo envisioned.

With improved communication and transport, trade and financial liberalization, and a greater willingness of developing countries to receive foreign investment, the nature of international trade has changed. Production activities and investment have dispersed across nations. The result is that the association between trade and wages has become far more complex than ever imagined by the early trade theorists.

But another important drawback to the debate is the widespread and limited view that wages are set according to the marginal productivity of labor, ignoring the role of institutions in determining labor demand and wages. Because of the complex nature of present-day international exchange and the social relations involved in determining employment and wages, it is important that analyses of rising wage inequality in Chile consider institutional factors, including labor relations, changes in labor legislation as well as the value of the minimum wage. Yet an excessive reliance on econometrics has meant that these variables have often been ignored, as they are difficult to quantify. Moreover, as explained, econometric studies can only show if there is a significant correlation and how much that correlation is. They cannot explain "why" or "how."

The industrial relations literature, on the other hand, stresses the role of institutions and corporate strategies in determining wages. These studies move beyond marginal productivity of labor to explain rising wage inequality. Although the studies are based on the experiences of industrialized countries, they offer a promising avenue of research for my analysis of Chile. With this in mind, I review, in the next chapter, changes in Chilean labor market institutions, standards and relations. This will provide an important background for the case studies that follow.

Chapter Three

Working in Chile: Reform, Repression and Flexibility Since 1973

INTRODUCTION

In 1974 Chile abandoned the import-substitution model that had existed in the country since the end of World War II, to become the first Latin American country in the post-war period to embrace free trade and free market principles. With the exception of a brief liberalization period in the late 1970s during Argentina's military government, the rest of Latin America would not follow in Chile's steps until nearly two decades later.

The adopted policy of market liberalization included opening up the economy to international trade, removing price controls and freeing the interest rate. The private sector was to hold the development reigns, aided by widespread privatization of formerly government-run industries, the adoption of the value-added tax and privatization of the social security system. Meanwhile, the government was to concern itself with setting the macroeconomic conditions that it believed necessary for growth, namely the reduction of inflation. Fundamental to the liberalization program of the military government were accompanying policies to enhance flexibility in the labor market. The military government threw out the existing labor code when it assumed power in 1973, replacing it in 1979 with a wholly revised code that restricted unions and collective bargaining. This hampered the ability of workers to negotiate wage increases, particularly in an environment of worsening unemployment.

The abandonment of the import-substitution model (ISI) in 1974 was prompted, in part, by a belief among Chilean economists that the closed economy model was exhausted. Corbo and Meller (1982), participating in an NBER study on employment generation under ISI, argued that ISI had failed in Chile because, "while manufacturing output was growing at an annual rate close to 6 percent in the 1960s, manufacturing employment grew by slightly more than 3 percent annually" (p.83). In a classic capital-labor trade-off analysis, the authors argued that eliminating the preferential exchange rate on capital goods imports "would have contributed significantly to creating employment in Chile's manufacturing industry" (p.117). An open economy would have forced Chilean manufacturers to prefer workers to imported machinery, generating jobs and the development of the country's export sector.

Behind the economic arguments against the inefficiency of the ISI model existed a politically charged resentment towards the gains labor had made in the country. Following the passage of sweeping labor reforms in the 1920s, the Chilean left acquired institutional legitimacy in the political life of the country, which overtime grew, making the Chilean left the strongest in Latin America. This strength culminated, decades later, with the 1970 election of the socialist government of Salvador Allende. On September 11, 1973, following three years of economic turmoil that led to truckers' strikes and discontent among the petty bourgeoisie and capitalist classes, the military ousted the Popular Unity and assumed control of the government.

To the surprise of many, the military regime, headed by army General Augusto Pinochet, remained in power for seventeen years, until it allowed democratic elections in 1990. Throughout its tenure, the repression of labor was a trademark of the regime. At the beginning, the repression was backlash to the power labor had attained during the previous half century in the country; eventually, however, the repression became a fundamental component of the government's market liberalization program, of which flexible labor markets was one of the central pillars.

This chapter reviews the economic and labor reforms undertaken by Pinochet's regime. Because the macroeconomic and trade reforms suffered fits and adjustments as a result of two severe recessions in 1975 and 1982, analysis of the reforms is framed around a discussion of the macroeconomic environment. The second part of the chapter reviews, in detail, the military government's repressive policies toward the labor movement in the period immediately following the coup and after 1979 with the institution of the new labor code. The discussion is followed by a review of the labor reforms instituted following the return to democracy in 1990. Despite more than a decade of democracy, the labor movement remains weak, in part, due to restrictions remaining in the revised labor code. This analysis of the limitations placed on worker bargaining power lays the foundation for examination of rent sharing, undertaken in chapter 6. The discussion of labor reforms ends with a review of the conditions of work in present-day Chile.

LIBERALIZATION POLICIES AND ECONOMIC PERFORMANCE

Soon after the military government assumed power in September of 1973, it announced its economic goals of inflation reduction, reduced government control in the everyday workings of the economy and the opening up of the economy to international competition.[1] The government's plan was to tackle the high inflation rate through money-based stabilization, rather than relying on repressing inflation through price controls and an over-valued currency (De Gregorio, 1999). The exchange rate was devalued 300 percent in October 1973, while the authorities began the process of unifying the six separate exchange rates. Price controls on nearly 3,000 products were eliminated. Tariffs, which averaged over 100 percent at the time of coup, began to be lowered. By June 1976, the average tariff rate had been reduced to 33 percent and all quantitative restrictions were eliminated. By 1979, all items, except automobiles, had a nominal import tariff of 10 percent (Edwards and Lederman, 1998).

In line with its ideology of increasing the role of the private sector in the economy as well as a fiscal need to generate revenues to lower the budget deficit, the government also began an ambitious privatization program. Between 1973 and 1975 firms that were under government inspection but not legally acquired by the State during the years of the Popular Unity were returned. Between 1974 and 1981, firms and banks nationalized during the Popular Unity years were sold into private ownership (Saez, 1993). The privatization process was hurried and the government did not pay much attention to the concentration of ownership, leading to the emergence of industrial and financial conglomerates, known as *grupos*. By 1979, the ten largest *grupos* controlled 135 of the 250 largest corporations and almost 70 percent of assets traded on the stock market.

In May 1974, the government deregulated the financial system, granting banks the authority to borrow funds and make loans at freely determined interest rates. Moreover, entry of foreign credit was allowed. Yet despite the belief that financial liberalization would lead to a lowering of interest rates, lending rates on short-term credit ranged from 121 percent in 1975 to 35 percent in 1978 (Ffrench-Davis, 1999). Many industrial firms within the *grupos*, however, were not affected by the higher interest rates, as they could access favorable rates from their banking partners.

Macroeconomic Environment and Firm Performance

During the first decade of the military regime, macroeconomic policy centered on controlling inflation, leading to a highly volatile macroeconomic environment. The first step in reducing inflation was cutting the deficit. Government spending was slashed by 25 percent while a ten percent temporary increase in income taxes was instituted. At the same time, a highly restrictive monetary policy was put in place. These policies, along with a decline in copper prices, led to a fall in GDP of 12.9 percent in 1975. Although inflation was reduced in 1976 and 1977, it was still high—84.2 percent in 1977—leading the authorities to alter their inflation-fighting policies via manipulation of the exchange rate, first through a policy of pre-announced devaluations and later, in June 1979, by fixing the peso to the U.S. dollar. These policies were successful at first. Inflation was cut in half in 1978 while GDP growth rebounded, growing at about 8 percent per year until 1981 (Muñoz, 1992).

The macroeconomic environment was unfavorable to domestic industries adjusting to the liberalization program as well as to emerging export industries. The policy of using the exchange rate as nominal anchor led to severe appreciation of the currency between 1978 and 1982. Moreover, the emergence of high interest rate spreads coupled with the fixed exchange rate policy, led to speculative behavior on the part of the *grupos* and other investors, who borrowed abroad at international rates and then invested in Chile. Meanwhile, domestic firms that were unable to access foreign interest rates suffered from interest rates of 30 percent and above. The high interest rates led many industrial companies to increase their involvement in financial activities at the expense of fixed capital investment (Mizala, 1992).

As a result of the financial difficulties, domestic production suffered during the 1970s. The recession of 1975 led to a sharp fall in domestic demand, which was followed by an import boom, primarily of consumer goods, during the period of peso appreciation. Corbo and Sánchez (1984) surveyed the responses of ten firms to trade liberalization and structural adjustment, and found that during the late 1970s the firms responded to liberalization by streamlining the activities of the firms, producing fewer product lines and closing inefficient plants, with little added investment. During the years of the peso appreciation, the firms did not have any more room for efficiency improvements: "[appreciation] was equivalent to a second, and more intensive, trade liberalization that proved very difficult to surmount" (p. 60). Mizala (1992), using industrial survey data, reported that in 1977 nearly 50 percent of the firms surveyed attributed declining sales to lack of domestic demand, while 19 percent blamed import competition. By 1980 insufficient domestic demand was reported by 21 percent of firms, with 40 percent of firms attributing declining sales to import competition. This difficult adjustment period caused the number of industrial firms to decline by 13 percent between 1967 and 1979.[2]

The effects of the turbulent macroeconomic environment are clearly illustrated in the case study of a consumer-durables producing firm in Chile (Katz and Vera, 1997). During the years 1974–1981, the company undertook a number of defensive steps. First, it merged with another large competitor and cut 1,500 jobs (from a combined total of 3,900 jobs) and later, it deverticalized production, concentrating on final assembly of the good. This strategy increased the use of imported parts, leading to further rationalization of the staff from 2,500 workers in 1975 to 1,300 by 1980 and a deskilling of the work force with the move to assembly work. Defensive steps included merging the firms and cutting costs via staff reductions to better face import competition. Then, during the appreciation of the currency, it integrated relatively cheaper input parts, while again cutting costs through staff reductions.

The Debt Crisis

Chile entered the 1980s with a large trade deficit, sustained through the inflow of foreign capital. During the international financial crisis of 1981–1983, these inflows quickly reversed, leading to a severe balance of payments crisis in the Chilean economy. A steep jump in world interest rates coupled with a sharp fall in copper prices and declining export earnings in uncompetitive industrial sectors, meant the authorities had insufficient reserves to defend the currency. The government was forced to abandon its fixed exchange rate policy, devaluing the currency by almost 100 percent in June 1982. An economic crisis erupted. Over 800 firms declared bankruptcy while numerous financial institutions faced eminent failure.

The financial and economic crisis of 1982 led to a severe contraction in domestic product of 14.1 percent. GDP growth would not resume until 1984 and would not reach its 1981 level until 1987. Though all sectors were negatively affected, the industrial sector suffered the greatest losses. During the difficult adjustment years of 1974–1981, industrial firms had gone into debt as a survival mechanism. Unable to take out more loans and faced with an increase in their debt (particularly if the debt was in dollars), many firms were forced to close their doors. Industrial GDP declined 21.0 percent in 1982, while 160,000 of the sector's workers lost their jobs in that year alone. The crisis brought about a period of severe disinvestment, which reached its trough in 1984 with investment at 45 percent of the 1979 level (Katz and Vera, 1997).

The economic crash of 1982 had a devastating effect on the country's labor force. In 1982, unemployment surpassed 20 percent with an additional 5.1 percent of the labor market employed in the two government jobs programs, the PEM, the Minimum Employment Program, and the POJH, the Program for Head of Household. By 1983, 391,000 Chileans, or

10.3 percent of the labor force, worked for the government jobs programs. All sectors of the economy contracted severely, except the "other services" sector, which became a refuge for 170,000 displaced laborers. In 1982, construction shed 90,000 jobs (52.9 percent of its labor force); commerce shed 143,700 jobs (23.1 percent); and financial services shed 15,600 jobs (Edwards and Edwards, 1991).

The economic contraction, coupled with the 1982 abolition of the wage indexation policy, led to a fall in real wages and stagnant wage growth. Real wages would not recover their 1980 level until 1988 (Infante and Klein, 1992). The loss of wage indexation during a decade when the annual inflation rate fluctuated between 20 and 25 percent meant that workers had to negotiate increases, even to retain their same level of earnings (Meller, 1992). Yet workers lost their bargaining power because of the high unemployment rate, which averaged 15.1 percent in Greater Santiago during the 1980s,[3] and because of the repression of labor rights.

Policy Responses to the Crisis

The crisis of 1982 forced a short-term reversal in the economic and legal policies of the military government. The newly privatized banks, which had borrowed heavily abroad during the late 1970s and early 1980s, saw their debt multiply with the devaluation and could not meet their payments. By January 1983, the government, under pressure from the international lending banks, intervened by liquidating two banks and nationalizing others, despite earlier rhetoric that it would not bail them out (Edwards and Edwards, 1991). Nationalization of the external debt created an increase in the deficit, a problem the regime dealt with in two ways: first, by raising the uniform tariff rate from 10 to 35 percent,[4] and secondly, through a new wave of privatizations instituted to increase government revenues.[5] In the area of labor reform, the government eliminated backward wage indexation, based on the idea that a fall in real wages would lower unemployment.

In order to jump-start investment and economic recovery, the government reformed its tax system, lowering taxes on wage income and placing incentives in the capital gains tax in favor of retained profits (Yañez, 1992). The regime changed its investment policies as well. In 1985, the government shifted its fiscal policy towards public investment, leading to a growth in government spending of more than 7 percentage points of GDP between 1985 and 1989. Expenditures on housing and social policies were also increased as the military government faced the upcoming plebiscite on the continuation of military rule. In 1988, a majority of Chileans voted in favor of democratic elections in 1989 rather than continue military rule until 1997. The results set the stage for the return to democracy.

Figure 3.1: Real GDP Growth, 1980-2000, percentages

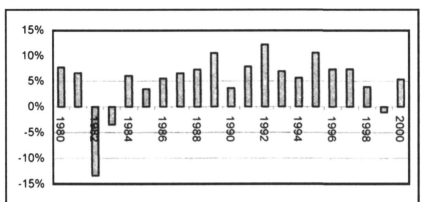

Source: Banco Central.

Economic Recovery and Growth

The Chilean economy began recovering from the debt crisis in 1984 leading to an extended period of strong and sustained growth that lasted until 1999, when GDP fell by 1.1 percent as a result of the Asian financial crisis (See Figure 3.1). During the 1990s, GDP growth averaged 8.9 percent real annual growth.

Much of the growth in real GDP was fueled by an increase in investment, attracted by the continued privatization of the basic services sector, by the stable macroeconomic environment and by favorable prospects for both market-seeking and resource-seeking multinationals. Between 1990 and 1998, FDI totaled almost $24 billion, nearly a ten-fold increase in investment over the 1980s. Increased investment had the negative effect of causing currency appreciation, which hurt the tradable goods sector. The government tried to control short-term capital inflows through the use of an "encaje," which obligated the investor to deposit 30 percent of investment into the central bank, thereby lowering the return and discouraging short-term investment. Because investors only bore a cost if their inflows were held in the country for less than one year, the policy succeeded in attracting capital inflows that were more stable and longer-term, and had the added benefit of mitigating currency appreciation.

One of the central goals of the military government's liberalization program was export expansion and diversification, and the government was largely successful in this respect. By 1990–1996, exports comprised 36 percent of GDP compared with 12 percent in 1965–1970. By 1996, the share of processed natural exports had grown to 33 percent of total exports compared with 23 percent in 1984. Traditional natural resources, of which copper was the most important, declined in share from 71 to 57 percent. Successful new "miracle" sectors developed including wood pulp, wine, fishmeal, and fruit and vegetable processing. Nevertheless, there was little expansion of non-traditional exports, aside from processed natural resources. Manufactured exports not based on natural resources accounted for just 10 percent of exports by 1996 (OIT, 1998).

To encourage non-traditional exports, the government instituted an incentive program to generate investment. In 1974, the government began refunding the value-added tax on imported inputs used for re-export. In 1985, the government introduced the "simplified drawback," which gave a rebate of up to ten percent of the value of the exports, if the export was a non-traditional good.[6] In 1988 the "drawback" was introduced. The program allowed firms to recover tariffs paid for importing inputs used in the manufacturing of export goods. A special customs law was also developed that delayed tariff payment on capital equipment, stimulating the incorporation of more modern machinery and technology into production. The government agencies, ProChile and Fundación Chile also played an important role in developing the export sector. ProChile's programs encouraged the development of industry associations seeking access to new markets, while Fundación Chile helped integrate new technologies into export industries, playing a critical role in the development of the salmon industry (Agosin, 1999).

The expansion of the export sector led to a 4.5 percent annual rate of job growth in processed natural resource manufacturing between 1988 and 1995 (Schurman, 2001). Overall, the rate of unemployment in the economy fell as economic expansion fueled job growth in all sectors except electricity, which was in the process of being privatized, and personal services, which had served as a refuge for the underemployed during the debt crisis. By 1992, the unemployment rate in Greater Santiago was at six percent, a rate not seen since before the military coup.

Real wages also started to rise. For the average Chilean worker, the 1970s and 1980s were both "lost" decades. The two economic crises, the economic opening, the elimination of wage indexation and the restrictions on collective bargaining caused real wages in the economy to plummet (See Figure 3.2). It was not until 1992 that workers earned the same wages they had been making in 1970.[7] In the 1990s real wage growth was sustained, averaging 4.2 percent during the decade. Some of the wage gains in the 1990s were attributable to the increases in the minimum wage, which averaged 7.9 percent real growth during the same period. The strong growth in GDP, job expansion and real wage growth had favorable social effects. In

Figure 3.2: Real Average Wages, 1970-2000, Index 1989=100

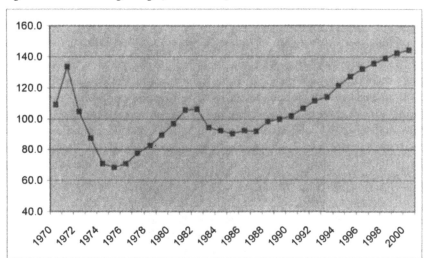

Source: Cortázar (1997) and INE.

1987, 45 percent of the population lived in poverty. By 1996, the number of Chileans living below the poverty rate had fallen to 23 percent.[8]

LABOR MARKET FLEXIBILITY AND ITS CONSEQUENCES

The economic policies and macroeconomic mismanagement of the military government caused a sharp increase in unemployment and a drastic fall in real wages until the 1990s. The uncertain economic environment served to discipline labor. Whatever disciplining the market failed to do, the military government did via its reforms to the labor market and its violent suppression of unions. Flexibilization of the labor market was one of the central pillars of the liberalization program. Its principal goals were to increase flexibility in hiring and firing, with the objective of eliminating rigidities and hence mismatches in the labor market; and to depoliticize labor relations, removing the historical affiliation between unions and political parties that had existed in Chile since the 1930s.

The legacy of the military government's reforms lives on in Chile today. Union affiliation rates continue to be low, and many workers are restricted from bargaining collectively, hampered by legal impediments under the current labor code. The contemporary weakness of the Chilean labor movement is in large part the result of the limitations of the 1979 labor code imposed by the military government as well as the successful crippling of labor during the military's 17-year rule.

Repression and Curtailment of Labor Rights under the Military Government

When the military assumed control of the government in September of 1973, it immediately suspended all existing labor contracts, outlawed unions and banned collective bargaining. Labor was essentially without rights and without recourse for reinstating those rights. Existing contracts specifying salaries, benefits and other remuneration were no longer valid. The government also abandoned the requirement of just cause in firing, though employers were still expected to provide severance pay equal to one month's pay per year of service. In practice, however, there was little enforcement of remaining legal provisions (Romaguera et al., 1995).

The decision to ban unions, and suspend collective bargaining and the right to strike, was made for political reasons (Cortázar, 1997). Unions in Chile were highly politicized and formed one of the principal bases of support for the Popular Unity government. Indeed, 81 percent of blue-collar union members supported the Popular Unity while 16 percent were Christian Democrats.[9] Since workers could no longer collectively negotiate wage increases with their employers, the government extended its system of wage indexation to the private sector. Government-mandated wage readjustments were based on past inflation, which in a period of declining inflation, led to real wage growth.[10] During the financial crisis of 1982, the government abandoned its policy of wage indexation.

In 1979, the government decreed a new labor code, following the threat of an international boycott if the government did not re-establish freedom of association (Ruiz-Tagle, 1985). Written by then-Minister of Labor, José Piñera, the new labor code reflected the three "basic pillars of the new economic model: free markets, free trade and limited state intervention in the economy" (Meller, 1992, p.74). Meller (1992) explains that for the economists who developed the 1979 labor code, a free labor market with freely chosen economic agents required the following elements: freedom of labor, voluntary union membership and union autonomy, and freedom to dismiss (employment at will). The labor laws were written to guarantee these provisions. By enhancing labor mobility, the government also believed that unemployment would be reduced (Edwards and Lederman, 1998). The business sector was particularly pleased with the reforms. A 1984 study of business leaders' perspectives on the reforms introduced by the military government ranked "introduction of new labor legislation" as the most favorable reform (Corbo and Sánchez, 1984).

Table 3.1: Important Changes to Labor Legislation during Three Distinct Political Eras

Provision	Pre-1973	Military Government*	Return to Democracy
Closed Shops	Allowed	Not allowed	Not allowed
Topics for Negotiation	No exclusion	Excluded from negotiation topics that "limit the ability of the employer to organize, direct and administer the firm."	Exclusion not removed
Industry-Level Collective Bargaining	Allowed	Not allowed	Allowed only if all parties agree. In practice, not used.
Length of Strike	Unlimited	60 days	Unlimited
Replacement of Strikers	Not allowed	On 1st day.Striking workers can be permanently replaced.	On 1st day if employer offered CPI increase. On 15th day if CPI increase not offered. Striking workers can only be temporarily replaced.
Workers abandoning strike	Not allowed	Could return to work after 15 days.	After 15th day if CPI offered. After 30th day if CPI not offered.
Federations/ Confederations	Allowed	Not legally recognized, though existed in practice.	Allowed
Causes for Dismissal	Difficulty in proving just cause ("non-removability law"); required payment of severance. Collective dismissal required prior authorization from government.	Did not have to specify cause yet required payment of severance. No restrictions on collective dismissal.	Economic reasons are just cause, yet still requires payment of severance. Unjust cause increases Severance payment by 20%. No restrictions on collective dismissal.
Severance Pay	1 month salary per year of service.	1 month salary per year of service limited to 5 months total in mid-1981.	Limit extended to 11 months.

Table 3.1: Important Changes to Labor Legislation during Three Distinct Political Eras (continued)

Provision	Pre-1973	Military Government*	Return to Democracy
Temporary Workers	Entitled to same legal rights as permanent workers.	Not allowed to join unions or to bargain collectively.	Allowed to join unions, not allowed to bargain collectively.
Subcontracting	Limited to activities that were not central to the firm.	No limitations	No limitations

*Unless otherwise specified, the law refers to the changes introduced in the 1979 Labor Code. Between September 1973 and 1979, the existing labor code was dismissed and workers did not have the right to due process.

Source: Author's compilation based on Cortázar (1994,1997); Romaguera et al. (1995), Ruiz-Tagle (1985) and Cox Edwards (1993).

The 1979 Labor Code drastically changed conditions compared with the pre-1973 labor code. The pre-1973 code reflected the labor reforms first instituted in the 1920s, which came about following a decision of the Chilean ruling class "to abandon the failed policy of simple physical repression of organized labor," opting instead to "curb labor's revolutionary potential through legislative means by integrating organized labor into the institutional life of the nation" (Bergquist, 1986, p.49)[11] (See Table 3.1). Though the 1979 code allowed freedom of association, it contained a series of provisions aimed at weakening the power of labor organizations. Union membership was deemed voluntary, thus outlawing closed shops and permitting multiple unions within a firm. Union financing had to consist entirely of member dues since contribution of funds to the union was not permitted in collective bargaining (Meller, 1992). Collective bargaining was limited to the firm level.[12] If a collective bargaining agreement covered workers from more than one company, even if all parties agreed to it, it was considered invalid under the 1979 code. National confederations of workers, which played an important role in energizing the labor movement during the 1960s and early 1970s, but which had been banned since 1973, did not regain legal recognition in the 1979 code, though they continued to exist in practice.[13] The legislation also failed to guarantee adequate protection against arbitrary dismissals of union leaders and imposed a maximum amount of hours that elected union leaders could devote to union activities (Cortázar, 1993).

Besides restricting the domain of unions, the new legislation limited the areas that could be included in collective bargaining agreements. In particular, article 12 of the new code excluded from negotiation any area that "limited the ability of the employer to organize, direct and administer the firm," thereby removing any possibility for workers to play a management role (Ruiz-Tagle, 1985, p.50). More debilitating to the formation and success of unions, however, was the provision that limited strikes to sixty days. At the end of sixty days, if an agreement had not been reached, the labor relationship was terminated and workers lost their right to collect severance. Strikers, however, could be rehired under the same terms and conditions as existed when the collective bargaining agreement had expired. This meant that their salary would not be adjusted for inflation (Meller, 1992).

The labor code also allowed for temporary as well as permanent replacement of striking workers from the first day of the strike. At any point during the strike, individual workers could abandon the strike and return to work under the conditions of the last offer made by the employer. The legislation weakened the effectiveness of strikes. Coupled with the difficult economic environment and political repression of union leaders, the new law created a sharp reduction in the number of workers participating in strikes in the 1980s. Between 1980 and 1985, less than one percent of workers (0.4 percent) participated in strikes, compared with 16.3 percent during the Popular Unity years and 12.5 percent in the second-half of the 1960s, under the Christian Democratic government of Eduardo Frei Montalva.[14]

The 1979 labor code also restricted the participation of workers in collective bargaining to workers with permanent contracts.[15] Temporary workers could no longer bargain collectively and thus lost the right to strike. The provision hurt agricultural workers in particular, since many are employed on seasonal contracts. Agricultural workers had been rallied into joining unions during the agrarian reform and accounted for 22 percent of union membership in 1972; by 1992 their share had fallen to 9.7 percent.[16] Yet despite the drop in membership, the 9.7 unionization share overstates the negotiating power of agricultural workers since a much fewer number had the right to collective bargaining.

Another important provision of the 1979 labor code was the elimination of restrictions on subcontracting. Prior to 1973, subcontracting was limited to activities that were not central to the firm. The removal of the subcontracting restriction meant that a firm anticipating a strike could arrange to subcontract production to another firm for the sixty days that the strike could last. Also, firms could hire workers through a third-party intermediary. As these workers were not technically working for the firm, they could not belong to the union.

The military government also removed restrictions on individual contracts. Before 1973, people in a variety of professions, ranging from dockworkers to bakers to hairdressers, were required to obtain authorization to practice their professions. These restrictions were eliminated, as were provisions regarding special compensation for specific workers, such as miners and oil workers (Meller, 1992).

After 1982, the government abandoned its policy of wage indexation, removing any remaining state interference in determining the market price of wages, including the minimum wage. During Allende's term, the real value of the minimum wage nearly doubled from 237 in 1970 to 474 in 1973, based on an index that sets the real value of the minimum wage in 1989 at 100. In 1974, the minimum wage fell drastically from 474 to 97. From 1974 until 1982, wages, including the minimum wage, were indexed to past inflation.[17] Because inflation was falling during this period, the policy of backward-looking wage indexation led to a 40 percent increase in the real value of the minimum wage between 1974 and 1982, allowing the real minimum wage to partially recover to 142 by 1982. Amidst the 1982 financial crisis, the government ended its wage indexation policy, causing the minimum wage to free-fall to 84 by 1987.[18] By the end of the military regime in 1989, the real value of the minimum wage was nearly sixty percent less than its value in 1970 and approximately equal to its level in 1974 (See Figure 3.3).

Figure 3.3: Real Minimum Wage, 1974-1989, Index 1989=100

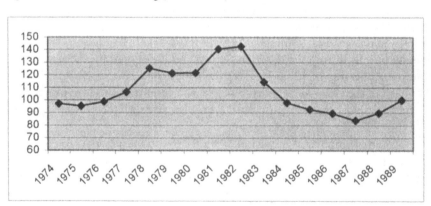

Source: Cortázar (1997).

Improvement of Labor Rights Following the Return to Democracy

Elected democratically on a platform of "growth with equity," the government of Patricio Alywin, which assumed office in March 1990, sought to improve the economic situation of workers in Chile through increases in the minimum wage and reforms to the labor code. Because of the importance assigned to ensuring a smooth transition to democracy, the government, a few weeks after its inauguration, invited national business and labor representatives to discuss and sign agreements concerning these reforms. The agreements, known as the "Acuerdo Marco Nacional Tripartito," were signed by the National Workers' Confederation (CUT),[19] the business sectors' Production and Trade Confederation (CPC), and the government. Besides the reforms agreed to by the three parties, the document was also symbolically important since it was the first time the three parties had participated in negotiations. At the negotiations, the CUT acknowledged the importance of the private sector in economic growth and development, while at the same time identifying as its objective giving workers access to the fruits and opportunities of economic growth (Campero, 2000).

The tripartite agreement led to the passage of several labor laws in 1991, 1992 and 1993. The most immediate improvement for workers was the increase in the minimum wage. During the last eight years of the military government, the minimum wage lagged behind the average wage and the rate of productivity growth of the economy. Its increase was of primary concern to the CUT, and its low real value made the increases acceptable to business (Cortázar, 1997). During Alywin's administration, real minimum wages rose an average of 6.6 percent a year. The two succeeding Concertación governments continued the policy of increasing the minimum wage, so that by 2000 it was 90 percent above its 1989 level.

Other labor laws that were passed as a result of the tripartite agreements concerned dismissal of workers, union organization and collective bargaining (See Table 3.1 for a comparison with the 1979 labor code). The revised labor code required employers to specify the cause of job dismissal, and it outlined acceptable reasons for dismissing labor without severance pay.[20] Although employers were still required to pay severance without having to specify cause of dismissal under the 1979 code, the new legislation was intended "to prevent purely arbitrary actions on the part of the employer that might be harmful to labor relations and the worker's dignity" (Meller, 1992, p.80). The severance pay limit of one month's pay per year of service was also increased to eleven months, from the five-month limit imposed in 1981.

The new labor law granted the right to form unions at the national level, recognizing the legal existence of the CUT and industry federations.

Industry-level collective bargaining was also allowed, but only if all parties were in agreement. Yet because of the strictness of the provision, less than one percent of collective bargaining agreements have extended beyond the firm level (Marshall, 1997). The new legislation facilitated union financing by allowing automatic paycheck deduction of union dues for the union as well as for any federation or confederation it belonged to. It also required that workers who were not in the union, but who receive the benefits of collective bargaining, pay dues equivalent to 75 percent of their cost. The intention of this legislation was to limit free-riding (Cortázar, 1993). In addition, greater protections were granted to union officers.

The most important change concerning collective bargaining was the removal of the sixty-day strike limit. Strikes can now continue indefinitely. Moreover, employers are no longer able to replace striking workers on a permanent basis and a greater delay is granted before the temporary replacement of workers can occur. Now if the offer made by the employer does not include an adjustment for inflation, the firm has to wait until the fifteenth day of the strike to fill the worker's slot with a temporary replacement. If an inflation increase is granted, then they can temporarily replace the striking workers on the first day. Similarly, a striker can return to work on the 30th day if an adjustment for inflation was offered or on the 15th day if an inflation-adjustment was not offered. Just as before, when more than fifty percent of striking workers return to work, the strike is legally declared over and the last offer of management is accepted de facto. In cases where no decision can be reached, the legislation encourages the use of mediation in labor disputes and states that final labor decisions be decided by forced arbitration, if necessary (Meller, 1992).

It is useful to consider what was not included in the legislation. Public sector workers and temporary workers, who were banned from joining unions during the military government, gained the right to form unions, but not to bargain collectively. Instead they are allowed to sign what is known as a "convenio colectivo" or collective agreement. The agreement, which is negotiated between management and a democratically elected group of workers—either as unions leaders or as a "negotiation group"— can be used to obtain wage increases and improved working conditions for the represented group of workers. Yet the negotiating power of the workers is very limited, as workers do not have the recourse to strike if the negotiations do not proceed as planned (Asesorías Estratégicas, 2000). Another important limitation that remains in place is the prohibition of closed union shops. Disallowing closed shops puts the burden of membership on the union and can lead to free riding by workers who do not join, but reap the benefits of there being a union. It can also weaken a union's ability to negotiate with management, as the union has a smaller membership.

The initial euphoria for business, labor and government to work together on labor reform legislation waned by the end of Alywin's term in office in 1994. In 1995, 1996 and 1997, the parties were unable to reach an agreement on the minimum wage, which was finally decided solely by the government (OIT, 1998). Disagreement remains on issues such as future increases in the minimum wage and supra-firm collective bargaining.

Weakness of Contemporary Labor Movement

The return to democracy in March 1990 energized the labor movement, causing an immediate upsurge in unionization from 507,000 workers in 1989 to 701,000 by 1991. Yet soon after, the euphoria declined. From the high of 22.4 percent of salaried workers in 1991, the unionization rate steadily fell, dropping to 15.3 percent in 1999, and then recovering slightly to 15.9 percent in 2000. In 2000, the unionization rate stood at less than two percentage points above the rate in 1986, despite the reforms to the labor legislation that gave greater protection to union leaders and strengthened worker bargaining power. As a percentage of all workers, including those in the informal and public sector, the unionization rate in Chile was 10 percent in 2000.

The fall in unionization rates exemplifies the present weakness of the Chilean labor movement, despite more than a decade of democracy. The low membership level is a symptom of larger problems that pervade the labor movement at multiple levels. Difficulties exist at the firm level in organizing workers and creating a more productive dialogue between management and labor. The contemporary Chilean labor movement has also failed to articulate a vision for labor relations in the country. Based on a handful of interviews with labor leaders and government officials, survey data, as well as secondary information, the following section gives a brief analysis of the sources of union decline since the return to democracy.

Difficulties in Organizing at the Firm Level

The ENCLA 1999 survey, conducted by the Ministry of Labor's Dirección del Trabajo, covered a wide range of labor-related topics that are useful for analyzing the impediments to union organization. The survey covered 1,300 firms across various economic sectors and regions of the country, and included the responses of managers, labor leaders (if a union existed), and randomly chosen workers. One of the reasons for the low unionization rate has been the increase in small firms in Chile. In 1966, for example, there was an average of 55 employees per employer in the secondary sector, yet by 1994, the average had dropped to 21 (Espinosa, 1996).[21] Small firms offer less receptive environments for forming unions for a variety of reasons, such as the tendency for paternalistic relations between manager and worker, as well as the increased ease workers have in communicating with management. Labor laws also inhibit the creation of unions in small firms, as a minimum of eight workers is needed to form a union, and the eight must represent at least half of the workers eligible to join. Not surprisingly, the study found that large firms, defined as those with 200 workers or more, had a unionization rate of 56.8 percent, a much higher rate than found in medium-sized firms (38.4%, 50–199 workers) or small firms (9.7%, 10–49 workers) (Dirección del Trabajo, 2000).

Part of the reason for the increase in the number of small firms is the increase in subcontracting. Subcontracting has become increasingly important in the mining sector, the most unionized sector in the economy. During the 1990s, CODELCO, the state-owned mining company, implemented a policy of subcontracting the digging of mines. In 1989, 92 percent of mining employees belonged to the core firm, while by 1995 this figure had fallen to 67 percent (Dirección del Trabajo, 1997). Partly as a result, unionization in the mining sector fell from 69 to 49 percent. In 2000, it was down to 47 percent.

In firms where a union did exist, the ENCLA survey found that 58.8 percent of workers are members of the union, a low affiliation rate. According to the survey, labor leaders in firms with unions attribute the low affiliation rate of workers to: (1) fear (40%), (2) a belief that they will not benefit from joining the union (30%), and (3) a belief that they receive more benefits from not joining union (13%). Workers responding to the survey from firms where a union does not exist gave similar reasons for why a union did not exist. In the workers' responses, "fear" drops from 40 percent to 18.5 percent, a smaller, but still substantial share of the workforce (See Table 3.2).

Table 3.2 Workers' Reasons for Not Having a Union, 1999, Percentages

Don't see benefit in having union	37.1
Receive more benefits from not having union	31.8
Fear about negative consequences on their employment	18.5
Other reasons	12.7

Source: Dirección del Trabajo (2000).

Nearly 70 percent of workers that are not part of a union either felt that they would not benefit from having one or that they would receive more benefit from not having one. This attitude can partly be explained by the apparent failure of unions to deliver gains to its members. For example, between 1998 and 2001, collective bargaining agreements averaged a one-percent increase above the rate of inflation at a time when average real wages in the economy grew by 1.8 percent.[22] As revealed in the case study of the cosmetics industry, some firms engage in the anti-union practice of granting higher wage increases to those workers that do not participate in collective bargaining. This practice is a clear example of why some workers feel that they receive more benefits by not being in the union.

Even when there is a commitment on the part of workers to form a union and bargain collectively, the union often faces an uphill battle. In February 2000 the workers of Servipag formed a union with the hope of improving their wages and benefits.[23] Servipag is a subsidiary of the Banco de Chile, started in 1990, as a place for phone, electricity and gas customers to pay their monthly bills. The company has 49 offices throughout the country, typically located in shopping centers. There are 480 workers at the branch offices and 90 workers at headquarters. The workforce is predominantly female, with completed high school education, but no experience in banking. Since 1990, the cashiers have earned the minimum wage with bi-yearly adjustments for inflation. They do not receive benefits commonly received by Chilean workers such as holiday bonuses, there are no increases for tenure, the uniforms are of low quality, and the lunch coupon of C$1,900 (Chilean) pesos (roughly US$3.50) is significantly less than the C$3,000 pesos received by workers in headquarters. Also, overtime is in practice mandatory, as well as quite extensive, given the long hours of the retail sector. Frustration with the attitude of management, low wages and poor working conditions led to the formation of the union, despite the difficulty in organizing, given the dispersion of the workforce across branches.

The goal of the union was to obtain salary increases, if not in monthly pay, then at least in bonuses for Christmas, Independence Day and vacation. Union officers explained that when these holidays arrive the workers lack the resources to enjoy them because of their low wages. In October 2001 the union presented its demands to management, asking for an increase in pay from the minimum wage of C$100,000 to C$140,000; bonuses; an increase in the lunch coupon to the level of headquarters' staff; and day care for children up to the age of four (Chilean law requires that companies pay until the child is two years old). According to the union officers, management had a "hostile attitude" towards the union from the beginning. They rejected the demands of the union outright, instead offering an adjustment for inflation, as had been given continually since 1990. The union members went on strike from 7 November 2001 until 17 January 2002. Despite repeated attempts on the part of the union to meet with management, there was no discussion during this period.

As the company had offered the union an adjustment for inflation, it was able to replace the striking workers on the first day of the strike with temporary workers. The temporary staff then received training from those workers that did not participate in the strike. In an effort to get management's attention, the union protested on January 15th outside of the company's headquarters, causing traffic problems and infuriating the company's neighbors. That day, management informed the union that they were considering their demands. On the 17th, however, they once again refused their demands. Unfortunately, more than 50 percent of the striking workers had already returned to work, which by law, meant the strike was officially over. The union was forced to accept management's offer of an inflation adjustment. The contract was signed for a two-year period, the minimum under Chilean law.

The union felt that part of its failure was due to its inexperience in collective negotiation. Union representatives were unfamiliar with the labor code, and their lawyer "abandoned them early on."[24] For example, the union had the right to have their advisors present during the negotiations, yet management did not allow it. The union could have reported this violation to the Dirección del Trabajo; it did not. Another obvious mistake was not protesting sooner in front of headquarters. After two months of not receiving pay, particularly during the holiday season, it is understandable that the drop-out rate of strikers increased.

Since the strike, the goal of the union has been to become better organized and informed in preparation for future contract negotiations. Yet this will be difficult since after the strike only fifty percent of workers belonged to the union. Lack of union membership along with some workers' willingness to stay on and train temporary replacements are significant debilitating factors to their efforts. The union officers attribute the low affiliation rate to (1) fear of the company and losing one's job, (2) a free-rider attitude and (3) allegiance to the company. In the weeks following the end of the strike, the principal concern of the union officers was that some workers that had been heavily involved in organizing the strike were being fired. The three union officers are protected from being fired by the "fuero laboral" clause of the labor code.

The collective bargaining process in Chile is a highly regulated and complicated process, dating back to the changes put in place by Marxists within the labor movement, between 1930 and 1970, to insure their control of the unions. As Bergquist (1986) explains,

> Successful manipulation of the [labor relations] system required detailed knowledge of the law, patience and tact—requirements that sapped the energies and resources of unions, impelled them into dependence on expertise supplied by middle-class professionals of the Marxist parties, and favored the emergence of leaders who proved resistant to innovation (such as worker control) when opportunities finally arose under the Marxist government that came to power in 1970 (p.72).

These conditions remain present in Chile. Union leaders need extensive legal knowledge, outside advisors and patience. Under the current collective bargaining procedure, a union must present its demands in writing to management, during a five-day period that begins exactly 45 days before the current contract is set to expire.[25] It must also certify to the Labor Office that the employer was notified. Within 10–15 days, the employer must give a written response to the workers' demands, failure to do so leads to a fine, and continual failure means eventual acceptance of the workers' demands. Upon receipt of management's offer, the workers can either accept their proposition or enter negotiations until the date set by law, at which time the workers must vote to accept the agreement or strike. If the majority of workers participating in negotiations vote in favor of a strike, it begins three days later. If the workers do not strike, the management's final offer takes effect (Asesorías Estratégicas, 2000).

According to Campero, a well-known sociologist and advisor to the Lagos administration, the rigidity of the bargaining process works in favor of management.[26] As he explains, because the timeline is so strict, management can anticipate when a strike is going to occur and can make the appropriate arrangements to prepare for the strike. For example, it could increase inventory or make arrangements to hire subcontracted employees during the strike's duration. Or, as in the case of the Servipag strike, management can contract temporary workers to begin work the first day of the strike.

The rigidity of the collective bargaining process makes it necessary for the union to receive outside counsel, particularly if its officers are new to the process. In recent years both the CUT and the Dirección del Trabajo have begun offering training to union officers. The union of Servipag workers plans to participate in this training, and the unions in the cosmetics and agroindustry sectors have already availed themselves of such training. Nevertheless, the difficulty of the process has led some unions to sign collective agreements (*convenios colectivos*) rather than the collective contracts (*contratos colectivos*) governed by the regulated collective bargaining process. In 1996, 25.7 percent of unions negotiating a contract signed a collective agreement (Asesorías Estratégicas, 2000). As mentioned earlier, negotiating a collective agreement prevents a union or negotiation group from striking.

In order to increase union affiliation, Campero recommends three reforms to the current labor code: simplifying the collective bargaining process, giving temporary workers the ability to bargain collectively, and restricting or eliminating the ability to replace striking workers. It is clear from the experience of the Servipag union that these reforms would have increased their chances of obtaining their demands.

Lack of Dialogue between Workers and Management

Another impediment to the success of the contemporary labor movement is the lack of dialogue between unions and management, beyond discussion of wages, and at times, working conditions. The effect of this lack of communication is that if workers do not want to risk fighting for a salary increase—particularly if unemployment is rising or high—there is little reason for having a union. Or, if the dialogue has been limited to wages and working conditions, workers may be encouraged to bypass unions and instead create "negotiation groups," thereby eliminating the need to pay monthly dues, while at the same time retaining the right to a regulated bargaining process that permits strikes.

The lack of dialogue stems partly from the provision in the 1979 labor reform that prohibits bargaining about the operation of a firm. This provision, which remains in effect but can be easily circumvented in practice, thwarted the development of "European-style" labor relations that could have fostered improved participation of the workforce in the activities of any given firm. Alburquerque (1999) explains that fear and distrust on the part of some employers about losing their right to property has led them to be more protective about the operation of the firm, causing them to cling to this legal restriction. Workers respond to this managerial attitude by showing little commitment to company and job loyalty. The result is mutual distrust, whereby management seeks to control worker input and lessen costs to the firm, and labor tries to bypass controls and maximize its earnings. Cooperative labor relations do not emerge from such an environment of distrust, as leaders of both labor and management are considered "successful" only if they take a hard line towards the other party (Alburquerque, 1999).

The lack of dialogue on topics other than salary and basic working conditions is evident in the results of the 1999 ENCLA survey. Because of the economic crisis, the Dirección del Trabajo included a question in its survey on consultation of management with workers concerning the crisis. Although more than 80 percent of the firms responded that the economic crisis had affected the activity of their firms, only 35.5 of firms had met with workers to discuss the crisis. When management did meet with staff, the topics discussed were limited to how cutbacks would affect workers, for example, the need for layoffs, reduction of work shifts, reduction of bonuses, as well as policies to save on raw materials and other production inputs.

Similarly, in a 1996 survey concerning consultation of management with union and workers on matters concerning the firm, less than half of firms frequently or occasionally accepted suggestions from workers regarding product quality or the production process (Dirección del Trabajo, 1997). Moreover, most workers were not consulted concerning shifts, overtime, or job transfers (See Table 3.3).

One impediment to worker involvement identified in the 1999 ENCLA survey is that in 65 percent of the firms, there exists no formal mechanism for the workers to participate in dialogue with management, either as a union or some other alternative. The study concludes that "there exists a backwardness in the country with respect to new management techniques that would provide workers a greater involvement and understanding of the production processes that competition in the modern world demands" (p.90). The lack of dialogue makes it difficult for workers to identify with the successes and difficulties of their firms and may prove a disadvantage as the country faces increased international competition.

Table 3.3 Management's Consultation with Unions and Workers, 1996

	Frequently	Occasionally	Rarely	Never	Don't know	Total
Shifts	17.7	11.0	9.7	52.9	8.7	100.0
Overtime	22.4	10.4	6.7	55.1	5.4	100.0
Transfer of job activity or location	9.0	8.4	8.4	62.8	11.4	100.0
Accepts suggestions on how to better do job	24.4	25.1	16.4	32.4	1.7	100.0
Accepts suggestions regarding quality	27.4	17.7	11.7	39.2	4.0	100.0
Accepts suggestions regarding hygiene and security	38.4	20.7	15.1	25.1	0.7	100.0

Source: Dirección del Trabajo (1997).

Problems with the Vision of the Labor Movement

Roughly 60 percent of unionized workers, or 350,000, are affiliated with the country's workers' confederation, the Central Unitaria de Trabajadores (CUT). Half of the CUT's affiliates are public sector workers. Affiliation with the CUT has declined since the beginning of the 1990s when 75 percent of unionized workers belonged to the CUT. According to the 1999 ENCLA survey, of the firms with unions, only 29.2 percent of unions belonged to the CUT and 28.8 percent belonged to a federation. The survey interprets this finding as stemming from the inability to bargain at the supra-firm level, but also proposes that "the union movement explore its own inherent dynamics in inhibiting the association of unions." Despite the inability to negotiate salaries at the supra-firm level, "there are innumerable issues that can be suitably treated by supra-firm-level unions" (p.75). For example, they suggest that federations and confederations discuss with employer groups issues such as safety and hygiene in the workplace, training, incorporation of new technologies, flexibility of work schedules, and re-skilling. The issues are particularly important for those workers that cannot be represented by the union of the firm, such as subcontracted workers (Dirección del Trabajo, 2000).

Interviews with labor experts reveal dissatisfaction with the CUT in planning and articulating a vision for Chile's contemporary labor movement. As Campero explains, the CUT is "out of touch with economic reality," they are "unable to deal with issues at the grassroots," their "discussion is very traditional, appealing to morality and ethics" rather than trying to understand the workers' new environment.[27] Campero believes that part of the CUT's difficulty in addressing firm-level issues is that it associates Chile's present-day economic model as a child of the dictatorship, and is therefore in continuous opposition to it (Campero, 2000).

Similarly, German Acevedo of the Ministry of Labor contends that there exists a tendency among union leaders to focus on larger issues, such as the economic model and trade policies, rather than on smaller, more concrete issues within the firm.[28] The focus on organizing against an economic model has kept labor relations from evolving. Magdalena Echevarría of the Dirección del Trabajo, also commenting on how "labor leaders are lost in old times," feels that the labor movement "has not been able to deal with new issues such as temporary workers or the subcontracting of personnel."[29] As she explains, the labor movement leaders know how to speak to the permanent, core union members, but not to anyone else, and in the process, they lose dynamism. She attributes part of the problem to lack of training in dealing with contemporary labor issues.

The "out-of-touchness" of the labor movement with contemporary issues results from the inability on the part of labor to break away from the model that existed prior to the military government. Frias, a longtime labor union analyst, explains how before 1973, the labor movement was aligned with political parties.[30] If the political party representing labor was in office, the government could pressure business to acquiesce to its constituent's demands. Yet since the return to democracy, government is no longer in a position to dictate to the business class. And although the government and the CUT share the same political party, the government does not need the labor movement as an electoral base. As a result, there is less dialogue between government and labor and less opportunity for the labor movement to influence change. Though this new system implies that the labor movement is now an autonomous actor, it has not adjusted to its new autonomous position, but instead waits for the government to align itself with the demands of labor (Espinosa, 1996). As this has not occurred, the labor movement has been reactive towards government and business. What labor should have done, according to Espinosa, was use the historical legitimacy won in the fight to democracy to create its own agenda, thereby forcing a response from government and business.

Part of the difficulty in adjusting to its new autonomous role lies within the leadership itself. The two presidents of the CUT in the 1990s, Manuel Bustos, followed by Arturo Martínez, were union leaders prior to the military regime and important figures in the fight for democracy during the 17-years of dictatorship. The CUT has not been able to attract "new blood," as Campero explains, because of the pervasive negative attitude within the movement. Young people have turned away from labor as a cause, favoring other causes, such as the environment. This lack of "new blood" is likely to further weaken the movement. Moreover, as Frias contends, when labor leaders with a "modern" vision come around, they face difficulty promoting their policies within the CUT. He believes this is unfortunate since the modern firm "offers opportunities to the labor movement that the CUT has not seized upon."[31]

A Low-Road Approach

The failure of Chile's contemporary labor movement to articulate a vision for labor relations in the country, beyond the extraction of higher wages, coupled with the management's protectiveness of its right to operate firms free from worker interference, has led to the predominance of "cost-based" labor relations strategies, as opposed to "value-added-based" strategies. Locke et al. (1995) identify these two labor-relations strategies in their multi-country study that analyzes the impact of changes in international competition and new technologies on employment relations in the industrialized world. The authors find that countries with weak labor market institutions are more likely to adopt a cost-based approach to labor relations, a result that can also be confirmed for Chile. Although it is not clear what the long-term implications are for the competitiveness of the firms adopting a cost-based approach, regarding labor relations, the strategy is "likely to lead to a downward spiral of wages, working conditions and labor standards and to reinforce adversarial relations at the workplace." Value-added strategies, on the other hand are "most likely to produce outcomes of mutual benefit to firms and their employers" (p.153). It therefore remains for the Chilean labor movement and the business sector to articulate and promote dialogue that can lead to more constructive labor relations to the benefit of all.

WORKING IN CHILE

The contemporary Chilean labor force is far more diverse than it was 30 years ago. Today's worker is better educated, has a more varied job history because of increased turnover, and is more likely than before to be female. But like many workers throughout the world, today's Chilean worker faces an uncertain future. Though unemployment has been reduced and labor force participation has increased, many Chileans continue to work for low wages, at long hours, and under precarious employment contracts.

Labor Supply: Who are the workers?

An important trend in labor supply in Chile is the increased participation of women in the labor force. Between 1987 and 1996, women's labor force participation jumped from 24.9 percent to 34.5 percent as opportunities increased in agroexport sectors that relied heavily on a female workforce (OIT, 1998). Female labor force participation remained at the 35 percent level into the early 2000s, which is low when compared internationally: Argentina's female participation rate is 46 percent (urban areas); Brazil's is 54 percent, while the U.S. has a female participation rate of 73 percent (ILO, 2003).

Chilean workers have also become better educated. During 1957–1965, only 6 percent of the Greater Santiago labor force had more than 12 years of schooling. By 1991–1996, 22 percent of the labor force had more than 12 years of schooling of which 15 percent were university educated (17 years or more) (See Figure 3.4.) At the same time, the number of workers with less than 12 years of schooling was cut in half from 84 percent to 43 percent, as the government pursued its policy of universal secondary education (Bravo and Marinovic, 1997).

Figure 3.4: Labor Force by Years of Schooling, Greater Santiago, 1957-1996

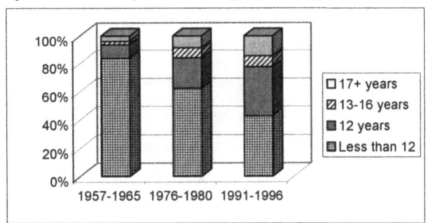

Note: Sample does not include mining and agricultural workers.

Source: Bravo and Marinovic (1997) based on Employment Survey, University of Chile

Another important feature of the Chilean workforce is the substantial share of workers employed in the informal sector. About one-quarter of Greater Santiago laborers characterize themselves as self-employed.[32] Of these workers, three percent are skilled professionals or technicians. Studies of the urban informal sector in Chile (Mizala and Romaguera, 1996; Berg and Contreras, 2004) show that the proportion of the labor force employed in the informal sector has remained constant since the 1970s at roughly twenty-five percent.

Hours, Overtime and Benefits

A worker that is hired (legally) in Chile is expected to work a 48-hour workweek at a monthly wage no less than C$105,000 (about US$190).[33] The long workweek has given Chile the dubious honor of being ranked the number one country in average number of hours worked per year, among the 49 countries ranked in the 2001 *World Competitiveness Report*. In that ranking Chile surpassed its long-time challenger, South Korea. Recognizing the excessive length of the workweek, the Chilean legislature passed a law in 2001 reducing the workweek to 45 hours in 2005. The goal is for productivity improvements to compensate for the loss of labor time.[34]

According to the ENCLA survey, 48 percent of firms operate six days per week while 51 percent operate five days. Manufacturing workers typically work a shift of six days a week, eight hours a day, plus overtime. Overtime is common in Chile, with two-thirds of workers performing overtime on a regular basis (Dirección del Trabajo, 2000). Employees who work more than 10 hours in a given day are eligible for overtime pay at time and a half. However, the first two hours of overtime are paid at the regular pay rate.

In 1981, the social security system was privatized and restructured from a government-run, pay-as-you-go system, to a private system whereby ten percent of a worker's salary is withheld and deposited into a retirement fund (AFP) of the worker's choosing. Upon retirement, the funds accumulated in the account convert into indexed annuities. In addition to the mandatory 10 percent contribution, workers pay a fee to cover the administrative costs of the AFP and to finance disability and survivors' insurance. The fee is quite high, fluctuating around three percent of earnings (Cortázar, 1997). Besides paying into their pension funds, workers must also contribute an additional seven-percent of their earnings to pay for health insurance. Employers do not contribute to either. Depending on the level of income of the worker, the worker can choose between a fully privatized health insurance system or the public system, FONASA. As the retirement and health insurance funds are tied to the worker, rather than the employer, the worker can switch jobs without affecting contribution to the funds.

Work Contracts

Under Chilean law, all employers must hire their workers under a contract signed by both parties. In practice, however, 25 percent of all salaried workers work without a contract. More violations of this provision occur in the agricultural sector, where 41 percent of workers are without contract, and in microenterprises (firms with five or fewer employees), where 49 percent of workers do not have a contract. Non-agricultural firms with more than five employees violate this provision less often, with only 12 percent of employees working without a contract (CASEN, 1998). Studies of the fruit export sector have documented the willingness on the part of low-wage seasonal workers to work without a contract, so they can avoid contributing to their retirement and health insurance funds (Barrientos et al., 1999). As the state guarantees a minimum pension that low-wage workers with sporadic employment are likely to rely upon, the remunerative gains from not having to contribute 20 percent of one's salary to the mandated funds are obvious. Nevertheless, working without a contract subjects the worker to a host of risks, such as not being paid for the job or for overtime, being paid less than the minimum wage and no access to childcare for children under the age of two.

Employment contracts can be permanent (indefinite) or temporary (definite) or by task. Regardless of the contract, workers must still earn the monthly minimum wage and must contribute to the retirement and health insurance funds. Within the non-agricultural sector, 83 percent of employees work under a permanent contract, 14 percent work under temporary contracts and 2 percent work by task. The seasonality inherent in agricultural work contributes to the increased occurrence of temporary contracts in this sector. At the time of the survey, October 1998, 39 percent of agricultural workers worked under temporary contracts and 3 percent were hired by task. Part-time employees can be hired on either permanent or temporary contracts. Their benefits accord to the type of contract they have, and do not differ due to number of hours worked. Part-time workers are also subject to the minimum wage, which is pro-rated according to the number of hours worked.

A temporary contract cannot exceed one year in length, unless the person is a manager or professional, in which case the fixed-term contract can last up to two years. A temporary contract can be renewed once; upon the second renewal, it converts into an indefinite contract. Hence, an employee can work two full years under a temporary contract if that contract is specified by time. If the contract is for a year, at the start of the third year, the worker becomes employed under an indefinite contract. If, on the other hand, the employee has been hired to perform a specific task, or for the production of a specific good that varies by season, it is easy—and legal—to circumvent the limited renewal provision, since the terms of the contract change. Thus, in the agroindustrial sector, workers are hired for the "apple juice season." Once apple juice production ends, only to be replaced by "peach juice production," the worker starts a new contract for the peach juice season. Because of the ease in continually renewing temporary contracts when hired for production seasons, agricultural and agroindustrial workers have been found to work for many years on temporary contracts (Henríquez et al., 1994).

Since the benefits system is organized around individual contributions, without an employer's contribution, there is less gain from switching to temporary and away from permanent contracts than one might expect. Nevertheless, there are some cost savings that give employers an incentive to hire workers under temporary contracts. They include:

1. Cost of having workers employed when the season is cut short for reasons beyond the company's control, such as a poor harvest;
2. Vacation pay;[35]
3. Customary benefits;[36]
4. Severance pay;[37]
5. Costs and risks associated with having workers form a union, which workers are legally entitled to do if hired under a permanent contract.

Thus, while seasonality naturally lends itself to the use of temporary contracts, there are also other reasons for why employers may workers on temporary contracts. Arguably the most damaging is the legal provision outlawing collective bargaining for temporary workers.

Subcontracting

Another way to increase "labor flexibility" is to hire workers indirectly through a third-party firm. The 1979 labor code removed the legal provision that prohibited the subcontracting of work for activities that were central to the firm. Gradually, after 1979, subcontracting began to gain importance in the economy. The ILO distinguishes between two types of subcontracting: (1) the subcontracting of production of goods or provision of services and (2) the subcontracting of workers. In the first type, a business relationship is established between two economic units, in which one sells the good or service and the other buys it. The seller decides autonomously the conditions of its workforce. Theoretically there should be no difference in the conditions of work if the good or service were produced inside the core firm or outside, unless the reason for subcontracting it is to lower costs through wage cutting, rather than for reasons of specialization (Echevarría and Uribe, 1998).

According to a survey of 58 leading firms in Chile conducted by Price Waterhouse, 50 percent of the managers surveyed would outsource only if it were to cost less than providing the service in house. This finding contrasts with a similar international survey cited in the study, which showed that only 27 percent of managers outsource to lower costs (Price Waterhouse, 1997). The Price Waterhouse study laments the views of the Chilean managers, explaining how outsourcing allows firms to "concentrate on their core competence, outsourcing everything that is not absolutely strategic, so as to not distract from the resources and capacity of management" (p.11). Thus, according to Price Waterhouse, outsourcing should be about a business relationship between two economic units that allows firms to focus on their product or service, rather than simply as a cost-saving strategy.

If a firm views subcontracting as a way to lower costs—as was the case for half of Chile's leading managers—then subcontracting is less about the product or service being provided and more about the subcontracting of workers. In this case, the service provided by the subcontracted firm is the provision of workers and the administration of the labor contract. By subcontracting the job, the core firm achieves greater numerical flexibility, undermining the job stability and high-wage advantage of the primary labor market (Harrison, 1997). The 1999 ENCLA survey found that 6.4 percent of workers in the firms studied were hired through a third party.

The incidence is quite high when compared with the European Union, where only one percent of workers are on third-party contracts (Dirección del Trabajo, 2000).

The subcontracting of workers can occur through different channels, with different implications concerning the precariousness of the work contract.[38] It can occur through more traditional forms like temporary agencies, such as Manpower,[39] or it can involve the use of a "jobber" (*enganchador*), who finds and hires workers for the firm, but retains legal authority over the work contract. Another even more precarious hiring practice is to pay workers an "honorarium,"[40] whereby the worker performs a service and then bills the company. Use of an honorarium implies a legal contract that assumes that both parties are on equal footing; it is covered by civil law rather than labor law, which recognizes the inequality between the two parties. It is highly problematic because workers are not covered under any labor protection, not only regarding health and retirement benefits, but if there is an accident of the job. Echevarría believes that the 6.4 percent figure given of the number of subcontracted workers reported in the ENCLA survey is an underestimate since employers do not disclose hiring on honorarium as they would be subject to a fine by the labor department.

Another type of subcontracting is via creation of subsidiaries within a firm. An extreme example of this form of subcontracting is the Chilean supermarket chain, Unimarc. The Unimarc parent office has a very small staff made up of a few managers. The company created a subsidiary for its cashiers and another subsidiary for its shelf stockers. There are tax advantages to having the company organized as a holding company, though the policy has implications for workers. First, the company can control how much they pay in profit-sharing, since they can declare losses in the firm that supplies the labor and profits in the firm where management is employed. The company can also circumvent fulfilling other legal obligations, such as the provision that if there are more than 25 women in a firm, it must provide childcare. The creation of subsidiaries also limits the power of unions, since collective bargaining is restricted to the firm level, which under this organization would be the firm composed of cashiers, for example.

CONCLUSION

The 1995 World Development Report on *Workers in an Integrating World* argues for the need to include labor market reform at the beginning of market reforms since "labor market adjustment is almost always slower than that of goods and capital markets" (p.102). Failure to reform the labor market can "hamper the process, as a sluggish labor market response leaves the partially reformed economy vulnerable to shocks during the transition" (*ibid.*). In Chile, unlike many other countries that have liberalized, labor market reform came before the opening of the economy.

Before the military government announced that it was seeking to open the economy to international competition, it dismissed all existing labor contracts and outlawed unionization and collective bargaining. These actions represented a backlash to the policies of the Allende government, which included nationalization of an array of private industries and mandated high real wage growth. Thus when the military government assumed power following the coup of September 1973, it reacted against the power labor had attained during the previous decades and particularly during Allende's tenure. Union leaders were persecuted and with unionization banned, workers did not have a collective recourse to negotiate employment security or wage increases. The sole institutional mechanism for wage increases was the government's periodic announcements adjusting wages for inflation, yet even in these instances, inflation was often underestimated. Workers had to bargain individually with employers, but with unemployment high, this often proved difficult. The difficult bargaining environment continued until the late 1980s, as unemployment remained high despite the legalization of collective bargaining at the firm level in 1979 following the adoption of a new labor code.

Labor thus faced two impediments: an uncertain macroeconomic environment that forced them to cling to their jobs and a political climate that repressed and then restrained their actions. It was under this environment that Chile inserted itself internationally. Jobs were lost in import-competing sectors and new jobs were created in non-traditional agroexport sectors. Yet the jobs of the globalized Chile differ in some important respects with the jobs of the past. Agroexport sectors, based on natural resource processing, are seasonal jobs that employ the bulk of the labor force on temporary contracts. Under the 1979 labor code, temporary workers are prohibited from collective bargaining. Firms can also subcontract core firm activities, allowing employers opportunities for greater numerical and wage flexibility. Thus, more than before, the minimum wage has become the only institutional form of wage increases for large groups of workers. Following the return to democracy, the minimum wage recovered the value lost during the 1970s and 1980s and contributed to increasing real earnings.

The labor movement, however, has not recovered the place it once held prior to the military government. The unionization rate stands at ten percent, just slightly above the rate during the military regime. When firms do have unions, many workers do not join. Relations between unions and management still focus on issues such as wage increases with little input from workers on how to contribute to the overall goals of the firm, as business leaders have continued with their cost-based approach to labor relations, impeding better dialogue. Unfortunately, the CUT has failed to develop an agenda that can motivate the rank and file and improve labor relations and labor participation throughout the country.

The effect of the constrained labor relations environment in an era of increased competition from abroad is evident in the two case studies that follow. Chapter 4 on the cosmetics industry and Chapter 5 on agroindustry elucidate how flexible labor laws and a weakened labor movement have become part of the competitive strategy of these industries.

Chapter Four

Foreign Competition, Corporate Strategies and Wage Suppression in the Cosmetics Industry

INTRODUCTION

The Chilean cosmetics industry, an import-competing industry, opened to external competition in 1974, when the government decided to integrate the economy internationally, lowering tariffs from an average rate of 105 percent to 10 percent by 1979. Although the industry received its first external trade shock in the latter half of the 1970s, it was not until the 1990s that imports overtook domestic production. By 2000, the wholesale value of cosmetics imports was US$100 million, a substantial share of a US$680 million domestic retail sales market. This chapter details the evolving strategies of the Chilean cosmetics industry to cope with the new competitive environment and the effect these strategies have had on the industry's workers.

The analysis of how an import-competing industry is affected by the policy shift from protected trade to free markets is more complex than the predictions of neoclassical trade theory. Free trade, after all, is a dynamic process. Tariffs and other trade barriers may be removed, but it takes time for foreign competitors to enter a market and for domestic firms to react to the new competition. Even then, strategies continuously evolve as a result of numerous external considerations such as technological improvements, a changed labor-relations environment and new management strategies.

Using the Chilean cosmetics industry as a case study, this chapter analyzes how workers are affected by the industry's transformation from local and protected to globalized. In my analysis, I discuss workers with different levels of education and training, performing different functions within the firm. In particular, my study distinguishes between workers employed in multinational subsidiaries as opposed to domestically owned firms.

Domestically owned firms are largely limited to the internal market and thus make technological and product line choices with this constraint in mind. Because of this constraint, their production is more labor-intensive. Multinational firms, on the other hand, have come to view their operations in Chile in terms of a larger regional strategy, as a result of the lowering of trade barriers in Latin America in the 1990s. Thus, competitive decisions concerning production, hiring and the concentration of resources are made within the context of regional considerations. The result has been a shift in production of multinational subsidiaries outside of Chile to markets with a larger domestic base. This shift differs from the previous strategy of multinationals of setting up local factories across Latin America in an attempt to avoid tariffs during import-substitution industrialization. Within this already complex environment, the military government's reforms to increase labor market flexibility have altered the bargaining power of workers within firms, granting management greater ability to control real wage growth.

THE COSMETICS INDUSTRY: AN OVERVIEW

The cosmetics industry is a fast-moving, consumer-goods industry that includes skin care, hair care, fragrance, makeup and personal hygiene products. In 2000, the world cosmetics industry was valued at US$122.2 billion (Koser, 2001). Throughout the world, the industry is characterized as having both strong multinational and local presence. In a 1993 classification of the participation of multinational affiliates in domestic markets, the 'toilet preparations and perfumery industry' was the only industry to achieve dominant participation by multinational affiliates (over 50 percent) while maintaining a low ratio (less than 33 percent) in local sales and employment (Dunning, 1993).

The Chilean cosmetics industry is composed of approximately 50 companies engaged in production and distribution. Roughly sixty percent of the Chilean market is foreign-owned, either through country affiliates, distributorships or licensing agreements. Firms sell their products to three consumer segments: selective (4 percent), semi-selective (20 percent) and mass-market (52 percent); the remaining 24 percent of the population do not have the resources to purchase cosmetics products (U.S. Department of Commerce, 2000). The Chilean Cosmetics Industry Chamber of Commerce estimates industry sales for 1999 at US$680 million, or approximately one percent of Chile's GDP. Per capita spending on cosmetics products is

US$45. Chile leads South America in per capita cosmetics spending, with a slight edge over Argentina, but substantially higher compared with Brazil (US$22), Uruguay (US$13) and Colombia (US$10). In comparison, residents of industrialized countries spend approximately US$150 annually per capita on cosmetics products.

The Chilean cosmetics industry has grown substantially during the 1990s, averaging 8 percent real growth in the second half of the decade. With increases in income, consumers have not only purchased more products but have also increased the range of products used, as well as upgrading to more selective goods. As a 1995 U.S. Department of Commerce study on the Chilean cosmetics market explained, "[cosmetics] products, once inaccessible to most of the population, have now entered the more 'basic' products list" (p.4).

Within Chile, the industry is turbulent, as changing multinational strategies have affected local investment patterns over the decades. In the 1980s and 1990s, most investment was brownfield, involving the acquisition of leading domestic manufacturers and distributors. With increased competition in the 1990s, many Chilean firms closed. It is important to keep in mind, therefore, that the industry has, and will continue, to evolve. This study is based on firms that still existed in the early 2000s, but their presence in the industry may be quite different in the future.

Firms Studied

In 2000, there were 50 cosmetics manufacturers and distributors, and 39 "soap and cleaning detergent" factories operating in Chile.[1] My sample includes 9 companies with 7 factories and represents upwards of thirty percent of the Chilean cosmetics market.[2] Table 4.1 gives a brief summary of the characteristics of the firms participating in the study. Firms were selected to achieve a balanced representation of multinational and domestic firms, and firms of various sizes; within these categories the selection was random.

Although there is a substantial difference in the volume of sales, domestic firms play an important role in the industry. For example, an ACNielsen survey of makeup units sold in the Greater Santiago area in January-February 2000, ranked a domestic firm as the leading seller with 33 percent of units sold, followed by the multinational M2 with 16 percent, and the domestic firms, C2 with 9.6 percent and C4 with 4.3 percent. Yet as M2 charges higher prices, it led the ranking in dollar sales. Thus, Dunning's classification of the world cosmetics and toilet preparations industry as dominant in multinational participation but with low concentration in local sales and production is consistent with the experience of Chile (Dunning, 1993).

Table 4.1 Characteristics of Participating Firms

FIRMS	Entry	Principal Products	Local Production?	Total Emp.	Prod. Emp.	Consumer Segment	Sales* ($US mil.)
Multinationals (100% Foreign-Owned)							
M1	1952	Hair dye, hair care	Not since 1998	151	4	Selective, semi-selective, mass market	n.a.
M2	1984	Hair care, hair dye, makeup, cream, fragrances	Just hair care products	500	500	Selective, semi-selective, mass market	$57
M3	1983 (2nd entry)	Hair care, personal hygiene, diapers, cleaning detergent	Just diapers	400	250	Selective, semi-selective, mass market	$150
M4	1977	Makeup, cream, fragrances, hair care (60% of sales are in cosmetics)	Subcontract production locally	470	0	Mass-market (door-to-door sales)	$105
Chilean-Owned							
C1	1979	Hair care, hair dye, toothpaste, liquid saccharin	Yes	170	70	Semi-selective, mass-market	$6
C2	1917	Cream, makeup, fragrances	Yes	180	80	Semi-selective, mass-market	n.a.
C3	1956	Makeup, nail polish, fragrances	Yes	45	22	Mass-market	n.a.
C4	1938	Cream, makeup, suntan lotion, fragrances	Yes	95	45	Selective, semi-selective, mass market	n.a.
C5	1986	Aerosol, cream, powder, hair care, nail polish	Yes	239	166	Maquila – doesn't sell final goods	$3.5

*Multinational sales are for Chilean subsidiary.

Source: Interviews with company managers. Sales data for multinational firms from ECLAC's Database on Transnational Companies, 1999; M3 and M4's sales data include non-cosmetic items; most managers declined to share sales information during interviews.

The Manufacturing Process

The manufacturing process of an industry indicates the technological limitations and opportunities for upgrading, capital-labor trade-offs and employment needs of an industry. Cosmetics production follows the "small batch" production model, meaning the factory is "organized as a succession of workshops dedicated to the production of small batches of standardized or semi-standardized items." This differs from plants "organized in line that produce in mass one item, or part of an item, standardized and homogenous" (Katz, 1986, p.20). In-line production is also commonly referred to as "continuous flow production;" likewise, small-batch production can be thought of as "discontinuous."

The organization of the shop floor as continuous versus discontinuous flow production will affect the physical configuration of the plant, the type of equipment used, the organization of the productive process, and the relative shares of skilled, semi-skilled and unskilled workers. It is not necessarily the case that a continuous-flow production facility uses fully automated equipment and has a higher capital-to-labor ratio. Production model, level of automation, and the capital-to-labor ratio are three separate concepts that, though often intertwined, can be separated. Different degrees of automation exist within small-batch facilities. A firm's choice of production model and technology depends on: (1) the type of product elaborated, (2) the size of the market or the forecast production volume, and (3) the relative price of production factors.[3]

The number of hours spent on specific activities differs greatly between continuous flow and small-batch production facilities. In continuous flow production, the goal is for 70 percent of working hours in the factory to be spent on operation activities. Quality inspections are conducted without stopping or slowing operations. Input, intermediate and final products move through the different stages of operation continuously, without slowing the process. Since the goal of continuous flow is to maximize capacity utilization in order to recover the sunk costs of the machinery, factories organized along these lines often operate 24 hours a day, seven days a week, or at least strive to do so.

The following example of facial cream production illustrates the discontinuous nature of small-batch cosmetics production. Production of cosmetics products involves mixing different chemicals and then packaging the resulting product in containers. Different workshops within the factory are dedicated to the production of different products, or the same product, but at different stages in the transformation process. In the production of facial creams, a "compounder" (or *fabricante*) is in charge of emptying different pre-measured bags of chemicals into a reactor. The reactor, which is powered by heat from the broiler, mixes the ingredients under extremely high temperatures (for four hours in the case of facial cream), followed by a final cold-temperature mixing. During the four hours of mixing, the compounder monitors the temperature via a displayed read-out to ensure the temperature is within the targeted range. After the mixing, the vat is stored in a separate sealed area of the factory, typically for several days. The reactor must be cleaned before it can begin processing another product. During storage, the company's in-house laboratory staff performs quality control tests on the batch. Once the facial cream is ready to be poured into bottles, the vat is transferred from the storage area to the filling lines. The barrel of cream is placed on a funnel-like object that fills empty jars, which pass through on a short assembly line. "Envasadoras" (literally, female bottlers) then place the tops on the jars. The products are individually bar coded and then packaged into boxes for distribution. Storage workers retrieve the boxes from the filling area and take the boxes to the outgoing warehouse to await distribution.

In the example of cream production, there are two operations: mixing chemicals in the reactor and filling bottles; and four separate transport activities: bringing the raw materials to the reactor to be mixed, transferring the mixed product to the storage area to undergo inspection and await filling, transferring the batch to the filling line, and finally, transferring the packed boxes to the storage area to await distribution. There is also one inspection made and three different times when the goods are stored (storing the raw materials, the intermediate goods, and the final goods).

In general, discontinuous flow production is characterized by greater relative employment of skilled and semi-skilled as compared with unskilled workers. At its extreme, this is conceptualized in the historical debate over the benefits of skilled craft production, as utilized in Western Europe at the beginning of the 20th century, versus mass-production technologies, employing scores of unskilled workers, as developed in the United States (see Piore and Sabel, 1984).

Compounders, who are in charge of specific transformation processes, have more responsibility than line workers in charge of just one task, and by definition, utilize more skills, though these skills are learned on the job. In the case of the facial cream production, for example, the compounder responsible for the reactor must prepare and clean the machine prior to using it and then must ensure that the correct raw materials are placed in the reactor, or else risk damaging a vat's worth of products. Nevertheless, small-batch cosmetics production in Chile employs a significant number of envasadoras (roughly three-quarters of the production staff), an unskilled occupation that can be automated for standardized product lines. Yet Chilean cosmetics factories choose not to automate these positions, since the companies produce a diverse range of products and bottle cap machines would have to be constantly adjusted for the size and shape of the bottle being filled. Only with a narrow, mass-produced product range, or high labor costs, would it make sense to automate this task.

In the United States, cosmetics production is also organized in batches, though batch size is typically larger and thus offers greater economies of scale. Small-batch production requires that time be spent setting up the lines; cleaning, sanitizing and setting up the filling equipment; performing quality control checks; training line workers; and tearing down the lines. These activities take about the same amount of time regardless of the size of the run; making large runs much more cost effective than small runs (Baker, 2001). It also becomes more worthwhile to mechanize certain tasks with larger runs.

Backward and Forward Linkages

Most cosmetics firms in Chile, both locally and foreign-owned, are horizontally structured. The principal backward linkages of the industry are the bottles or jars that hold the products and the raw chemical ingredients used in production. Large plastic receptacles are supplied locally as it is not cost effective to transport bottles full of air, though small plastic containers, such as those used in make-up products, or bottle tops, can be cost-effective to transport. The quality of locally produced plastic is considered to be good. The firms that produce the containers have the ability to produce an extensive selection of shapes of bottles and tubes, with concomitant printing capabilities. All cosmetics firms contract outside suppliers to produce containers, with the exception of two large domestic manufacturers, who produce shampoos, soaps and lotions for the low end of the market, and manufacture their own plastic bottles. The grade of plastic bottles that they produce is noticeably worse than the grade of plastic used by the firms who rely on outside suppliers. As their market segment is low-end, however, they compete more on price than on appearance, allowing them to use lower-grade plastic.

Chemical ingredients are, and always have been, imported from abroad, as the volumes produced by raw material machines are too large for the Chilean market. For example, one machine that makes the ingredients used in lipsticks produces enough for 32 million units per year, yet the entire Chilean lipstick market is 6 million units per year. For this reason, nearly 95 of the raw materials used in production are imported from Europe and the United States. Chemical raw materials account for roughly ten percent of firms' costs. In the last half of the 1990s, the price of raw material inputs fell by 10–15 percent as a result of technological advances that lowered production costs. The emergence of large distributors who consolidate orders for different purchasers, both domestic and foreign-owned, and ship the orders in much larger amounts, lowered transport costs, also contributing to lower raw materials prices.

Important forward linkages for the industry are advertising and related services as well as the retail outlets that sell the products. An image-conscious industry such as cosmetics traditionally dedicates substantial resources to marketing and publicity, hiring advertising companies and retaining in-house marketing staff.

Intensifying Competition

Although initially alarmed by the government's 1974 announcement that tariffs would be reduced to 10 percent by 1979, Chilean cosmetics firms actually faced little competition from imports during the 1970s and 1980s. The economic crisis of the 1980s, coupled with the temporary increase in tariffs following the crisis, resulted in an average decade fall of final good cosmetics imports of 4.2 percent. During the 1970s and 1980s, cosmetics and personal hygiene imports were limited to high-end niche products, such as name brand perfumes sold in department stores. In the 1990s, imports diversified in terms of product range, as well as consumer market group. A strong economy, along with multinational fervor to capture new markets, led to a real annual increase of final good cosmetics imports of 66.5 percent between 1990 and 2000. By 2000, imports totaled US$100 million, a significant portion of the US$680 million cosmetics retail sales market (See Figures 4.1 and 4.2). Increased imports of economically priced, mass-market products in the 1990s threatened the survival of companies that had previously been untouched by import competition.

Figure 4.1: Cosmetics Imports, Finished Goods, 1980-1989, US$ Million 2000

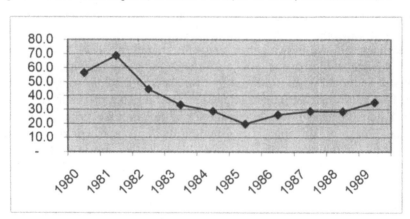

Source: Author's calculations based on data from Banco Central.

Figure 4.2: Cosmetics Imports, Finished Goods, 1990-2000, US$ Million 2000

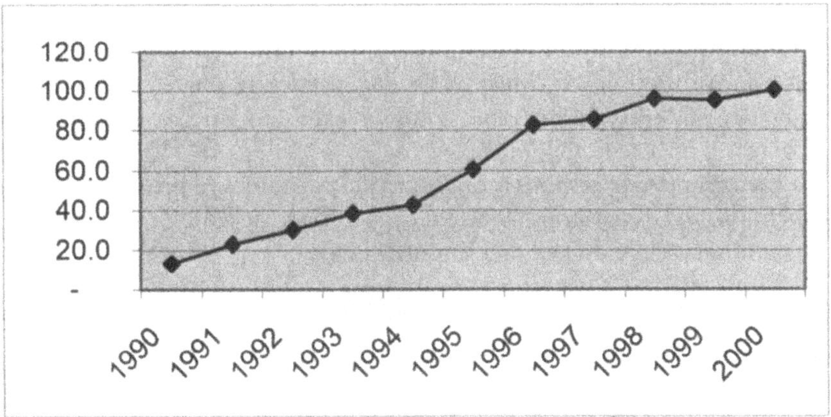

Note: Because of a change in classification of cosmetics products in 1990, the two periods had to be separated and a growth rate could not be calculated for 1990.

Source: Author's calculations based on data from Banco Central.

During the same period, cosmetics companies faced cost pressures on the retailing end, with the growth of "hypermarkets," as well as supermarket and pharmacy chains. The U.S. supermarket model was introduced into Chile in the 1960s, yet it was not until the mid-1980s that supermarkets—defined as having three or more checkout lanes—began to take hold and expand in square footage. At the end of the 1980s, over 40 percent of the population shopped at supermarkets; by century's end, 63 percent of the population shopped regularly at supermarkets. According to the supermarket industry association,[4] supermarket penetration cannot surpass 70 percent of the population since rural areas constrain supermarket growth. Hypermarkets, which have 10,000 m² of floor space, first opened in Chile in the mid-1990s with the entrance of the multinationals, Jumbo and Carrefour. In the early 2000s, there were 21 hypermarkets in the country and they accounted for 28 percent of supermarket sales. Nearly 20 percent of sales went to the industry leader, D y S, which also holds an additional 9 percent market share through its regular supermarkets. To compete with D y S and other giants, small supermarket chains have formed an association, called M.A.S., which centralizes purchasing and produces a generic line of products.

Industry domination by a few large supermarket chains as well as the consolidation of buying power of the smaller, traditional supermarkets means that retailers have exerted pressure on cosmetics firms to keep prices down. Large chains and hypermarkets also rent their shelf space, a practice foreign to the traditional retail outlets. Though renting shelf space only accounts for 5 percent of a supermarket's revenues, it adds to cosmetics firms' costs, as does the policy of requiring the firm to restock the product. More importantly, the increased purchasing power of the retail sector keeps prices, and profits, down. Meanwhile, independently owned pharmacies and markets with long-established relations with domestic cosmetics firms are going out of business.

The competitive responses of cosmetics companies to growing import competition and retail consolidation have varied, depending on whether they are domestically owned or a multinational.

COMPETITIVE STRATEGIES: THE FERVOR OF THE MULTINATIONALS

Multinational activity, in Chile and elsewhere, has undergone two expansionary waves in the last half of the 20th century. The first wave has been referred to as the "golden age of multinational expansion," and lasted from the post-war period until the global economic downturn of the mid-1970s and early 1980s (Bailey et al., 1993). The second wave began in the late 1980s, when multinationals re-surged again, primarily through mergers and acquisitions of national and multinational companies.

Multinational entrance into Chile has followed the global pattern, though the first wave came to an earlier halt, as the 1970 election of the socialist government of Salvador Allende raised fears that multinational firms would be expropriated. Following the debt crisis of the early 1980s, multinationals established operations in Chile by purchasing existing factories or distributorships, and taking advantage of the opportunity to purchase struggling, and in some cases, bankrupt Chilean firms at reduced prices.

Regionalizing Production

The competitive strategies of multinational companies in host countries are not solely the result of the economic policies and political environment of the host country, but also depend on the economic policies of other countries in the region, as well as on companies' internal policies. Although free trade reforms were initiated in Chile in 1974, it was not until the 1990s that neighboring countries adopted similar policies to reduce final good tariffs. Factories that had opened in Latin American countries to "tariff-hop" during import-substitution industrialization closed in the 1990s after the region embraced free trade, making it possible to establish regional production centers to serve the different country markets.

In 1998, M1 closed its Chilean factory of 32 years.[5] The decision to close the factory was part of a regional strategy for Latin America, centered on Brazil, the company's third largest market outside of Germany, where it is headquartered. A regional management office was established in Brazil in late 1998 to achieve "efficient management of the entire region's business and closer proximity to the markets" (1999 annual report). Part of this strategy centers around the harmonization and development of regional products. This means that the same product—both contents and packaging—is sold in Brazil, Chile and the rest of Latin America.[6] The strategy involves centralizing regional production in Brazil and Mexico, with Brazil supplying South America and Mexico supplying itself, the Caribbean and Central America. In 1999, the factory in Colombia closed and the Argentine factory was expected to close by the mid-2000s. The Brazilian factory has been expanded and modernized to serve all of South America, and is five times larger than the closed Chilean factory.

In 1991, the Chilean factory employed 100 production workers. When it closed in July 1998, it employed 75 workers. After closing, four workers were kept to place labels on the imported goods. Other operations, such as administration and sales, were little affected by the factory's closing. Production equipment was sold second-hand to domestic cosmetics firms and the factory was reconfigured as administrative offices and storage.

The decision to close the Chilean factory came from company headquarters. The Chilean subsidiary fought the decision up until the actual closure and management is still not pleased with the decision, as it has raised its costs. Since the shutdown the subsidiary has been importing products primarily from Argentina, but increasingly from Brazil as well. Importing is costly because of transportation costs and the expense of holding larger inventories. Though shipping from Argentina takes three days, compared with ten days from Brazil, shipments from both countries must pass over the Andes, which often causes delays, especially in the winter months. Inventories were especially high prior to the harmonization of products within the region, as other factories had to make special production runs for the Chilean subsidiary and thus demanded that they purchase greater quantities. With product harmonization, the subsidiary can purchase smaller lots, thus lowering inventory costs. Yet harmonization also means that the subsidiary has had to spend additional monies on marketing to "introduce the new look" to the Chilean consumer. Lack of in-house production has also resulted in a loss of flexibility in production decisions. So far, the benefit of modernizing the Brazilian factory and increasing the economies of scale has not been enough to compensate the subsidiary for the added expenses of shipping, holding larger inventories and reduced flexibility. Only if the product cost were to fall enough to compensate for these added expenses would the regional strategy prove beneficial to the

Chilean subsidiary. Thus the Chilean subsidiary is essentially subsidizing the Brazilian operation, which has benefited from the company's regionalization and harmonization strategy as its overall costs have fallen.

M2 opened a subsidiary in Chile in 1984, during the second wave of multinational expansion.[7] In the 1960s the multinational had entered into an agreement with a local cosmetics company to distribute the firm's products. In 1984, the multinational purchased that same local cosmetics company, which included a small production factory. M2 felt that the Chilean market had strong potential for growth, which, coupled with a favorably perceived regulatory environment, led the firm to invest. In addition, the time was ripe for acquisition, as many Chilean companies had gone bankrupt during the economic crisis of the early 1980s, making cheaply priced factories and manufacturing equipment readily available to foreign investors.

The Chilean subsidiary is one of eight subsidiaries in Latin America and one of four subsidiaries—along with Argentina, Brazil and Mexico— that has a factory. The Chilean factory employs 60 production workers to produce shampoo and conditioner, the only product line not imported into the country. Hair dye, makeup, cream, and lotion are all imported. In other Latin American countries that are not large enough to warrant establishment of a subsidiary, the company's products are sold through a distributing agent. Country presence is part of the firm's "global brands strategy," the principle that "a women should be able to find her product anywhere in the world." Like M1, this strategy involves harmonizing products in order to increase purchase volumes and control costs. Harmonization has led the firm to concentrate on 10 global brands, which now make up 85 percent of sales, while a "whole list of [other] brands has disappeared."[8] The global brands strategy imposes strict quality standards and packaging requirements on all production centers.

In 1996, M2 purchased a leading global mass-market makeup company and introduced the brand later that year into Chile. To introduce the brand, the firm bought Chile's leading makeup company. Almost immediately after purchase, the multinational discontinued the Chilean makeup product line, replacing it with the product line of the global makeup company that M2 had recently purchased. In early 2000, the Chilean factory was closed. Fifty workers were laid off with severance pay, while 20 employees were transferred to other divisions within the subsidiary. The makeup line, which presently leads the Chilean market on the basis of sales,[9] is imported from a single factory in the southern United States. The general manager of the Chilean subsidiary explained that the factory was closed because it was not profitable to produce the makeup in Chile. The

Chilean market is small and only requires 3–4 million units per year. In order to be profitable, at minimum, the factory would need to produce 12–14 million units per year. The southern U.S. factory, which employs 1,150 workers, produces 100 million units per year, enough for its product line around the world. Indeed, fifty percent of its sales are outside the U.S.

The multinational's decision to purchase the Chilean makeup company in 1996 was made not in order to locate production in the country, but rather, as the general manager stated, "as a way to buy the market." Though he would not expand on this point, it seems likely that the company purchased the trademark with its accompanying factory knowing that it would be more cost-effective to import the products from the Southern U.S. factory. Yet, by taking over the company it could capture the market without having to engage in a costly advertising battle. Interestingly, in January 2000 this same multinational purchased the leading Argentine mass-market makeup company, with 1999 sales of $17 million. The acquisition was intended to give the company a key position in the Argentine market (Company Press Release, January 27, 2000) and follows the CEO's strategy of "continuing to make regular small to medium-sized acquisitions. . . . that will complete either our brand portfolio, our technology families, or our geographical presence."[10]

M3's presence in Latin America began in Mexico in 1946, with the opening of its first Latin American subsidiary.[11] In the 1980s the company expanded its operations through numerous acquisitions, including a pharmaceutical line and three leading cosmetics and perfume companies. The acquisitions "fuelled the company's globalization plans, dramatically expanding [the company's] international presence" (company web page). By 1993 over 50 percent of the company's sales were from outside the United States, leading the company to reorganize in 1995, from a U.S. and international division, to four regional divisions covering North America, Latin America, Asia and Europe/Middle East/Africa. The new structure required each region to report to a single operating officer.

M3 had operated in Chile during the 1960s, but sold its operation in 1970, following the election of Salvador Allende. The company had lost its factory in Cuba in 1961 and feared additional expropriations. In January 1983, M3 once again began operations in Chile. When the company re-entered the market, it bought an existing medium-sized, family-owned cosmetics company, which according to other firms, had been quite successful. The factory operated under M3 until 1995, producing the company's line of shampoo, conditioners and deodorants. An additional factory, which at present produces eight of the company's twenty diaper products, was opened in the 1980s and remains in operation.

M3 has production facilities in most countries in the region, as a result of its pre-1990 strategy to establish factories in various countries to avoid tariffs. When tariffs began to drop throughout the region, the company began to regionalize operations. Nevertheless, many of the country factories have been kept in operation by having them specialize in certain products or certain lines of products, which are then exported to other Latin American countries. As the company sells roughly 300 products ranging from laundry detergent, to toiletries and cosmetics, to snack and pet food, the company is better able to disperse operations than its competitors. Shampoo and conditioner are now imported from Mexico into Chile, while deodorant is imported from the U.S. The locally produced diapers are exported to Colombia, Venezuela, Peru and Argentina.[12]

An exception to the strategy of regionalizing production is the case of M4, a direct-sales multinational, which subcontracts production to local Chilean manufacturers in order to offer a more diverse product line. Direct sales means that the products are sold door-to-door by representatives who order products from the company based on the sales they have made, earning a mark-up on the product. Since the selling strategy is more personal, the company offers a wider range of products. Sixty percent of the company's sales are in cosmetics products (makeup, cream, perfume, hair care), while the other 40 percent is in clothing and home furnishings.[13] The general manager explained that oftentimes, color demands are unique to a country, making it difficult to supply the product from abroad, since the foreign factory would have to make special runs for the subsidiary's color specifications. For this reason, the company produces 90 percent of its products domestically through local contractors.

M4 first began selling its products in Chile in 1977, importing from Argentina and then Brazil. When the decision was made to produce locally, the company felt that the small size of the Chilean market did not warrant establishing a company-owned production facility and opted instead to subcontract production. The multinational created a locally owned firm to produce according to its design, standards and specifications. The equipment and raw materials were provided by the multinational. The local producer then charged the multinational a "vendor charge" based on the number of units produced in a given year. This plant also supplied the Bolivian and Peruvian markets. In 1999, the multinational began subcontracting production to another factory and renegotiated its contract with the original local producer, selling them the equipment. Both subcontractors operate as maquilas in that the multinational supplies the bottles and raw ingredients importing them from its distribution centers. The firms then mix the materials and fill the bottles, and the multinational arranges to pick up the finished lots and deliver them to the company's distribution center. By externalizing production, M4 gains flexibility in responding to volatile changes in demand.[14] Ninety percent of the company's cosmetics products are produced locally, with the other 10 percent imported from the U.S. and Mexico. Imported items, such as eyeliners, require more advanced machinery for production.

The decision by multinationals to import finished goods or manufacture locally is affected not only by a company's internal strategy, but also by trade policies within each country as well as within the surrounding region. For the Chilean cosmetics industry, trade liberalization throughout Latin America in the 1990s determined the decision to regionalize production, rather than Chile's liberalization in the 1970s. Other considerations, such as the size of the domestic market, transport costs, and exchange rate volatility also play an important role in the decision. Most cosmetics companies establish regional production sites, sometimes to Chile's benefit, but typically not. One example of a beneficial choice is the May 2000 decision by another multinational (Lever) to invest $20 million in restructuring and expanding its Santiago factory to serve, along with Brazil, as one of two regional toothpaste production facilities in South America. The Chilean facility will produce for the domestic market as well as export to Peru, Colombia, Venezuela, the Caribbean and Central America.[15]

Standardization, Larger Runs and Material Purchases

By consolidating small, national factories into regional production centers, multinational firms also increase their leverage with suppliers. With regionalization, factories can purchase chemical raw materials in mass allowing them to negotiate a much lower price. This is true both of common ingredients that can be sold and delivered in tank-wagon trucks rather than the more costly drums, and of high-cost "magic" ingredients, such as botanical extracts used in shampoos. Concentration levels of the magic ingredients are minimal (less than one percent), yet chemical producers sell them in units of ten kilos, nine of which may be not be needed by a small production facility.[16]

In addition, increasing the size of the production run lowers per-unit costs. As mentioned previously, runs require similar set-up and tear-down times regardless of whether they are large or small; thus the larger the run, the lower the per unit cost. Also, by standardizing products, the factory can design machinery to automatically fill and cap containers, decreasing the number of *envasadoras* employed. The trade-off with automation is that it offers the firm less flexibility in product type and design. Companies must identify key products, and then develop a product look and packaging that will sell across countries.

Once a multinational's product designs are finalized, the goods are produced at the regional production center and exported to neighboring countries for sale and distribution. In the process, country subsidiaries narrow their operations, concentrating solely on the marketing and sale of the product in the home country. Factories are closed and the relatively well-paid, low-skilled factory workers find themselves out of work with only a severance check in hand. Unions cannot help these workers as they too cease to exist. Sales workers, product promoters, marketing specialists and general administrative personnel are left behind to peddle the newly harmonized goods. The defunct factories are dismantled and the equipment is sold locally to other cosmetics manufacturers. With few exceptions, regional strategies by multinationals have contributed to deindustrialization in Chile.

Loss of Backward Linkages

The decision to shut local factories has also affected the local plastic and glass container industry, an important backward linkage generated under ISI. "Plásticos" is a family-owned and run, plastic-resin-transformation company that opened its doors in 1950, specializing in the production of plastic bottles for the cosmetics and food industries.[17] Eighty percent of the company's sales are to multinational companies. Since 1997 business has suffered. In 2000, they laid-off 100 workers, reducing their staff to 240. Although the Chilean recession of the late 1990s contributed to falling sales, most of the company's financial problems were caused by the loss of contracts with multinational firms, which have regionalized their operations outside of the country. At the same time that Lever consolidated its toothpaste operations in Santiago to serve Western South America, it moved the region's deodorant production to Brazil. Plásticos had manufactured their deodorant bottles and lost this business with their move. Similarly, the company lost its contract with M1 when it closed its Chilean factory.

In general, exporting is not an option for large plastic bottle manufacturing since it is not cost effective to transport empty containers. Small plastic containers, such as those used in makeup products, or bottle tops, can be cost-effective to transport. Plásticos produces tops for a multinational that distributes products in the U.S. and Mexico, as well as for another multinational that sells to Argentina and Brazil. Nonetheless, the volume gained from exporting bottle tops does not compensate for the loss in local bottle production. Exporting, as seen in this example, will not solve the problems created by multinational regionalization.

Because firms rarely ship plastic containers overseas, Plásticos enjoys some protection from imports, but not from increased local competition. In 1994 an Australian packaging multinational expanded its ventures in Chile by purchasing and upgrading a local Chilean plastic-resin transformation manufacturer that had been Plásticos' main competitor. Plásticos responded by taking out loans to purchase new machinery, taking advantage of available cheap credit. Though the machinery purchases have allowed them to blow more sophisticated molds and have improved overall productivity, the high debt ratio combined with declining sales has placed the company in a vulnerable financial position. The president of Plásticos sees a grim future for the industry as a whole, stating that the Australian multinational's investment had not fared well either. And though the president lamented the possible demise of his grandfather's business, he admitted his willingness to sell the company if someone were to offer to buy.

Increase in Forward Linkages: Advertising

Forward linkages from the cosmetics industry have not been affected by the closing of local factories. An important forward linkage, advertising, has benefited from the multinational policy of maintaining distribution and sales offices in the country and from the increased competitive environment. An image-conscious industry such as cosmetics traditionally spends much of its resources on advertising. According to data from the manufacturing census survey, spending on advertising has grown significantly since 1990, tripling between 1990 and 1997, after growing slowly during the 1980s.

The Chilean advertising industry been boosted by the introduction of new products into the market by both multinational and domestic firms. For example, in 1998, M3 introduced its washing detergent into the Chilean market, directly competing with another well-established multinational. This resulted in a publicity war and an increase in advertising spending on detergent from US$500,000 in 1998 to US$1.8 million in 1999 (Martinez, 2000).

Increased spending on advertising has also resulted in a rise in the hiring of advertising-related workers by multinational firms. During the 1990s, M2 introduced its entire product line into the Chilean market, leading to a substantial increase in its local marketing and sales staff. Between 1990 and 2000, employment at the Chilean subsidiary increased from 200 to 500, despite the closing of the local makeup factory and with it, the loss of 50 production jobs. The general manager did not foresee further increases in staff for the 2000s since all of the company's principal products had been introduced into Chile.

FACING COMPETITION: THE COMPETITIVE STRATEGIES OF THE DOMESTIC FIRMS

During the 1980s, most domestic firms were isolated from competition with multinationals, as domestic firms sold to the middle and low-end consumer market, while multinationals sold to the high-end consumer market. The somewhat isolated position eroded in the 1990s as multinationals refocused their competitive strategies, creating direct competition for local firms. In 1996, for example, M2 revealed its intention to increase sales in Chile through its "trend towards mass-market products," which included the introduction of a mass-market makeup line.[18] This represented a break from it original strategy of the early 1980s, in which the company competed in the high-end market segment with lotions and perfumes imported from France and in the upper-middle-end consumer segment through its locally produced line of shampoos. By the mid-1990s, the firm had dropped its shampoo prices to compete with Chilean shampoo producers for the mass-market consumer segments. At the same time, an American shampoo company opened a factory in Peru and began shipping to Chile, which allowed it to lower its prices. The multinational's decision to enter the mass market directly affected Chilean companies that had previously been untouched by multinational competition.

The competitive strategies developed by domestic firms to face increased import and multinational competition consisted primarily of diversifying the product base to offer a broader range of cosmetics products, as the small domestic market limits specialization. Companies also responded by improving their stock of machinery, sometimes importing new equipment from abroad, but mostly taking advantage of the cheaply and readily available second-hand equipment of closed multinational factories.

Product Diversification as the Predominant Competitive Strategy

Small batch production allows, and indeed, facilitates product diversification. With little extra investment, firms can increase the range of goods they offer, diversifying their risk and staking out market share in new areas. Product diversification also allows better use of excess capacity in the factories. Chilean cosmetics firms typically operate 48 hours a week, in accordance with the normal workweek, with some overtime when preparing for the peak holiday season, but with a great deal of downtime otherwise. Thus firms are easily able to expand output.

Product diversification can also help companies at the retail end since they must rent shelf space at the supermarket and pharmacy chains. By offering smaller quantities of more products, firms increase the possibility of sales compared with filling the same shelf space with fewer product lines. Although a wider assortment of goods requires more frequent re-shelving, this is less costly than holding inventories of the same product on rented shelf space.[19]

C1, which has been in business since 1979, specializes in the production of shampoo, hair dye, creams and liquid soap.[20] Its 2000 sales were approximately US$5 million and it employed 170 workers, placing it in the category of medium-sized enterprise according to Chilean classification. In 1995, the firm was forced to lower its shampoo prices in response to competition from multinational firms. The company's owner realized that if the company did not make changes it would go out of business, so the leadership began looking for products that were not sold in Chile, but that they felt would sell well in the country. They introduced the U.S. Sesame Street brand shampoo into Chile by obtaining the license to produce the product in Chile. For another shampoo, a high-priced U.S. brand, rather than obtaining the license, C1 produced a similar-looking product, a practice known as benchmarketing. Also, pet shampoos were scarce in the country so they began making a dog shampoo to sell at pet supply stores. In 1995, the company branched out to non-cosmetic product areas by producing a liquid artificial sweetener to sell in supermarkets. The company had noticed that there was only one brand of liquid saccharin offered in the country and it was only sold in pharmacies. C1 was able to under price the competitor and offer the product at supermarkets. By 2000, they had fifty percent of the market, despite the entrance of new competitors.

C2 first began operations in 1917, selling a line of facial cream that retains a strong consumer following. When the present owner bought the company in 1995, the company was losing money and was nearly insolvent.[21] The owner diversified the product line, introducing makeup and perfume, as well as expanding the types of lotions offered to include body lotions and skin treatments. The company also invested in updating the "look" of the product by redesigning the packaging and undertaking marketing campaigns to introduce the new look and product line to its traditional consumer base. The strategy was a success, leading to a 13 percent growth in sales between 1996 and 2000.

C3 began operating in 1956 as a distributor of pharmaceutical accessories.[22] In 1960 it opened a factory to manufacture perfumes and colognes for sale at local pharmacies. Over time the product offerings of the company expanded to include makeup, lotion, shampoo and deodorant. In 1974, when the owner heard that the tariff rate, which had just been reduced to 30 percent, would drop to 10 percent, he was certain his company would go out of business. Although competition steadily grew, it was not until the 1990s that C3 felt the pinch of globalization. At this time, C3 was manufacturing 4,000 tons of shampoo per year, but had to stop selling it, as it was no longer profitable to produce with the decline in price. It also stopped distributing another high-volume sales item, a deodorant line imported from England. Instead, the company diversified into areas with smaller markets, focusing on the low-end decorative cosmetic segment, which offered the firm greater protection from multinational competition. It expanded its range of decorative cosmetics and also began importing hair and makeup accessories. By 2000, the company was selling over 300 types of cosmetic products, of which imports accounted for twenty percent of the firm's sales. C3's competition is other Chilean firms, and it competes on the basis of price, quality and product presentation. No monies are dedicated to advertising.

C4 differs from the other domestic firms in that it manufactures more exclusive products for sale at department stores.[23] Because it concentrates more on the upper-end segment of the market, it began to feel the effects of import competition earlier, in 1985, and particularly during 1985 to 1990. C4 was founded in 1938 and in the 1960s was bought by its present owners, who also own a small pharmaceutical company. The present owners transformed the company from an importer of perfumes and colognes for sale on the domestic market, to a manufacturing company that produced perfumes and colognes domestically. During the next twenty years the company grew, selling perfumes and colognes on the local market. In the second half of the 1980s, C4 was losing business to multinationals and decided to refocus its competitive strategy.

The company expanded the range of products beyond perfumes and colognes to produce facial creams, suntan lotions and a complete line of makeup. One advantage that they identified over multinationals is that they can develop and test a product on the market much more cheaply and quickly than a multinational, which must get approval from headquarters. The company formed a product development committee that uses market research information to develop new products for under-served areas in the market. Because of this strategy, their product portfolio has increased to target a wide range of socioeconomic classes. Their principal audience, however, remains semi-selective consumers who shop at department stores. Here their focus is on selling at prices one step below imported cosmetic products.

Third-Party Production

Another way to increase sales is as a third-party manufacturer for other cosmetics companies, for generic pharmacy and supermarket brands, or for hotels. For this reason, C1, C2 and C3 have all taken on manufacturing subcontracting, although C4 has not.[24] In 1996, C1 began seeking out additional manufacturing jobs and now produces a generic toothpaste brand for a local pharmacy chain and a generic sweetener for a supermarket chain. In 2000, third-party production represented 10 percent of the company's revenues.

C5 began operations in 1986, producing its own brand of aerosol products for retail sale.[25] A year later the company faced financial difficulties and decided to switch from being a final goods maker to a third-party "maquila" (in-bound assembly) company, producing goods for multinational and domestic cosmetics companies. It has retained this model since then, though the company does use excess production time to produce aerosol products for retail sale, accounting for approximately seven percent of company revenues.

C5 is one of two companies in Chile licensed to produce aerosols, as aerosol production must follow strict safety and environmental standards. Nearly 40 percent of the company's sales come from aerosol production; the other 60 percent comes from a wide range of cosmetics and consumer goods that the company produces, such as fragrances, lotions, hair care products, deodorants, powders, makeup and nail polish. C5 produces many different brands and types within each product category; for instance, the company currently produces 45 different types of aerosol products. Such product diversity is directly related to the firm's business model. The company presently has 30 clients who provide the raw materials and packaging, while the factory concentrates on mixing the raw materials, pouring them into the containers, and then packaging goods for delivery. Many clients change the products or their packaging, which contributes to the diversity in production. C5's principal client is M4. C5 is highly dependent on M4 for business and, according to the manager, would most likely fail if they were to lose this client.

Exports: Growing, but Still Small

Like third-party production, exporting offers domestic firms a way to increase output and revenues, and in the process, take advantage of the installed capacity of the factory. C1 initiated exporting in 1995 and by 2000 was exporting to ten Latin American and Caribbean countries. Exporting accounts for ten percent of sales and according to its owner, allows C1 to increase sales for little marginal cost. C2 began exporting in 2000 to Peru, Bolivia and Costa Rica and has plans to export to Argentina and Ecuador. Exports in 2000 accounted for eight percent of sales; the goal is to increase exports to 25 percent. As C5 is a maquila, it does not determine if the produced goods will be exported, which is the clients' decision. One multinational that subcontracted aerosol production to them began exporting from Chile to Peru, which increased their business. Yet they have also lost business from multinationals moving their operations outside of Chile. Previously they had manufactured an aerosol hairspray for M2, but they lost this business when the firm shifted to importing products from its Mexican factories.

Lagging in Innovation

Domestic cosmetics firms are not the technological innovators heralded in Piore and Sabel's (1984) seminal study of craft production. Domestic cosmetic firms follow recipes. Like the manufacturing firms of South Korea and other successful late industrializing countries described in Amsden (2001), the Chilean cosmetics manufacturers copy the technology and processes developed in industrialized countries. The in-house laboratories focus on quality control and provide little process innovation. The research and development that does occur is slow and often filled with stumbles.

During C1's search for new products, it noticed that there was little competition in the hair dye industry. Hair dye is a high-margin product. Though the product is difficult to develop, once it is developed, it costs little to manufacture; leaving significant profits that can be dedicated to advertising to ensure continuing sales. C1 thought that if it could develop its own line of hair dye products that was up to the quality standards of the multinationals, it could undersell the competition and capture some of the market. In 1995, the company began developing a domestic line of hair dyes, with the effort spearheaded by the owner's daughter, a trained chemical pharmacist like her father. Developing the formula required rounds and rounds of experimentation, which is why hair dye formulas are closely held secrets ("like Coca-Cola," as the owner explained). In order to develop the product, the firm had to invest in specialized machinery and pay royalties to an international consultant who advised them during development. The father and daughter went through endless rounds testing the products, on themselves and other family members, a fact attested to by the owners' purplish-brown hair tone. After four years of trials, C1 released the product in 1999. The four-year gestation period far exceeds the six-month development period typical for multinational firms and is indicative of the hurdles that small and medium-sized companies face in becoming technology leaders.[26]

Because hair dye is a high-margin product, C1 can compete with the multinationals on the basis of price or quality, but it does not have the resources to compete through advertising. Of the two leading sellers in Chile, C1 believes its product is of better quality than one of the leading brands, and the same quality as the leading brand. The product sells at half the price of the leading brand (C$1,790 versus C$3,490). C1 captured 12 percent of the market in the first year after its introduction.

Technological Upgrading

With small-batch production, technological upgrading becomes limited to integrating machinery that is more productive, but does not differ greatly from its predecessors. The equipment may produce better quality products at a faster rate, but the organization of work does not change. The small size of the domestic market, and the associated competitive strategy of product diversification, limits the type and degree of automation within cosmetics manufacturing. Given that production has not been standardized and thus cannot be automated, it would be incorrect to interpret technological upgrading as a capital-labor trade-off.

Attempts by domestic producers to fully automate have failed. In the case of C5, for example, the need to adapt machinery to different bottle shapes and sizes limits automation. In 1998 the company bought a fully automated aerosol-making machine from Argentina, capable of producing a month's supply of products with the click of a button. The machine proved to be insufficiently flexible for the needs of the company since it was designed to produce more than the firm needed, yet required much labor time for cleaning with each of the product changes. The company stopped using the machine shortly after it was purchased. Management now recognizes that semi-automated machinery is more appropriate for its production model.

As technological upgrading in the cosmetics industry does not primarily concern capital replacing labor, increases in output have generally been accompanied by increases in employment, even when the machinery is more productive, such as upgrading from manual to semi-automatic equipment. The following example from C4 illustrates the type of machinery investments undertaken by domestic producers. In 1999, C4 purchased a new reactor from Argentina that produced two and a half times the volume of their older reactor, which dated from the 1970s. The digital temperature display on the new reactor is more accurate and more readable than the mechanical temperature display of the old one; the reactor itself is also easier to clean. C4 still uses the old reactor, which is located in the workroom next to the new reactor. Compared with the old reactor, the new one improves quality through its improved temperature control, its ability to make larger batches, and its ability to mix the batches more quickly. In sum, it is more productive. Yet at the packaging stage of production, more *envasadoras* are needed to fill and put the caps on the jars, and then package the boxes to prepare them for delivery. In the aggregate, the labor saved from having a better reactor is cancelled out by the labor intensity of the packaging operations, leading to an increase in employment. Yet overall productivity is greater and the final product is of higher quality.

Overall, the decision to upgrade machinery has been motivated, as the owner of C1 put it, by the need to manufacture "new and better quality products." C1 took out loans in order to purchase the machines needed to produce hair dyes. The machinery imported was both new and used, from Argentina and the United States. C1 also took advantage of available second-hand machinery to upgrade its factory. When M3 shut down its shampoo plant in Chile and switched to importing from Mexico, C1 bought some of their machinery. They also bought machinery from a Chilean firm that had gone bankrupt. Fifty percent of the machines in their factory today were not there five years ago. C1 did not buy the machinery to lower its labor costs. This is not to imply that labor costs are of no concern, but that the cost of machinery far exceeds the savings. As the owner stated, "machinery is expensive—more than the savings gained from having three fewer workers."

Similarly, when C2 decided to introduce a line of makeup, it needed to buy the appropriate machinery. The company bought new machinery from China and used machinery from M2, which had closed its makeup production factory in early 2000. Through its purchases, C2 was able to improve output. The old compact (powder makeup) machines made one compact at a time; the new machine can make 25. But as in the example of the more productive reactor, a worker is still required to fill the plastic holders with the compact colors and then shut the plastic tops. In the end, more workers were needed for the labor-intensive tasks, causing the number of production workers to increase from 60 to 80 between 1996 and 2000.

Plant data from Chile's National Annual Manufacturing Survey supports the interview testimony that cosmetics manufacturers have increased their employment of unskilled production workers since the late 1980s (See Figure 4.3). In cosmetics plants, the relative employment of unskilled to skilled workers has increased because of the production model and product diversification. Between 1980 and 1995, the number of unskilled workers (*obreros*) increased by 83 percent, from 2,043 in 1980 to 3,745 in 1995; the number of skilled workers (*empleados*) increased by 49 percent, from 1,643 in 1980 to 2,441 in 1995.

Figure 4.3: Employment of Skilled and Unskilled Workers, Cosmetics Manufacturers, 1979-1995

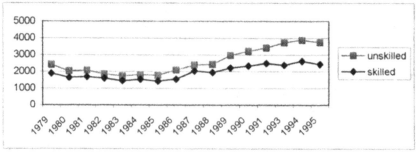

Note: 1992 is dropped because of a drop in the sample for this year.

Source: ENIA, SIC 3523.

Employment gains have been accompanied by gains in productivity. Between 1980 and 1995, output per employee, measured in 1999 US$, increased from $74,700 per employee to $112,200, an annual rate of growth of 3.3 percent. Similarly, value added per employee increased annually by 3.8 percent and by 1995 was $69,000 per employee (ENIA, 1995).[27]

Spillovers from FDI: Quality, Presentation and Advertising

Most Chilean consumers would agree that in the 25 years since trade liberalization, the quality and appearance of cosmetics products offered in Chile has improved substantially. Many of the improvements are the result of the external opening of the economy—the increase in import competition as well as the rise in foreign direct investment—though some improvements are associated with a general upgrading of cosmetics products throughout the world.

The increase in import competition coupled with the availability of cheaply priced machinery from closed multinational factories motivated domestic firms to upgrade their machinery and in the process, improve product quality. Another source of investment has been in product presentation. Domestic producers recognized that without a significant price advantage they would have trouble competing with multinationals, since the latter had better product presentation. Though domestic firms have concentrated more on maintaining a price advantage, the firms have also made some investments in improving the "look" of their products. When the present owner of C2 purchased the factory in 1995, his first order of business was to modernize the product's look, which at the time dated from the 1970s.[28]

Apart from product appearance, another related expense is advertising. Domestic firms have increased advertising spending, yet remain cautious about dedicating too much money, preferring to use the savings from advertising to offer lower prices. As the target customer's selectivity increases, the firm must dedicate more revenues to advertising and general product promotion. C4 sells to the most exclusive clientele, upper and upper-middle level consumers, and thus dedicates more revenues to marketing, product promotion and sales than other domestic firms. C3 sells to the lower-middle income consumers and does not spend any money on advertising. Though it has invested in new packaging, C3 relies on its lower prices to sell its product. C1 and C2, which sell to upper-middle and lower-middle income consumers, have increased the amount of spending on advertising and product promotion, but are still cautious. Both have hired more product promoters, known in the industry as *promotoras*. Promotoras are young women who explain and pass out samples at shopping centers and events. Both Chilean and multinational firms use promotoras, a practice that became popular in the country in the early 1980s. Between 1995 and 2000, *promotora* was the fastest growing occupation in C1, rising in number from 8 to 35. Still, C1 has mostly relied on price difference to sell its hair dye product. It spends little money on advertising, instead focusing on having the promotoras introduce the product to consumers. C2 dedicates 25 percent of its US$6 million budget to marketing and sales efforts. Yet the owner recognizes that their marketing expenditures are dwarfed by those of large multinationals, which spend up to fifty percent of their much larger budget on advertising and dominate billboards, television and print media. C2's owner felt strongly that competing with multinationals in terms of equipment was not the difficult part ("what is produced there can be produced here"), but rather not being able to keep up with the multinationals' spending.

IMPLICATIONS FOR LABOR

The analysis of the competitive and defensive strategies of cosmetics firms reveals certain general trends in labor demand, depending on whether the firm is multinational or domestic. Multinational corporations that moved production outside Chile dismissed low-skilled production workers and the few skilled laboratory personnel, while maintaining their relatively higher-skilled administrative, marketing and sales staffs to distribute the products in Chile. Also, multinationals have subcontracted non-core service positions, further reducing their direct hiring of low-skilled workers, though they still hire them indirectly. The net result has been a large upward shift in the relative demand for skilled compared with low-skilled workers among multinational cosmetics subsidiaries operating in Chile.

Domestic firms have hired more production workers as companies have focused on manufacturing, accepting subcontracting jobs from multinational firms and retailers. Moreover, technological investments have been labor augmenting because of the competitive strategy of product diversification coupled with the characteristics of small-batch production. Product quality and output have improved, yet the net effect has been a rise in demand for low-skilled production workers. Furthermore, investments in increased marketing and product promotion have generally favored a low-cost approach with the hiring of low-skilled *promotoras* to introduce the products, rather than other more costly forms of advertising. Chilean cosmetics companies have taken a low-skilled, labor-intensive approach that has increased overall relative demand for low-skilled labor.

The competitive policies of multinational corporations and the defensive responses of domestic firms have had direct ramifications on who is or isn't hired by these two competitor groups, as summarized in Table 4.2.

Table 4.2: Cosmetics Industry Jobs: Gender, Skills, Pay and Labor Demand

Job Title/ Duties	Sex	Skill/ Schooling	Pay (Domestic Firms) US$	Labor Demand	
				Multi-nationals	Domestic
Management	Both	High-skilled. University degree.	$7,300/month (technical director at C5) $5,500/month (HR manager at C6)*	Unchanged	Unchanged
Marketing and Sales	Both	Marketing staff has university degree. Sales staff has high school or more.	Marketing: $1,400- 2,600/mo. Sales: $1,200- $1,600/mo (C4)	Increase	Increase dependent on consumer segment: more exclusive = increased demand
Quality Control	Mostly Female	University or technical school studies.	Head of QC = $1,800/month; Assts. = $550/month (C5)	Decrease – job loss with closing	Increase from expansion and emphasis on product quality.
Fabricante/ Compounder	Male	Semi-skilled. OJT.	$500/month	Decrease – job loss with closing	Increase with greater output
Mechanic	Male	Semi-skilled. OJT. May have technical school studies.	$500/month	Decrease – job loss with closing	Increase with greater output
Envasadora/ Filling & Assembly	Female	Unskilled, some high school.	$275/month	Decrease – job loss with closing	Increase with greater output
Storage and Distribution	Male	Unskilled, some high school.	$275/month	Decrease from outsourcing and computerization	Some increase, though controlled w/ computerization

Table 4.2: Cosmetics Industry Jobs: Gender, Skills, Pay and Labor Demand (continued)

Job Title/ Duties	Sex	Skill/ Schooling	Pay (Domestic Firms) US$	Labor Demand	
				Multinationals	Domestic
Non-core services (cleaning, security, grounds, cafeteria)	Cleaning & Cooking= Female; Security & grounds= Male	Unskilled	$250/month	Decrease from outsourcing	Unchanged
Promotora/ Product Promoter	Female	Unskilled, appearance most important.	$275/month	Increase; needed for selling at department stores	Increase; emphasis on low-cost promo- tional efforts

*C6's management did not participate in the study, but its union leader did.

Note: Wages are US$ per month and were calculated at C$550 = US$1. Data are averages for the category and are based on interviews with general managers and union wage information.

Source: Author's compilation based on interviews, factory visits and union contracts.

Apart from the direct effect on hiring as a result of firms' respective competitive strategies, firms have also changed their employment policies to achieve their competitive goals. Employment policy can enhance the flexibility of the firm towards its employees by increasing the degree of functional flexibility, numerical flexibility and wage flexibility of the workers (Harrison, 1997). In the process, the bargaining power of management over labor may strengthen.

Functional flexibility refers to the efforts by managers to redefine work tasks and re-deploy resources in order to facilitate and accelerate change. Through polyvalence, or the broadening of work tasks, managers increase the workers' substitutability, while at the same time facilitating their adaptability to new tasks. Numerical flexibility involves redesigning jobs so as to substitute part-time, contract and other contingent workers for better-paid, full-time workers. A second type of numerical flexibility is the outsourcing of production, maintenance, catering, clerical and other activities that were formerly undertaken in-house. Finally, wage flexibility refers to the various efforts by managers to reintroduce greater competition among individual workers, particularly in positions where workers have been sheltered from wage competition by unionization (Harrison, 1997).

Functional Flexibility

The present structure of manufacturing within the Chilean cosmetics industry limits mobility between jobs, though not between tasks performed in a specific job. Sex segregation within job duties, specifically within production jobs, means that *envasadoras* concentrate solely on filling and assembly jobs, though because of the diverse product range, the task itself may vary every few hours. Perceptions about gender, particularly the manual dexterity of female workers, has led cosmetics manufacturers—both in Chile and elsewhere—to hire along gender lines. Mechanics, compounders and storage workers are male. Mechanics and compounders are semi-skilled jobs filled by long-tenure workers who learned the needed skills through on-the-job training and, in some cases, through supplementary technical courses. Mechanics are responsible for adjusting machinery for different production runs and for doing in-house repairs. Compounders are responsible for mixing batches; the slightest mistake can cause the ruin of expensive raw materials. Other men are hired for the storage and distribution department. Female envasadoras do not have the training to perform the jobs of the mechanics and compounders, and are perceived as not having the physical strength for jobs in storage and distribution. Likewise, men are perceived to lack the manual dexterity for filling and assembly jobs and are not likely to acquiesce to doing "women's work." The result is a socially enforced rigidity between occupations, despite the legal ability to institute greater polyvalence. Union contracts do not specify limits on tasks performed within jobs and there are no clauses for paying workers more if non-job related tasks are performed. However, functional flexibility is not a strategy practiced by Chilean managers.

Numerical Flexibility

Numerical flexibility, as discussed above, can involve either replacing full-time workers by part-time or temporary contract workers, or by outsourcing activities and services so as to focus on core activities within the firm. The case studies provide evidence of substantial multinational outsourcing of non-core services and production, in contrast to Chilean firms, which have kept most activities in-house. There was no evidence, either in multinationals or domestic firms, of replacing full-time workers with part-time workers, or of the use of temporary rather than permanent contracts. Temporary contracts were only used to hire workers for the busy season, as intended by the law.

All of the multinationals interviewed outsource non-core activities. Basic services such as cleaning, gardening, security, the cafeteria, delivery and stocking of merchandise, and *promotoras* are contracted to third-party businesses. Typically the firms receiving these contracts are well-established multinationals such as Wackenhut, the U.S.-owned security firm, and Sodexho, the French-owned catering company. Multinational firms explained that non-core activities were outsourced to allow them to concentrate on their core business. Domestic firms explained that they did not outsource because it was more expensive than retaining the workers in-house, despite the administrative costs of having a larger staff.

Though it may be cheaper for the Chilean firms to retain these services in-house, this is not the case for multinationals, which pay roughly double the going wage for unskilled workers, according to interview testimony. Production workers at M2's domestic shampoo facility earn on average US$540 per month, and no employee makes under US$375 per month, according to the general manager. In comparison, the average wage for envasadoras at domestic firms was $275 per month. When M1 produced in Chile, "workers would line up to work there" because of the higher wages, according to the President of the Federation of Cosmetics Workers. Similarly, M3 stated that it pays above industry average for all occupations. Unfortunately, few interviewees could convincingly explain why they pay more without appealing to tautologies on how workers seek jobs with multinational firms because the multinationals pay well and in turn, they pay the workers well because they are good workers.

A possible explanation of why permanent unskilled workers at multinationals are paid above-market wages is to improve internal equity in the firm. Abraham and Taylor (1993), in their research of firms in the United States, argue that large firms pay higher-than-market wages to unskilled workers with the goal of improving internal equity. In the case of Chile, managers of multinational subsidiaries affect the distribution of wages at their affiliate. Multinational managers earn similar salaries with adjustments for cost-of-living, whether they are at headquarters or the subsidiary. Having the subsidiary manager earn an international wage creates two disparities: (1) the difference between the subsidiary manager's salary and that of the domestic competition and (2) the internal difference between the subsidiary manager's wage and the wages of the staff hired on the local labor market. With lower wages for low-skilled workers in developing countries as compared with developed countries, the difference in wages between unskilled and skilled workers widens within the firm as the skilled manager's pay is influenced by international trends. In order to lessen this disparity, multinational firms may raise the pay of workers at the bottom to narrow the gap and improve internal equity. Internal equity could therefore explain why multinationals operating in Chile paid higher wages to their production staff.

Another possible explanation is that multinationals pay more because they are in a labor market that is foreign to them and they need to create incentives to attract people. Since there is a history of backlash against multinationals in Latin America, it is in the best interest of the multinationals to pay more than the local firms. If they paid less or the same as the local firms, the investments would more likely be frowned upon by government officials, particularly if they were making brownfield investments. As a result, the higher wages of multinational firms may have given them an incentive to outsource non-core tasks.

While benefits may accrue from having core workers earn higher-than-market wages for efficiency wage or other reasons, there is "little obvious return to paying high wages to workers who are easily monitored, easily replaced, and/or performing work that is peripheral to the organization's main objectives" (Abraham and Taylor, 1993, p. 4). Thus the pattern in Chile of contracting out non-core activities on the part of multinationals is consistent with the econometric findings of Abraham and Taylor for the United States, that the higher the wages paid by a firm, the more likely they are to outsource janitorial services. Because the multinationals pay higher wages, the cost of subcontracting for multinationals is relatively less than for domestic firms. For the multinationals, outsourcing is a savings, while for domestic firms it is a cost.

The decision by multinationals to subcontract non-core activities has the long-run effect of undermining the creation of internal labor markets. M1 reorganized its staffing beginning in 1995 and especially after the arrival of a new general manager in 1997. Prior to the reorganization, "the firm acted as a typical Chilean company . . . almost feudalistic . . . the organization was very classical." Turnover was very low, with most people working all of their lives at the company. They would "start off in the warehouse, then move to the factory. . . . one person even made it to become sales manager." There were "very few professionals . . . trained in modern business practices." During the reorganization, more professionals (i.e., persons trained at business schools) were hired. The accounting and human resources department were modernized and reduced in size. Overall, the staff was cut by 20–30 percent. Prior to the reorganization, the average age of workers in the firm was mid-40s with many years of tenure; after the staff changes the average age dropped to 35 with an average of 2 years in the company.[29]

Cleaning, gardening and security services were the first activities to be outsourced, followed by product delivery and distribution in 1997. Promotoras, who the company began using in 1983, have always been hired through an outside agency. When M1 outsourced delivery, it sold the trucks to the firm given the delivery contract. M1 pays this firm a fixed amount every month for the deliveries. Management decided to subcontract delivery for three reasons: (1) to concentrate on the business of the firm; (2) to reduce administrative costs by having fewer workers; and (3) pressure from headquarters to lower headcount. According to one manager, the last issue reflects headquarters' desire to improve the statistic of "sales per employee." The company's annual report confirms that a great deal of attention was given to this statistic. A graph in the report showed sales per employee increasing steadily from 107,000 euros in 1994 to 154,000 euros in 1999. In the Chilean subsidiary, the number of in-house workers fell from 246 in 1996 to 145 in 2000, and the number of subcontracted workers increased from 127 to 149. Part of the drop in in-house production is due to the closing of the factory in June 1998, which terminated the employment of 75 in-house production workers. The rest of the drop stems from additional outsourcing of non-core service workers.

The reorganization focused on bringing in new and younger talent, often with business school training, and eliminating routine service, delivery and production jobs within the firm. The changes undermined the company's internal labor market in two respects. First, outsourcing means that these workers—who often rotate between assignments at different companies—are much less likely to be promoted to positions of greater responsibility within the company since they are not actually company employees. And secondly, because of the present managerial preference for workers with business school training, on-the-job training is less likely to lead to promotions.

Wage Flexibility and Labor Relations

Though domestic firms make less use of numerical flexibility practices than multinationals, wage flexibility is an important element of their competitive strategy. The weak bargaining environment evident since the 1973 coup has facilitated controlling the wage growth of low-skilled workers, contributing to a widening dispersion of pay between the skilled and low skilled.

C5, the domestic maquila firm, is located in a poor town, just past Santiago's city limits. An entry-level envasadora makes five percent above the minimum wage, or C$105,000 per month[30] (slightly less than US$200), as well as bonuses for attendance, punctuality and production increases that can amount to an additional 30 percent of the wage. On average, envasadoras earn C$140,000 per month plus bonuses. The 16 administrative staff earn an average of C$475,000 pesos per month, although this distribution is skewed between secretaries and the company directors. For example, the technical director who is a chemical pharmacist and is second in the company earns C$4,000,000 per month (US$7,270), which is 28 times the average production wage. Over time the wage gap between skilled and unskilled workers in C5 has increased because of the general manager's policy to "favor the skilled workers." Of the 235 persons employed during 2000, the general manager considers 45 skilled. This includes the administrative personnel, the quality control staff, chemical technicians (who have post-secondary training from a technical school), and machinists. The machinists are skilled tradesmen who can repair and adjust the machines as needed. Although the manager stated that skilled workers were not difficult to find, he prefers to limit turnover among the skilled staff, particularly those positions where the employee works with explosives or is responsible for the mixing of large batches of raw materials. Thus, safety considerations affect the manager's remuneration policy, widening the distribution of wages within the company.

Efforts by low-skilled workers to counter the favoritism towards skilled workers at C5 have failed. Recognizing that the company's ease in replacing them made it difficult for them to negotiate salary increases, low-skilled production and service workers formed a union in 1992 in an attempt to bargain collectively and secure greater wage increases. Management signed a collective bargaining agreement with the organized workers and negotiated individually with the workers who did not join the union. Non-union workers received greater salary increases than stipulated in the collective bargaining agreement, in a deliberate and successful attempt on the part of management to destroy the union. The strategy to destroy the union is based on an account by the general manager of C5, who admitted his philosophical distaste for unions. Paying higher wages to non-union workers solely for not being union members is an anti-union practice, which the firm can be fined for, though proving guilt is difficult to do in practice.[31] Union members at C5 stopped paying their dues and the union fell apart just months after signing the two-year contract. There have been no attempts since then to unionize. Wages are presently negotiated collectively under a "convenio colectivo" (collective agreement).[32] In 2000, the workers signed a four-year agreement with the company that entitled them to bi-annual wage increases equal to the rate of inflation as well as individually awarded merit increases.

Based on data from the National Annual Industrial Survey for SIC 3523, between 1980 and 1995, skilled workers' wages grew at an annual rate of 4.2 percent, compared with unskilled workers' wages, which grew by 1.5 percent. Unskilled workers have not yet seen the returns from the productivity gains accrued during this period; rather, the gains have gone to skilled workers, despite a drop in their share of employment among cosmetics manufacturers from 45 percent to 40 percent over the 15 years. (See Table 4.3).

The wages reported in Table 4.3 are higher than the information given in the interviews, though the relative growth rate for the wages of skilled and unskilled workers is comparable to the case study findings. Average production workers' wages were similar across domestic firms at C$150,000 (US$275) per month, a reply I received from all of the domestic firm managers interviewed. The interview data is also corroborated by union contract information, which also confirms a similarity across firms in the wage increases, base salaries and benefits given. The similarity is likely due to the information exchange among industry firms, instituted through a biannual wage survey undertaken by the Cosmetics Industry Chamber of Commerce. Similarly, the National Federation of Cosmetics and Pharmaceutical Laboratory Workers shares wage and benefit information among union leaders in the industry and provides guidance during the collective bargaining negotiations.[33]

Unions exist in domestic firms that were established prior to 1973. Firms that opened after 1973 generally do not have unions; instead workers sign collective agreements. Where unions do exist, negotiations with management are limited to the collective bargaining negotiations, which by law, occur at most every two years. Management does not typically consult with the unions about production changes or machinery purchases or other matters concerning operation of the company. Union contracts concern wage increases and benefits for the upcoming two-year period. Contracts do not detail job duties for specific occupations, though they may specify different raises according to the job title. With the exception of one firm, workers do not directly benefit from increases in productivity.[34] In both the 1997 and 1999 collective bargaining contracts, this union was able to convince management to include a productivity bonus for production workers, to be paid every three months, if output was over a specified amount. The bonus was calculated on an hourly basis, thereby lowering overtime, with the goal of making workers more productive, and in turn, improving the quality of life of the production staff.

Table 4.3: Productivity and Wage Growth, Cosmetics Manufacturers, 1980 & 1995

	Output/ Employee	Value-added/ Employee	Skilled Wages	Unskilled Wages	Skilled Worker Emp. Share
1980	$74,738	$43,781	$14,394	$4,530	44.6%
1995	$112,192	$68,721	$23,497	$5,536	39.5%
Annual Gr. 95/80	3.3%	3.8%	4.2%	1.5%	-0.8%

Note: Data are 1999 US$ converted at US$1 = C$550. Skilled are white-collar workers, including technical workers involved in production. Unskilled are blue-collar production and service workers.

Source: Author's calculations based on data from the National Annual Industrial Survey, SIC 3523.

Multinational firms that invested in the country through the acquisition of already existing cosmetics firms, as in the case of M2 and M3, inherited unions that were later dismantled by the firm or closed when the factory moved abroad. M1's factory, a greenfield investment dating from the early 1950s, was unionized, yet the union dissolved when the company shifted manufacturing to Brazil.

When M2 purchased the leading makeup manufacturer in Chile in 1996, it inherited its factory of 70, largely unionized, production workers. The factory union leader was, at the time, also the president of the National Federation of Cosmetics and Pharmaceutical Laboratory Workers. According to the current president of the Federation, the factory union leader was offered a large severance package to leave the firm, which she accepted, resigning from her position as union leader and Federation president. By 1998 the union had dissolved. The general manager claims that it dissolved because the wages and benefits paid by M2, to both union and non-union workers, were higher than what they were receiving under their collective bargaining agreement. The current federation president claims that workers were given bonuses to quit the union. If the higher wages were paid to encourage workers to abandon the union, then this could partly explain the finding of higher wages among multinational firms. Whatever the motive for raising workers' wages, the union ceased to exist by 1998 and two years later the factory closed.

C2 is among the oldest cosmetics manufacturers in Chile, dating from 1917. It has a long-established union, though at present union membership is at a historical low, with only 20 percent of production workers belonging. When the present owner purchased the company in 1995, the company's two-year collective bargaining agreement had expired and was up for negotiation. As the company was financially stretched from expanding and modernizing the facility, management did not offer a wage increase. The workers responded by going on strike. Under Chilean law, if a company does not offer workers an increase equal to or greater than the previous year's rate of inflation, the company must wait 15 days before it can replace striking workers, otherwise it can hire temporary replacement workers on the first day. The workers returned to work on the 15th day and signed a contract that stipulated an adjustment for past inflation and raised worker's salaries by C$2,000, or US$4.50 per month (measured in 1999 US$). In 1995, there were 54 production workers, of which 38, or 70 percent, belonged to the union. By 2000, only 16 production workers belonged to the union, though the number of production workers had increased to 80, which meant that only 20 percent of the workers were union members. The union president at the time of the strike was promoted to Head of Production and left the union immediately. Since then there has been a vacuum in leadership that has caused union membership to drop.

The overall weakness of the Chilean labor movement, as discussed in Chapter 3, is apparent in the cosmetics industry (See Table 4.4). Worker apathy abounds, weakening the negotiating power of the few remaining unions. Anti-union practices also lessen the movement's strength, though the threat of retaliation on the part of management towards union workers is less of a concern for the cosmetics industry than it is in other industries. Allegations of anti-union practices involve paying non-union workers more or enticing union members to leave the union—not dismissing union members.[35] Though being bribed is preferable to being fired, it is just as effective at destroying a union than dismissal and is less disruptive to the firm. As mentioned earlier, it is also much more difficult to prove.

Table 4.4: Existence and Status of Unions in the Cosmetics Industry

Firm	Union?	What Happened?/ Condition of Union?	Anti-union practices?
M1	No	Dissolved with factory closing.	
M2	No	Dissolved 2 years prior to factory closing.	Allegations of anti-union practices by offering early retirement package to union leader and bonuses to workers to leave union.
M3	No	Dissolved with factory closing.	
M4	No	Subcontracts manufacturing.	
C1	C1	Workers sign collective agreement.	
C2	Yes	Only 20% of production workers are members.	Allegations of anti-union practices by promoting union leader to non-union position.
C3	Yes	Most of the 22 production workers belong. Negotiations concern wage increases.	
C4	Yes	Union exists for both white-collar and blue-collar workers. Negotiations concern wage increases.	Allegations of anti-union practices by promoting union leaders to non-union positions.
C5	No	Workers sign collective agreement.	Management admitted paying non-union workers more in a deliberate and successful attempt to destroy the union.

Source: Interviews with management and union leaders; collective bargaining contracts.

The ability of management to easily entice union leaders and workers to leave the union speaks to a general weakness and lack of loyalty among union leadership as well as the rank and file. When asked why certain workers did not join the union, cosmetics union leaders explained the decision as a combination of: (1) fear, (2) laziness, (3) cheapness,[36] (4) a belief that all union members are terrorists whose goal is to take over the company, and (5) loyalty to management. Another debilitating factor is the common practice, both in the cosmetics industry and in general, of management extending the collective bargaining agreement to non-union workers, encouraging free riding.[37] Finally, the ineffectiveness of unions to secure wage increases encourages members to drop out of the union, and in doing so, weakens the union even more.

Even well functioning unions with capable leadership often have difficulty securing rents for their workers due to the highly competitive external environment that the firms' face. During the collective negotiation period, management responds to the union's first wage request with a written statement that discusses the financial and economic state of the firm and gives a counter-offer. In August 1998, C4's union and management entered negotiations. At this time, Chile was beginning to feel the effects of the Asian crisis, though unemployment was still low, at 6.9 percent. In management's response to the union, management noted the negative impact of the Asian crisis on the Chilean economy and the drop in economy-wide demand, which had slowed company sales. Yet management put greater emphasis on the heightened state of competitiveness within the cosmetics industry, and in particular, on the market power of multinational firms:

> Nowadays competition is noticeably greater as a consequence of market liberalization; we not only face internal competition, but also a very strong competition from the most powerful transnationals of the sector . . . (Contract Negotiation Document, C4, 1998, translated from Spanish).

Management mentioned how a multinational (M3) had acquired the licenses to distribute products that C4 had been distributing, causing a fall in C4's sales and lower market share. In the end, the workers received wage increases of one percent in addition to the previous year's rate of inflation.

Domestic firms' strategy of keeping prices lower than those of multinationals means they are under constant pressure to control costs. At the same time, multinationals have attained more efficient product runs and cheaper raw materials through regionalization, allowing them to further lower their costs and expand sales to middle-income consumers. Price drops squeeze the rents of domestic firms, giving them less room to grant real wage increases to their workers. Unions have difficulty countering management's demands as their inability to retain members lessens their representation in the firm, hampering their negotiating power. The result is a lack of real wage growth for the industry's most vulnerable: easily replaceable, unskilled workers.

CONCLUSION

The case study of the Chilean cosmetics industry revealed differences in the competitive strategies of multinational and domestic firms (See Table 4.5). The decision by multinationals to regionalize operations resulted in the closing of local Chilean factories established during ISI, some of which had

Table 4.5: Summary of Competitive Strategies of Multinationals and Domestic Firms

	Multinationals	Domestic Firms
Operations	Shut local ISI factories and regionalize production.	Successful firms have expanded operations with accompanying growth in output.
Production Technology	Larger operations enable longer runs that lower per unit cost and facilitate automation. Company benefits from consolidating raw material purchases.	Similar production technology though upgraded to improve productivity.
Products	More narrow and standardized product line.	Diversify into new products to increase range of products offered.
Pricing Strategy	Price drop.	Price drop. Lower prices are principal lever of competition since domestic firms do not have the large advertising budgets.
Subcontracting	Subcontract production and non-core service jobs.	Firms have sought third-party production jobs either for multinationals or supermarket and pharmacy chains. Firms do not subcontract non-core service jobs.
Marketing	Publicity wars.	Semi-selective goods producers have increased their marketing budgets, though favor low-cost options such as promotoras.

Source: Author's compilation.

originally been Chilean-owned. The strategy to regionalize operations was not precipitated by Chile's trade liberalization of 1974, but occurred instead two decades later, when the trade barriers of other countries in the region were lowered. By regionalizing operations, multinational firms could consolidate purchasing and produce larger batch sizes, allowing the firms to lower their costs. The price drop gave these firms entrance into the mass-market consumer segment, directly forcing competition with local producers. It also resulted in the loss of production jobs, the majority of which were filled by low-skilled workers.

Domestic firms responded to the heightened competition by expanding and diversifying their product line, accepting third-party production jobs, and improving the quality of the goods they offered. To facilitate the improvements, firms invested in upgrading their machinery, purchasing both second-hand and new equipment. Due to the nature of small-batch production, technological upgrading has not been labor saving. Firms that have successfully increased their output have also had to hire more *envasadoras* to process the goods. The result has been a relative increase in the employment of low-skilled workers among Chilean cosmetics manufacturers.

But despite their increased relative employment, wage increases for low-skilled workers have not matched the gains that skilled workers have received. The lack of wage growth for low-skilled workers stems from pressure on domestic firms to keep costs low in order to under-price multinationals and retain market share. Employers can force the brunt of cost-savings on low-skilled workers because they are easily replaceable. Efforts on the part of low-skilled workers to counter unfavorable wage increases have largely proved unsuccessful, as many workers lack dedication to collective efforts, impeding the negotiating strength of the unions.

The findings from this case study of restructuring in an import-competing industry provide insight into the causes of widening wage dispersion in Chile under free trade. The methodology highlighted the role of foreign competition and corporate strategies on the demand for skilled and unskilled workers. My analysis of the production process showed that widening skilled/low-skilled wage dispersion is not the result of skill-biased technological change, despite machinery investment and productivity increases. On the other hand, foreign direct investment is associated with rising relative demand for skilled workers. Greater competition brings lower prices and better quality goods, to the benefit of Chilean consumers. Yet the more competitive environment forces domestic firms to cut their costs. Employers reward skilled workers, forcing cost savings onto replaceable and poorly organized low-skilled workers.

Chapter Five

When Moving Up the Value Chain Isn't Enough: Temporary Labor in Chile's Agroindustry

INTRODUCTION

Chilean agroindustry, defined as fruit and vegetable processing,[1] developed in the early 1980s as a dynamic new export industry reaping the benefits of available high quality raw materials and low-cost labor. The industry is an important link in the processed-foods value chain, supplying inputs to processed-food manufacturers in the U.S. Its connection with the multinational processed foods sector has stimulated investment in new machinery and higher quality control standards as well as the development of higher value-added products farther along the chain. Agroindustry thus embodies the goals inherent in Chile's export-led growth development strategy, as the exports are not just more diversified but also have a greater value-added component. Exports in 1981 were US$60 million, growing to US$600 by 1995, where they have since fluctuated. At the same time, employment tripled from 5,000 to 15,000 workers, comprising approximately 3.6 percent of employment in manufacturing. Because of its sales and employment growth, as well as its role as a forward linkage from the fresh fruit export sector, the sector has come to be associated with the Chilean "miracle."

Yet despite its success, increased competition on the global value chain from suppliers in China and elsewhere has impelled Chilean agroindustrial firms to reduce the costs of producing commodities or develop new products that are more sheltered from competition. This chapter analyzes how the competitive changes undertaken by Chilean agroindustrial firms have affected its labor force. As the analysis is based on firm-level research, an attempt is made to open up the "black box of the firm" to understand how a firm's varying responses to external competitive pressures can affect the welfare of its workers. In particular the chapter asks: Do workers benefit when agroindustry diversifies its product range or moves to more value-added products? How have workers fared in this industry and what are their long-term prospects? The research benefits from the industry's heterogeneous mix of firms, ranging from simple commodity production to full-package production. The analysis shows that regardless of a firm's competitive strategy, reliance on a temporary labor force, even when production is year-round, is a hallmark of Chilean agroindustry.

CHILEAN AGROINDUSTRY AND THE GLOBAL VALUE CHAIN

Most agroindustrial production consists of intermediate goods for the processed-foods commodity chain. Apple juice, for example, is sold in concentrated form to fruit and juice makers and retailers, such as Coca-Cola and Snapple Fruit Beverages in the United States, while dehydrated chilies, tomatoes and apples are shipped in large bundles to international food manufacturers like General Mills. Processed food manufacturers order small apple pieces for use in oatmeal and cereals, or buy full-size apple rings then repackage the products for final consumption. Similarly, canned peaches are sold in their destination market under the retailer's label. Chilean agroindustry is thus an example of a buyer-driven commodity (or value) chain, whereby companies organized in the chain are independently owned, but the bulk of value added is not in the production stages, but at the stages of branding and marketing. In buyer-driven commodity chains, retailers, branded manufacturers and marketers set up production networks in developing countries to supply imported inputs that are then marketed to northern consumers. The main leverage of the branded manufacturers and marketers is "their ability to shape mass consumption via strong brand names and their reliance on global sourcing strategies to meet this demand" (Gereffi, 1999, pp. 42–43).

Value chain analysis is a useful tool for understanding the inter-country distribution of income (Kaplinsky, 2000). Firms that control marketing and distribution on the buyer-driven commodity chain command steady and high rents because of barriers to entry. In contrast, firms involved in production have seen their rents fall, as more countries have developed their manufacturing ability and entered the sector. Thus, an important lesson from the value chain literature is that developing countries should upgrade on the value chain if they want a greater share of the profits. The upgrading trajectory is thought to consist of five stages, spanning operations limited to assembly (Stage 1), to Stage 5, when the firm is indistinguishable from firms in the advanced country to which it exports (Humphrey, 2004). Chilean agroindustry traverses Stage 2 (manufacturers that are also responsible for the sourcing of inputs) to Stage 4 (firms that design, produce and market their products under their own brand name).

Value chain analysis is also recognized as useful for understanding the growing dispersion of wages between skilled and unskilled workers in different economies (Kaplinsky, 2000). This is because value chain theory recognizes that workers are not just rewarded for their skills, as traditional economic theory suggests; rather the firm they work for in part determines their incomes. As value chain research has shown, it is those workers at the bottom-end of the commodity chain, such as female workers in export-processing zones, who suffer the most from poor working conditions (Carr and Chen, 2004). Yet, while the benefits to workers at different spectrums of the value chain are apparent, less apparent are the dynamic benefits when firms upgrade. This case study of Chilean agroindustry attempts to assess the benefits for workers from shifting competitive strategies, including upgrading on the value chain.

Structure of Agroindustry

The structure of agroindustry in Chile, including its relationship with local suppliers and the external market, is depicted in Figure 5.1. The figure illustrates the value chain from Chilean agriculturist, to agro-processor, to the food manufacturer or intermediary that purchases the products. The goods processed by Chilean agroindustrial firms are usually sold through international brokers, but in some cases are sold directly to the foreign food manufacturer or to a trader. Food manufacturers, working directly or through international brokers, set the demands for and standards of the products. Typically, before entering into a contract, the client will travel to Chile and inspect the facility to make sure the factory meets the standards of the buying firms. Contracts are usually one year long, though they sometimes extend for 18 months.[2] Though most of the products are sold through brokers, the manufacturers still get to know their clients. The clients offer advice on quality control and technology, and may even suggest new products to develop. During processing, products are continuously checked by the manufacturers' on-site quality control labs, thereby guaranteeing that the product meets client standards and preventing problems at delivery.

The relationship between the agroindustrial firm and the raw material providers parallels the relationship between the agroindustrial firm and the northern food manufacturer. Agroindustrial firms sign 1–3 year contracts with farmers. The contracts specify quality standards for the produce as

Figure 5.1: Agroindustry Value Chain

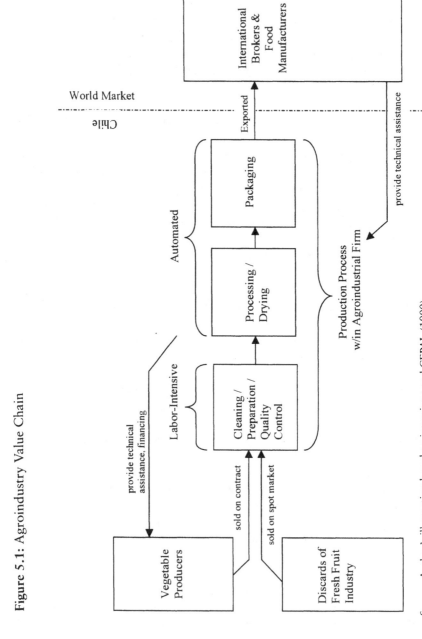

Source: Author's illustration based on interviews and CEPAL (1990).

well as the provision of services, such as credit, inputs and technical assistance, on the part of the manufacturer. In multi-year contracts, output prices are renegotiated yearly, though in the case of tomatoes, the agro-processors' association, FEPACH, sets a uniform price at which all tomatoes will be bought for the season (Peppelenbos, 2000). Many agroindustrial firms also employ agronomists to work closely with the farmers throughout the season, but particularly during planting. An important ongoing effort of the agroindustrial firms, which has received governmental support, is to develop better ties with agriculturists.

Figure 5.1 also shows the production process within the agroindustrial firm. With the exception of juicing, the first step of production is labor-intensive, involving the receipt, selection and preparation of the produce, while the next two stages of processing and packaging are automated. The line is organized as a continuous flow process. In order to achieve a high operational level, fruits and vegetables pass through the line without stopping. The final operation of the line is packing the products in plastic bags, which are then boxed for export and taken to the outbound storage area. If the product has advanced up the value chain to final good sales, there will be the additional step of packaging the products for individual retail sale.

The production line in agroindustry is highly capital intensive and self-operating, though the need for quality assurances requires line workers to perform inspections. The manual inspections can occur at the beginning, middle or end of the line, depending on the product being processed. Despite the different locations within the line, all inspections have several features in common. Workers stand, sifting for defects in the products, such as apple pieces that have brown spots, prunes with pits still embedded, or extraneous matter, such as pebbles. Workers hired to perform these jobs are almost always female, hired for their perceived attention to detail and manual dexterity.

Most agroindustry factories operate close to 24 hours a day, seven days a week, though for some products, production is stopped for one day during the week for routine cleaning. This production model makes the best use of the installed capital equipment, some of which is rented. More importantly, continuous flow assures that the fruits and vegetables are processed as quickly as possible in order to retain their freshness.

During the peak production season, line inspectors comprise roughly 70 percent of production jobs in agroindustry. Other production jobs include mechanics, as well as laboratory workers who perform continual chemical analyses of the products. The laboratory head is a university-educated food scientist, with assistants either holding the same degree or

Table 5.1: Characteristics of Participating Firms

Firm	Entry	Products	Markets	Importance in Sector	Peak Emp	Perm. Emp.	Sales, 2000 (US$)
A1	1941	Prunes	Europe, Latin Am.	#1 prunes	160	80	$12 million
A2	1987	Prunes, raisins, nuts	Latin America	#1 dried fruits (#2 prunes)	270	30	$14 million
A3	1948	Dehydrated apples, tomatoes; cherries	U.S., Europe	#2 dehydrated apples	575	50	$15 million
A4	1988	Dehydrated apples, tomatoes; apple juice	U.S., Europe	U.S., Europe	450	40	$28 million
A5	1994	Fruit and vegetable juices	U.S., Asia	#4 or #5 in juices	46	34	$4 million
A6	1906	Tomato paste; canned fruits and vegetables	Latin Am., Asia, Europe (Chile, 25%)	#1 in canned peaches; one of six tomato paste manuf.	1,060	90	$24 million
A7	1978	Frozen fruits & vegetables	Chile, 90%; U.S. (berries)	#2 or #3 in frozen veg.	450	125	$15–$17 million
A8	1989	Frozen fruits & vegetables	Chile, 75%; Latin Am.; U.S. (berries)	#1 frozen vegetables	650	155	n.a.
A9	1989	Prunes, raisins, nuts	Chile, 95%	#1 in sales to local market	80	75	n.a.

Note: If Chile is not included in markets, then the company only exports.

Source: Based on interviews with firm management, 2001.

degrees in technical studies. Other factory jobs include storage and distribution workers, who unload raw materials and bring packed boxes to outbound storage to await distribution. Depending on where a firm gets its raw materials, some also employ agronomists.

Firms Studied

This study of the Chilean processed fruit and vegetable industry includes a heterogeneous mix of agroindustrial firms, including four distinct types of agricultural processes: dehydration, freezing, canning and juicing. Most of the firms participating in the study are leaders in their sphere. The industry is very consolidated, with rarely more than six to eight producers in a given product line. Most firms do not diversify outside their product group; hence a juicer will experiment with producing new types of juices but does not generally venture into frozen goods.

Table 5.1 gives some basic information about the firms studied, including what they manufacture and their importance in the sector.[3] The seven firms for which there is sales information are considered large by the Chilean standard of annual sales greater than US$1.5 million. In terms of number of firms in the sector, the sample is roughly twelve percent of the industry, but in terms of market share it is substantially more representative, as many of the firms are leaders in their product group.

INCREASED GLOBAL COMPETITION AND STRATEGIC RESPONSES

Chilean agroindustrial firms seeking to increase their share in world exports have encountered a number of competitive bottlenecks. Overall industry sales in 2000 were US$474 million—30 percent below the real value reached in 1996—despite a drop in production of just 6.2 percent and a more favorable rate of exchange (See Figure 5.2).[4] The boom years of the 1980s and early 1990s have given way to more uncertain times. The industry faces a number of challenges including a not-always-level playing field in terms of tariffs set by importing countries, a protectionist backlash by competitors in developed countries, and "unfair" subsidies received by its competitors in other countries. The emergence of China as a low-cost competitor has hampered the growth of commodity sales since 1996 and poses a threat for the future growth of the industry, particularly in the areas of apple juice, low-humidity dehydrates, and tomato paste. Already the

Figure 5.2: Chilean Agroindustrial Exports, 1981-2000

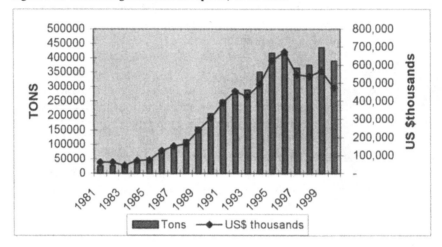

Source: FEPACH based on Banco Central de Chile.

world tomato paste market is flooded with low-grade Chinese tomato paste, restricting Chilean tomato paste manufacturers to the high-grade segment and removing an important outlet for times when the tomato harvest is of lesser quality than expected.[5]

For the Chilean fruit juice industry, of which apple juice constitutes around 60 percent of sales, the market has been very volatile, the result of a number of bad apple harvests and competition from China. Since 1996, Chilean apple juice exports have suffered, falling by 48 percent between 1996 and 2000. Other products face similar challenges. One cherry-exporting firm reported that in 2000, it began losing some of its long-term clients, who started buying from the Chinese. In May of 2000, it cost the firm $4 to produce a batch of dehydrated red and green peppers, whereas Chinese firms were selling the same batch for $3.90. As a result, incoming orders had fallen to one-fourth of their previous levels.

The current structure of the agroindustrial value chain saves the value-added for the final stages of production. There are more rents from branding and marketing than can be earned from technology, since there is no asymmetrical access to key product and process technologies (Gereffi, 1999). Technological advances are well known, and though some firms may lag behind others in adopting new technologies, these gaps can be closed quickly. In order to upgrade within the value chain, Chilean companies would have to use their learned production expertise to produce and sell their own branded merchandise at home and abroad. Unfortunately, this has proven quite difficult for Chilean companies. As a 1998 CEPAL study explained,

> The large multinational firms are the doors of access through which the developing country food industry is forced to enter, given that, in the consumer's eyes, the multinational firms offer a seal of guarantee for the products they offer . . . Because of this, it is practically inconceivable that Chilean producers, acting independently, could penetrate these markets, without being attached to the multinationals that dominate the sector . . . (p.257, translated from Spanish).

Due to their dependence on foreign buyers, Chilean agroindustry firms have little opportunity to move up the value chain. For example, one of the emerging trends in the food industry is "functional foods." These are foods that contain anti-oxidants, or are fortified with vitamins and minerals, and thus have high market appeal to health-conscious North American buyers. Developing functional foods is well within the capabilities of the Chilean agroindustry, yet the buyers do not want to buy functional foods from the Chileans. They prefer to purchase the product as clean as possible and then add the additives, thereby saving the value-added for themselves.[6] According to David Olsen, a buyer of international dried fruit for the U.S. market, the only way for a Chilean company to sell functional foods and other products with greater value-added in the U.S. would be if the company had an established U.S. connection to sell the product. Even then, the range of products that can be sold is limited, and as a result, Olsen states, "having the Chileans do finished products isn't realistic." A more promising route for selling greater value-added products is to begin by selling products in the home market and then branching out to other Latin American countries—a strategy that has been pursued by some of the firms in this study.

In sum, Chilean producers are facing increased competitive pressure in existing markets. While upgrading is one solution to these problems, there are barriers to this as well, in particular the proprietary control of brand names, lack of market demand for more value-added products as well as the escalation of tariffs when value added is increased. As a result, firms can improve productivity and become more competitive in existing markets at the same stage of the value chain or, if they want to upgrade into the more lucrative areas, they can upgrade production technologies to diversify products and markets or supply national and regional markets with higher value-added products. The research identified four main competitive strategies: (1) mechanization; (2) worker training; (3) moving away from commodities; and (4) production for the internal market. The first two strategies involve improving productivity to be more competitive against other producers at the same stage of the value chain; the second two strategies involve moving up the value chain to more lucrative activities. The strategies are described below; in the next section I discuss how the different strategies undertaken affect workers.

Mechanization to Control Costs

Fruit and vegetable processing is organized in a continuous line, with operators performing tasks at the beginning or end of the line, as well as monitoring the proper functioning of the machinery throughout the line. Most technological upgrading has consisted of buying better hydration tunnels to process the fruits and vegetables. The firms have also purchased machines that peel and cut apples, pit prunes, and make fruit and vegetable pulp. With the exception of the machine that washes the produce prior to its processing, as well as freezing chambers, the Chilean firms import their machinery. Firms typically purchase new machinery from the United States or Europe. Reconditioned machinery, commonly used in other Latin American industries, is not as prevalent in agroindustry, though it can be found in firms that sell to the domestic market, such as A7. Since agroindustrial production is primarily for export, it does not have the economy of scale restrictions of other Chilean industries. Moreover, the products must meet the higher quality standards of the world market. Meeting the goals of greater output and higher quality forces agroindustrialists to continually update machinery.

Data from the manufacturing census reveals that between 1980 and 1995, investments in new machinery, measured in 1999 U.S. dollars, increased from $3.5 million to $25.6 million. The strongest years of new investment were from 1990 to 1993, when many new firms were entering the industry. On the whole, the new investment has increased employment since more line workers are needed to inspect the product being processed. Thus, during the 1980–1995 period, new machinery investments averaged a 41.7 percent annual increase while employment grew by 8.8 percent annually. Productivity, calculated as gross value of production divided by employment, grew by 1.7 percent, most of which occurred after the heavy investment in new machinery, beginning in 1990.[7]

In most instances, technological upgrading has been a benefit for labor, as more workers are needed to sort the goods. This is the case in prune production, where workers who manually pit prunes were replaced by pitting machines. Though these workers' tasks were eliminated, the increase in output meant that more workers were needed to sort the pitted prunes, leading to an overall expansion of employment. A similar pattern of overall employment expansion occurred when dehydrating firms moved to automatic tunnel dryers away from ovens.

A4 is a subsidiary of one of Chile's most important conglomerates, with businesses in salmon and scallop farming, real estate, and fresh kiwi exports. The firm produces dehydrated apples, peppers (red, green and jalapeño) and tomatoes, as well as a variety of juice concentrates. Most production is of dehydrated apples, red peppers and apple juice. Its dehydrated fruit and vegetable sales totaled US$16 million in 2000, making it the country's leading dehydrates exporter, along with A3. Juice sales were US$12 million. A4's competitive strategy emphasizes controlling costs through technological investment and verticalization.[8]

There are three stages in processing dehydrated fruit: preparation, drying and packaging. Preparation is the labor-intensive stage; the other two stages are automated, with just a few workers who monitor the machines and separate newly dried goods that have stuck together. When A4 first built its factory in 1988, the company purchased new manual dehydrating equipment from the United States. Thus, in the beginning, the drying stage of production was also labor-intensive. Manual dehydrating machines operate like large ovens. When dehydrating apple rings, for example, the sliced apples are placed on large baking sheets (about four feet in diameter), slid into the doorless oven to bake, and then removed with special utensils. Frustrated by the output limitations of the manual ovens, the company purchased semi-automatic drying tunnels in 1990 and upgraded to a continuous dryer in 1994. They now have three continuous dryers. Upgrading from a semi-automatic to a fully automatic dryer in 1994 did not replace labor; rather it caused output to expand greatly, thus increasing employment while barely reducing labor intensity.

The expansion of output from using continuous dryers created a need for more workers in the preparation stage of processing. The line inspection duties ensure that once the fruit pieces are dehydrated, the product appears homogenous and meets the clients' standards.[9] Another preparatory task, which occurs at the beginning of the line, involves the manual removal of certain fruit and vegetable stems, such as the stems of red and green peppers.

By 1997, the factory was employing 1,200 workers during the peak months. The need to employ so many workers at the same time the fresh-fruit packinghouses were in full swing became problematic. Previously, their entire work force had come from the small town where the factory is located, in an agricultural region two hours south of Santiago. When labor needs increased, the firm was forced to hire workers from neighboring towns and transport them by bus to and from the factory. Another alternative would have been to raise salaries to entice packinghouse workers to come to A4, but the firm chose to not do this. The logistical difficulties of bussing in production workers for three different shifts a day, as well as the physical limitations in finding line space for so many workers, convinced the firm in early 2000 to purchase an optical sorting machine at a cost of US$800,000. A client had suggested they purchase the machine in order to cut costs. The machine, which uses lasers to detect and sort spotted apple pieces from good pieces, reduced peak employment from 1,200 workers to 450 workers, allowing the firm to recoup the cost of the machine in just one year.

Unlike other machinery that increases speed and improves product quality, optical sorting technology simply replaces labor. Based on software known as "machine vision," the machine is programmed to sort products using cameras, lights and information about the product's physical characteristics. Machine vision technology was first developed in the early 1980s in the U.S. and by the 1990s was used widely throughout the U.S. food-processing industry.[10] In Chile, however, only A4 has adopted the technology. The other firms are aware of its existence and have considered it, though most cited concerns about quality and excessive product loss from using this equipment. A8, on the other hand, has plans to adopt the technology within the next several years, for use in selection of exported berries for processing.

Optical sorting technology is the epitome of economists' conception of labor-saving technological change, as it replaces workers performing manual selection with a machine. Most of the growth in agroindustry employment has been in line workers that sort the products. Indeed, with the exception of optical sorting technology, technological upgrading in agroindustry has increased employment in the industry, because the greater volumes processed lead to employment growth in the labor-intensive task of sorting and selecting products.[11] With optical sorting technology, these workers' jobs can now be automated. According to Key Technology, a leading U.S. manufacturer of optical sorting machines with sales representation in Chile, their sense from potential customers in Chile was that the labor costs were still low enough not to warrant investment in the machinery, which partly explains why only one Chilean firm has adopted it.[12] Nevertheless, the existence of such technology may pose a threat to jobs in the future.

Training for Increased Productivity

Investing in machinery to increase output is one way to increase productivity. Another option is to invest in the workers themselves, so that they better understand the jobs they are doing and are better prepared to ensure and guarantee quality standards. Although training as a competitive strategy is not commonplace in this industry, A3 has made training the centerpiece of its competitive strategy. The strategy is important to analyze as it has certain labor market implications, which I discuss in the next section.

A3 processes dehydrated apples, tomatoes, green and red peppers and mixed berries for export. The company also cans and exports cherries and asparagus. Its competitive strategy is to invest heavily in training to increase adaptability, inspiring innovation and development.[13] The policy includes all of the staff, not just management. The company believes that by having a workforce that is both knowledgeable and involved in company decision-making, it can lower costs and increase productivity. The company has an intensive and continual training program. Between the months of February and October, workers participate in training programs, which rotate between the three work shifts, so that every six weeks, a worker receives three weeks of training of 1 1/2 hours per day. Topics include working in teams, quality control, safety, and process improvement. Training is not restricted to the area in which the worker works, but rather covers all of the company, thus ensuring that the workers understand the mission and processes of the firm.

The company also formed a group of eighty workers, who are dedicated to the company and committed to its improvement, regardless of their rank or educational background. At the monthly meetings, all eighty members must identify a problem, so that the group can discuss the problem and find an in-house solution. An important goal of the "Group of Eighty" is to share openly and discuss, in detail, the finances of the company. The belief is that by having these workers understand the financial constraints of the company, they may be more willing to accept changes, such as when the bonuses for the cherry season were eliminated. It may also make them more committed when issues do arise. For example, when the firm needed staff to work on Mother's Day to process a batch of raw materials that was going to spoil, workers of the group of eighty were more willing to come in as they understood more fully the financial implications of not processing the goods.

The company "look[s] for optimal efficiency between human and technical needs, rather than buying technology and then training the staff." In other words, the main competitive advantage is not the technology, but "having a workforce that is adaptable to changes in the competitive environment" (company document). The company, therefore, invests in processes and equipment jointly. They have some new technology—for example, they bought a continuous drying oven in 1999—but they also have some machinery that is thirty years old and manual, such as the oven-style dehydrators. Both dehydrators are used simultaneously in production.

According to management, the system of teamwork and regular meetings has helped them solve problems and improve technology without having to resort to costly solutions. When the sales staff informed the maintenance staff that the level of rejection of dehydrated grains and powders was high, the maintenance staff discovered that there was a problem with the grain measurer of the machine. The maintenance staff then developed a design to fix the grain measurer, which prevented replacing the machine. Similarly, a special forklift was designed in-house, as were the machines that wash the fruits and vegetables. A3's competitive strategy emphasizes communication and ingenuity among the staff rather than pure technological investment, like A4.[14] Thanks to the training program, workers are more adaptable, allowing them to perform a multitude of tasks as needed by the firm. Some of the line workers have been trained to do jobs previously done by supervisors, such as operating the metal detector at the end of the line, permitting a reduction in the number of supervisors. Worker training has been good for business. Attention to quality control, team work and process improvement enabled the company to obtain ISO-9002 certification in 1998, allowing them to sell to processed food manufacturers, such as General Mills and Kraft, which only buy products from firms that are ISO-certified.[15] A3 was the first Chilean agroindustrial firm to obtain ISO certification and did so one year before its technologically superior competitor, A4.

A5 opened in 1994 as a producer of fruit and vegetable juices and was furnished with new equipment from Europe and the United States.[16] According to the owner, and based on a visit he made to a juice factory in California, the technological sophistication of his plant is on par with industrialized countries. As they have not needed to make additional investments in machinery, productivity growth has stemmed from learning, by both management and workers, how best to operate the company. Plant workers, all of whom have completed high school, receive training from the manufacturing equipment suppliers and also take courses on machinery operation, repair and quality control at technical schools. Once the client base was well established, the company reduced the number of administrative personnel. It also found that it needed fewer supervisors in the plant and has eliminated some of these positions, thus boosting output per worker.

Juice production differs from other sectors in the industry in that it is highly capital intensive. Almost all parts of a fruit or vegetable can be used to produce juice, making line inspectors—who are so prevalent in other agroindustry sectors—unnecessary. Just a few operators are needed to run the equipment. At A5, 21 workers are employed in production, which amounts to about five workers per shift.[17] In 1999, the company instituted a wage system for the operators that ties pay to productivity, with productivity determined by monthly output.[18] The intention was to make the workers "feel like they are part of the company," so that they would respond quickly to problems that arise. Now, when the machinery stops working, they are quicker to fix it.

Moving Away from Commodities: New Products, New Markets

The role of technology in agroindustry's competitive strategies is not limited to cost minimization. New technologies allow firms to develop new products, enabling them to enter more lucrative markets. In the case of Chile's prune industry, investment into prune pitting technology has allowed prune-producing firms to process the more valuable pitted prunes demanded by the European market.

A1 was formed in 1941 as an association of 25 plum growers joining together to process and export prunes.[19] In 1994, the association incorporated, with each member given a share of the corporation. A1 is the largest prune processor in Chile, with nearly 50 percent of the total volume exported. In total there are 42 prune exporters in Chile, though four companies dominate the industry. Prune exports, measured in tons, have grown at an annual rate of 24 percent since 1981.[20] By 2000, nearly 22 million tons of prunes were produced annually in Chile, 95 percent of which were for export, making Chile the third largest prune producer, after the U.S. and France.

Although A1 is a well-established firm that has always exported, it did not become aggressive about its competitive strategy until the second half of the 1980s, and particularly during the second half of the 1990s. A1's competitive strategy has three inter-linked components: (1) upgrade technology; (2) sell to more lucrative markets; and (3) shift from intermediary to final-good sales. Upgrading technology is inter-linked with market expansion, since better technology is needed to sell to more lucrative markets. Before the mid-1980s most of the company's sales had been to Latin America, whereas by 2000, only 30 percent of their sales were to Latin America; Europe accounted for nearly 70 percent of sales. In comparison, 70 percent of total Chilean prune exports are to Latin America.

To sell to Europe, the firm had to invest in prune pitting technology and upgrade its quality control and health standards. In Europe, unlike Latin America, the market is mostly for pitted prunes. Manually pitting prunes is one option for entering this market, but the slow process limits the ability of a firm to increase output and sales at a significant rate. As the general manager stated, the German market was essentially closed to them without the prune pitting technology. To meet the higher health standards demanded by the European market, the firm instituted the HACCP[21] quality control system.

In 1986, A1 acquired its first pitting machine. It leases the machine for US$20,000 per year from the U.S. manufacturer, Ashlock, the industry leader of prune pitting machines. The company added more Ashlock machines, and by 2000, it had ten. In 1988, the company purchased a new plastic-bag-packaging machine from Italy in order to expand production of pre-packaged goods to sell directly to foreign retailers. In 1991 the company mechanized plum harvesting with the purchase of mechanical shakers, which shake the plums out of their trees.

Prior to investing in the pitting machines, prunes were pitted manually by women working at piece rates. The machines replaced these workers, yet as a result, output increased and many more jobs were created. Between 1995 and 2000, A1 increased production from 4 million to 10 million tons, while between 1997 and 2000, the number of production workers grew by 20 percent. Moreover, the final product has increased in value-added since 70 percent of the prunes are now pitted, which sell at a higher prices than prunes with pits.

Three partners founded A2 in 1987 with the intention of exporting prunes.[22] In 1993, the company expanded into raisin production. By 2000, the company was exporting $6.5 million worth of raisins, $6.0 million worth of prunes and nearly $1 million in nuts. A2 accounts for 22 percent of Chile's prune exports, 13 percent of raisin exports and 9 percent of nut exports.

When the prune factory opened 13 years ago, the machinery was Chilean. Like A1, the company has invested in prune pitting technology to increase output. A2 has eight Ashlock machines, though it still uses piece workers for 30 percent of its pitted prune production, for customers who specifically order manually pitted prunes. One Ashlock machine pits 10,000 prunes per day, which is equivalent to the daily output of 75 workers. But this did not cause a loss of 600 jobs (8 machines times 75 workers), since over time the effect of having the machines has been to raise output of pitted prunes. For example, prior to investing in the pitting machinery, A1 employed only 50–60 women to manually pit prunes. It was not until they invested in the Ashlock technology that their pitted prune production saw a rapid increase. Productivity growth, therefore, should be thought of as increasing output, rather than as shedding workers. Indeed, technological investments have for the most part been beneficial to low-skilled workers in agroindustry.

Another competitive strategy, which does not involve technological investment, is to develop new products that have lower price elasticities.

When A5 entered the market in 1994 to produce fruit and vegetable juices, it recognized that producing vegetable juice for the Asian market was an unexploited niche within the sector.[23] Since entering the market, A5's focus has been on selling and developing vegetable juice products to Asia, although two-thirds of their production is still fruit juices, most of which are sold to the U.S. Part of the owner's motivation for developing vegetable juices was to move away from processing fruit juices, which are subject to commodity price fluctuations. Plus, since 1996, Chilean apple juice exports have suffered due to a loss of sales to Chinese competition. Vegetable juice production also has the added benefit of allowing the company to extend its production season and make better use of the installed capacity.

Full Package Production

One option for Chilean agroindustrialists trying to escape commodity price fluctuations, as well as gain control of the more lucrative distribution and marketing ends of the value chain, is to move up the chain into full package production. Full package production—Stage 4 in the value chain—implies the manufacturer is producing the complete item, including obtaining the raw materials, and then delivering the product in a finished state, ready for retail sale. Thus, the product leaves the agroindustrialist's factory as a final good, with either the manufacturer's or the retailer's label placed on the package. The rents associated with product development, distribution and marketing are, along with retailing, the highest value-added activities in the value chain (Bair and Gereffi, 2001).

Both prune manufacturers (A1 and A2) have begun marketing prunes as packaged final products. The firms have bought plastic-bag packaging machines that allow them to package prunes under their brand name as well as under their brand name of that of the retailer's. A1 has also expanded its prepackaged products for direct sale to foreign supermarkets; it now has contracts with the leading direct retailers in Brazil. In 1993, prepackaged products accounted for only four percent of sales; by 1998 they had reached 20 percent of sales and were projected to reach 35 percent by 2003.

Another agroindustrial sector that manufactures full-package products and has been successful in upgrading is the tomato paste sector. Tomato paste manufacturers have diversified from just producing for export to develop their own brands of packaged tomato sauce for the domestic market. Tomato sauce production for the local market requires a lower quality grade of tomatoes than that required for tomato paste production for the international market, allowing the manufacturers to make use of poor-quality tomatoes. Perhaps the most ambitious attempt at development, sale and distribution of final good tomato-derivative products is by the country's largest agroindustrial firm, Iansa. In 1997, Iansa acquired a Brazilian processed-foods company whose main product line is tomato sauce and ketchup. With this acquisition, the company secured an important outlet for its tomato paste as well as a strong foothold in the South American processed-foods market. The company's goals are to expand sales of products at the high-value end of the value chain throughout South America (Silva Torrealba, 1999).

Leaving the Export Market: The Attraction of Local Sales

A7 and A8 both entered the frozen foods market to export frozen berries. Like other agroindustry sectors, exports of frozen produce began expanding in the mid-1980s with exports, measured in 2000 dollars, growing from just over US$2 million in 1985 to US$42 million by 1991 and US$75 million in 2000. Exports peaked at $94 million in 1996. But by the mid-1990s, both A7 and A8 had shifted their competitive focus away from frozen berries for export to frozen vegetables for the domestic and neighboring markets, as a result of falling profits.

A8 was started in 1989 with the idea of exporting frozen berries and asparagus.[24] With this in mind, the company built a factory near the airport to process frozen produce for export. In 1991, the company expanded through a merger with a firm that owned a frozen fruit processing plant in the south, in the heart of the country's berry-growing region. Yet after several years, the company realized it could no longer depend on the external market for growth and began investing to develop sales to the internal market.[25] In 1997, it purchased the leading domestic frozen foods manufacturer, which was suffering from financial problems. Though the equipment in that company's central-valley factory was outdated and required upgrading, by buying the company they now owned the leading frozen food brand in the Chilean market, giving them a platform for future domestic growth. The strategy proved successful. By 2000, the company had become the leader in the domestic frozen vegetable market, with 40 percent market share; fruit accounted for just 30 percent of production. The company expects sales to the domestic market to grow at five percent per year; it does not expect growth in the frozen fruit market. Its future growth strategy is based on developing new products and offering a wider variety of products to the domestic market. It also has plans to export frozen vegetables to South and Central America.[26]

A8 now has three factories: (1) the original Santiago factory, which operates year-round as a packaging facility, (2) the Southern berry and asparagus factory, which exports to Europe, the U.S. and Asia, and (3) the central-valley frozen vegetable processing plant. When A8 bought the central-valley factory, it invested in upgrading the technological capacity of the facility through the purchase of reconditioned equipment from the United States.[27] Frozen vegetable production is capital-intensive—at both the harvesting and processing stages—which is why both A7 and A8 prefer frozen vegetable production to frozen fruit production. Both companies have contracts with agricultural producers to grow vegetables, providing technical assistance at the planting stages as well as the machinery and labor needed to harvest the crops.

With frozen produce, the goal is to freeze as soon as possible after harvesting—within four to twelve hours—to retain freshness. Once the harvested vegetable gets to the factory, it is cut, grained and washed, in a highly mechanized process. After washing, the corn grains or peas pass through a machine that kills bacteria, then through tunnels that freeze the product at an exact temperature, and then finally it passes through bins that divide the products according to size. Afterwards, it goes to a freezer chamber where it is stored to await packing and transport. It only takes 12 people to produce 3,000 tons of peas: five to operate the machines and seven in quality control. A8's central-valley factory employs only 50 employees; at the time of purchase in 1997, it employed 250.

In comparison, frozen fruit production is highly labor-intensive. Harvesting is done by hand. Once the berries arrive at the factory, they are manually selected according to size and appearance. If the berry has a stem, as in the case of strawberries, the stem is then removed manually using a simple hand-held metal wire.

Like A8, A7 has also moved away from production for export to frozen vegetable processing for the internal market. A7 was established in 1978 to produce frozen fruits for the both the internal and external market; it diversified into frozen vegetables in 1983.[28] By 1996, exports comprised fifty percent of sales, yet the firm found itself in financial trouble and was forced to restructure. Restructuring involved labor shedding and moving away from exports towards production for the internal market. Now, exports make up just 10 percent of sales. According to the general manager, the financial problems were the result of an overvalued peso and rising labor costs. By putting greater emphasis on production for the internal market, the company could better control production costs by shifting away from fruits to vegetables, which depends on a more mechanized harvesting and production process. The strategy proved successful: since 1997, profit margins have averaged 22 to 23 percent. Sales in 2000 grew by 15 percent and were expected to grow by 8 percent in 2001.

When manufacturers cannot earn rents from production, they sometimes opt for packaging and reselling, where margins are higher and often more dependable. In the early 1990s, A9 decided to stop processing fruit and vegetables and instead focus on the packaging, marketing and distribution of dried fruits and nuts for the local market.[29] The company has contracts with many suppliers covering a range of products. It is the country's leading seller of dried fruit and nuts for the internal market; exports account for only five percent of sales.

A9 transports produce from rural areas to its Santiago packaging facility where the products undergo quality control tests and are then repackaged into smaller bags for retail sale. The goods are sold under A9's various brand names, or under a retail store's generic line, at local supermarkets and retail outlets. Some of the contracts with suppliers could be considered subcontracted "assembly" work, since A9 built the physical space, provides the raw materials and any necessary equipment, and pays an annually negotiated price, per kilo of good. A9's owner appreciated the flexibility of not being integrated vertically, because the firm can add and drop products at very little cost. In order to earn rents on the production side, it is necessary to specialize in just a few products to increase economies of scale sufficiently. Since A9's focus is on the internal market, it must offer a wide range of products. Due to this circumstance, limiting the range of products to lower per unit production costs is not a viable strategy.

IMPLICATIONS FOR LABOR

How have the different competitive strategies of the agroindustrial firms affected the demand for labor? Are workers better off if firms "move up the value chain" to higher value-added production versus focusing on technological upgrading to control costs? Do workers benefit when they are better trained?

Table 5.2 summarizes the employment effects of the four competitive strategies identified in the analysis. In general, the most striking finding about employment in Chilean agroindustry is its endemic reliance on a temporary workforce, even when workers are employed year-round. Regardless of whether a firm's competitive strategy emphasizes technological upgrading, training, higher-value added production, or production and sale for the internal market, labor market flexibility—in the form of temporary employment contracts—is the centerpiece of the firms' employment policies. Competitive strategies that extend the production season, either by developing new products or full-package products or because of an emphasis on training, increase the length of the employment contract, but unfortunately, do not lead to permanent employment for low-skilled production workers. Semi-skilled production workers, however, are more likely to be offered a permanent contract than if the competitive strategy had not been pursued.

Table 5.2: Summary of Employment Effects of Identified Competitive Strategies

Competitive Strategy	Firms	Employment Effects
Mechanization to Control Costs	A4, A6	Cost-saving is most important factor in decisions. Line inspectors can be replaced with optical sorting technology that automates their jobs. Heaviest reliance on temporary contracts.
Training for Increased Productivity	A3, A5	Requires that production season be extended. Leads to longer contracts and greater employment stability. May increase the permanence of contracts for semi-skilled workers, but not for low-skilled workers.
Moving Away from Commodities (new products, new markets, full-package production)	A1, A2, A5, A6, A7, A8	Leads to more stability in sales, improving employment stability. Particularly true in full-package production, which extends operating season. Does not necessarily lead to permanent contracts.
Production for the Internal Market	A7, A8 (and A9, just sales)	More capital-intensive since internal market has higher concentration of products that can be harvested and processed mechanically. Selling to internal market leads to growth of year-round packaging and sales jobs, which have permanent contracts. Processing workers still hired under temporary contracts.

Source: Author's assessment based on interviews, factory visits and secondary information.

If a factory only operates for part of the year, it is understandable that the manufacturing firm would employ workers only for the season, on temporary (also known as definite) contracts, as opposed to permanent (indefinite) contracts. Yet temporary contracts are also given to many workers employed year-round. For the eight agroindustry manufacturers included in the survey (excluding A9, which does not manufacture), the total number of jobs at the peak of the season was approximately 3,700. About 650 workers, a little less than 20 percent, had permanent contracts, while about 1,400 workers, or 38 percent, remained for most of the year.

By offering these workers temporary rather than permanent contracts, firms can save labor costs by dismissing the worker if the season is cut short for reasons beyond the company's control, such as a poor harvest. Moreover, they do not have to pay for vacation or other benefits that are customarily extended to permanent employees; and they are no longer legally required to pay severance. But one of the most striking implications of offering temporary contracts is that it removes the ability of workers to bargain collectively, therefore prohibiting the use of strikes in wage negotiation. With so few workers in agroindustry firms eligible to participate in collective bargaining negotiations, the ability of unions to negotiate wage increases has been severely hampered.

Under Chilean law workers can only renew temporary contracts twice, since upon the third renewal the worker is automatically granted an indefinite contract. In agroindustry, however, workers can be hired continuously under temporary contracts as the contract is for the processing of a specific crop, rather than specified for a length of time, as is done in other industries. For example, as mentioned in chapter 3, if a worker is hired for the peach juice season, when peach juice production halts, only to be resumed the next day by strawberry juice production, the worker begins a new contract "for the strawberry juice season." Because the contract specifies production of a different product, it is legally not considered a renewal. Alternatively, firms can bypass a temporary contract from becoming permanent by having a break between renewals.[30] The nature of the products allows the firm flexibility in dismissing workers early if the harvest is less bountiful than expected and ensuring that the workers continue indefinitely under temporary contracts. Through the use of temporary contracts, firms can facilitate adjustments to changes in production, thereby lowering labor costs. In the process a firm increases the numerical and wage flexibility of its labor force.

Another principal finding from the case studies is that the wages of low-skilled workers are not higher if the worker is employed in a firm that emphasizes training or a more extended product line versus mechanization. In general, low-skilled workers' wages are set at the minimum wage with bonuses for tenure, attendance and working the night shift, as well as overtime pay. By Chilean law, after the first 12 hours of overtime (60 hours), a worker earns time-and-a-half. Because of the need to process the agricultural products speedily during harvest time, it is common for workers to work a 72-hour week, 12 hours a day, 6 days a week, during the peak season.

Nevertheless, low-skilled workers' wages in agroindustry increased substantially in the 1990s as the return to democracy in 1990 led to a near doubling of the real value of the minimum wage during the decade. By 2000, the minimum wage was 90 percent above its 1989 level. While it could be argued that minimum wage increases were partly responsible for the profit squeeze of agroindustrial manufacturers, rising wages had the beneficial outcome of stimulating investment that increased productivity as well as forcing firms to develop new products. Moreover, the minimum wage increases simply precipitated a profit squeeze that was emerging as a result of competition from manufacturers in China and elsewhere.

Since low-skilled workers' wages have increased as a result of institutional increases in the minimum wage rather than as a result of a firm's competitive strategy, the principal benefit of working as a low-skilled worker in a firm that emphasizes training, or in a firm that has moved up the value chain in its production, is that the worker is likely to be employed for more months out of the year. Job duration increases because the firms operate longer. Thus a competitive strategy that lengthens job duration will increase a worker's yearly earnings, even if the worker's monthly or piece-rate earnings are unaffected.

Finally, the gender and social relations of the country facilitate the policy of employing a largely temporary labor force, contributing to the success of the agroindustrial sector. Upwards of seventy percent of agroindustry jobs are filled by female factory workers, known as *temporeras,* hired to inspect and sort products before or after they pass through the line.[31] The temporeras' jobs are essential to the production process, guaranteeing that Chile meets the quality standards of the markets it sells to. Most managers say they prefer women to men for the job because women are believed to have greater dexterity, attention to detail, and familiarity in choosing fruits and vegetables based on their experience in the kitchen. Some managers also mentioned that a man could not work in the middle of a group of women without breaking cultural norms. Another benefit, as pointed out by researchers studying the working conditions of the *temporeras* (Barrientos et al. 1999; Henríquez et al., 1994), is that society expects these women to return to their duties in the home after work at the factory terminates. As they are home during the winter months tending to their household duties, they act essentially as a "reserve army" waiting to return to the factory when the agroindustrial production season commences once again.

The inherent "flexibility" of the female labor force benefits the employment policies of the firms, but in the end hurts the women. According to my interviews, the production workers given permanent contracts were mechanics and supervisors, who are most often male. The laboratories, which are under the domain of women, employ the head of laboratory on a permanent contract, but release the skilled laboratory assistants from their contracts in the off-season months.[32]

Unlike the export sectors of many other developing countries, where women hired to work in factories are single and either leave or are dismissed upon getting married, Chilean *temporeras* tend to be middle-aged, married women (Newman, 1994; Barrientos et al. 1999).[33] By working in the factories only in the summer months, women can earn much needed income for their families without significantly disrupting the social contract between husband and wife.[34] More importantly, because of limited employment opportunities in the off-season, many women return to the factories year after year and are thus a reliable source of experienced labor. As the manager of A7 explained, before the season starts, they contact the *temporeras* that worked with them during the previous season and may even send them a basket of frozen goods. Workers who return for more than two seasons earn a bonus of five to ten percent of their pay, which to the manager did not seem like much, but, according to him, "it is recognition and it means a lot to the workers." Similarly, A2 stated that its workers are given a bonus to return and that they do indeed return.

Labor laws therefore work in tandem with gender and marital norms to maintain flexibility in the amount of time a worker is employed. Hiring women also enhances wage flexibility, since, on average, women in Chile earn 28 percent less than men, after controlling for worker characteristics and industry (Berg and Contreras, 2004). Indeed, it seems likely that the high share of women in agroindustry has been an unrecognized boon to the sector as management has been able to take advantage of the greater flexibility and lower cost of female labor.

Firm Experiences

Comparing the use of temporary labor between A3 and A4—which have vastly different competitive strategies even though they are the country's two leading apple dehydrators—illustrates the pervasive reliance on temporary work contracts in agroindustry. A4 is owned by a leading Chilean conglomerate and has invested in optical sorting technology and buying its own apple firms in order to control commodity costs. A3 is a family-run company whose intensive worker-training program and its program to build relations with suppliers have won it praise (including a management award) from the country's development agencies. A3's management believes that a well-trained workforce can guarantee the quality necessary to establish contracts with leading processed food manufacturers in the U.S. and Europe.

At A4, the factory is shut for five months out of the year. During the off-season, the staff is reduced from 450 to 70 workers in operation and administration. Of these 70, nearly 30 are mechanics and operators, considered semi-skilled by the plant manager. These workers are retained for part of the off-season months to do routine maintenance and cleaning jobs under a "maintenance contract." Although there is not enough work to keep them busy for the five months, the firm offers them an extension of their temporary contract during the off-season so that they do not leave for another company. However, the firm does not grant them a permanent contract. Unskilled line workers, who earn ten percent above the minimum wage, plus bonuses for attendance, working the night shift, and an end-of-season bonus, are dismissed when the season ends.[35] The remaining workers are in management and administration and have permanent contracts. Administrative staff have their salary adjusted for inflation three times per year and receive a "participation bonus" as well as bonuses at the end of season. Executives participate in profit sharing.

A3 employs between 550–600 workers for ten months out of the year (February-December), for three shifts a day, six to seven days per week. During the non-peak months of December and January, the workforce drops to 180 workers. Because of the investments made in worker training and the need for committed team workers, A3 has diversified its products and processes to keep the factory running, even though this has meant higher fixed costs and the production of some low-margin goods, such as canned asparagus. The result has been an increase in the length of the contract offered to workers and thus, greater employment stability. Yet even with the quasi-permanence of positions, particularly when compared with A4 and other firms in the sector, only 50 workers have permanent (indefinite) contracts. The staff with permanent contracts include the managers, area chiefs, supervisors and administrators. The rest of the staff, who work 10 to 12 months out of the year, rotate on temporary contracts defined by the good they are processing.

The continual use of temporary contracts is a complaint often voiced by workers of the company's Group of Eighty, the monthly worker-management roundtable that discusses problems in the company. Some of the Group of Eighty workers may be sent to China to help open a dehydration factory there, and "they wonder what the payback is for them of such a high degree of involvement." Although there are much more than 50 workers who stay on all year, management believes "it is too risky to give them indefinite contracts," even if it means that they might lose the workers. According to management, competition is too fierce and margins too low to be able to afford permanent contracts. Yet because of a lack of better employment alternatives—nearby fruit-packaging firms pay the same and also offer temporary contracts—workers stay at A3 and thus there does not appear to be a market-determined need to give them more stable employment contracts. An important advantage of the workers' staying at A3 is that the factory operates almost year-round, meaning that many workers have an extended duration of employment as compared with other job market prospects.

One implication of A3's compensation policies is that their workers are paid the same as other agroindustrial workers in their area, despite being better trained. There are three pay scales for the line workers, determined according to "the individual's contribution to the firm." Line workers earn the minimum wage or five to ten percent above. Previously the company gave a one-month bonus each year to all workers, but the salary structure has been changed to benefit the Group of Eighty workers, who for six years have been contributing extra time to the company without additional compensation. Now, the company will divide profits, above a certain amount, with the Group of Eighty workers. The extra month's pay has been eliminated. Managers earn roughly ten times the pay of the line workers. Compensation for the non-managerial staff for the training, flexibility and team effort of the workers has been based more on volunteerism rather than remuneration, as the training manager readily acknowledged.[36]

The training-intensive competitive strategy of A3 has an advantage over A4 in that it employs workers on longer contracts, which increases job stability and earnings, since they work for more months of the year. Still, the strategy has not resulted in permanent contracts. A4's strategy of controlling costs through mechanization is extreme in its reliance on temporary contracts, even for semi-skilled workers. In the long run, however, the more pressing concern for the workers is that A4's competitive strategy is based on controlling costs, including labor costs, making labor shedding an inherent goal. In the case of A6, for example, the heavy technological investments made in the mid-1990s coupled with more efficient management have led to a reduction in employment from 2,000 to 1,000 workers between 1995 and 2001.[37]

At A5, the training-intensive vegetable and fruit juice manufacturer, the likelihood of having a permanent contract is higher than at A3. The difference stems from the nature of juice production, which is highly capital-intensive and relies on a small number of semi-skilled operators to perform and monitor the manufacturing process. Since almost all parts of a fruit or vegetable can be used to produce juice, line inspectors, who are so prevalent in other agroindustry sectors, are unnecessary. At A5, 21 workers are employed in production, which amounts to about five workers per shift.[38] The workers are well paid, earning between US$7,000 and $9,000 per year, or about three to four times the legal minimum wage. Salary increases for these semi-skilled operators have matched the growth in productivity, growing annually at 2–3 percent above the rate of inflation. The men employed in production have completed high school as well as some technical school studies.

To assess the impact of training as a competitive strategy on employment, it is thus better to compare A5 with other juice manufacturers. Because A5 also manufacturers vegetable juices, it is able to extend production for four additional months, past the five months for juice processing, allowing it to offer a greater number of permanent contracts.[39] Low-skilled workers who receive deliveries and work in storage are hired on temporary contracts for the season. Yet only 26 percent of A5's workers are temporary, compared with over 50 percent at the country's leading juice manufacturer, Patagonia, and 38 percent at another juice company, Jucosa.[40] At A4, which produces juices in addition to dehydrates, all of the operators work on temporary contracts, which, as mentioned, are extended during the off-season as "maintenance contracts."[41] The workers at A5 have directly benefited from management's strategy to diversify the product line and extend the factory's time in use. With extended factory operation, management can emphasize training, which increases the value of the employee to management, leading to an increase in permanent employment for the semi-skilled.

From the analysis of firms that emphasize training as a competitive strategy, namely A3 and A5, we can conclude that semi-skilled workers benefit when companies emphasize training, whereas it does not help low-skilled workers. For low-skilled workers, increased contract length does not lead to permanent employment. Similarly other competitive strategies that extend job duration, such as moving to full-package production, also fail to offer permanent employment to its low-skilled workforce, as is attested to by the prune manufacturers, A1 and A2.

Unlike most other agroindustrial products, prunes can be processed year-round, since once a plum is dried it can last up to three years if it is stored correctly with regular fumigation.[42] The prune industry, therefore, does not have the seasonal constraints of other agroindustry firms. Moreover, both A1 and A2 have moved into full-package production, which extends the operation of the factory since the companies now bag, label and market prunes for sale at retail outlets. Nevertheless, A1 and A2 employ a large percentage of production workers on temporary contracts, despite the ability to operate throughout the year.

A1 employs 160 workers, 140 of which are production workers. The factory operates 24 hours a day, Monday through Friday, with day and night shifts. Of the 140 production workers, 60 have indefinite contracts. Management gives indefinite contracts to those workers whom it considers skilled and semi-skilled. This includes the machine operators, the line heads, and the laboratory personnel. Unskilled workers, employed as line inspectors or in packaging and storage, work on temporary contracts from one to eight months. Nevertheless, the possibilities for advancement are better at A1 than at most other agroindustrial firms, since a capable line inspector can be promoted to head of the line, a permanent job.

A2 has separate prune and raisin factories, which both operate from February to November, despite the ability, at least in the case of prunes, to operate year-round. The factories are open six days a week, with two eight-hour shifts. Ninety workers are employed in the prune factory, whereas the raisin factory employs 150 workers, because of the greater labor intensity of raisin inspections. Since the factory is shut for two months of the year, the workers are hired on ten-month temporary contracts, returning to the factory after their two-month break.

Finally, the competitive strategy of shifting production towards the internal market does not appear to have much of an effect on the temporary versus permanent contract balance for production workers, though it does aid the growth of other jobs. Production for the internal market involves more sales and administration workers since the companies must market and distribute the products across retail outlets in the country. These workers hold permanent contracts, are more skilled, and are more highly paid, though much of their pay is based on commission. At A7, for example, of the 450 workers in 2001, there were 100 in sales and administration, a far larger share than found in purely exporting firms. Similarly, at A8, the packaging plant operates all year preparing goods for retail sale to the local market, employing 90 workers with permanent contracts. Still, having extended company operations throughout the year has not helped production workers become permanent employees. Of the 330 production workers at A7, only 25 have permanent contracts, including the head of operations, the head of maintenance, the head of refrigeration, two shift heads, and 15 other workers who do maintenance and low-level supervision. In keeping with the company's "policy of not putting more people in the plant" there has not been an increase in permanently employed factory workers, despite employment growth.[43]

Piece-work and Homework

An employee, whose output is not controlled by the speed of the line but instead depends on effort, is often paid at piece rates in agroindustry firms, regardless of the type of competitive strategy the firm pursues. Typical piece-rate jobs include manually pitting prunes, de-shelling nuts, and removing strawberry and red pepper stems. A2, A3 and A8 all employ piece-rate workers for these jobs, which are overwhelmingly filled by women. At A2, thirty percent of prunes are still pitted manually upon the clients' request, despite the firm's investment in automatic pitting machines. The workers who manually pit the prunes are paid at a per kilo piece-rate. Although piece-rate earnings are oftentimes higher then pre-set salaries, the extra output derived from piece-rate work often comes at the cost of physical strain for the worker (Schurman, 2001). One of the benefits of moving to automatic prune pitting was that piece-rate manual pitters were replaced with line inspectors earning monthly salaries.

Homework also exists in the industry. About thirty percent of nut de-shelling at A2 is subcontracted as homework, typically to family members of the factory workers. It is not as common as in-factory piece-rate work, as most fruits and vegetables would be damaged if sent to a person's home. By subcontracting production to the worker through piece-rates and home-work, the already flexible employment relationship in agroindustry becomes even more flexible. Although piece-rate workers employed in factories must by law also earn the minimum wage, employers can circumvent the legislation by paying employers an "honorarium."[44] A9, which subcontracts nut de-shelling to a third-party contractor, does not believe that the earnings of the workers who remove the shells have increased, since the kilo-price paid by A9 has remained constant over the past decade. Nut de-shelling cannot easily be automated without ruining the appearance of the nut. In the case of A9, approximately 60 women contracted by a local jobber perform nut de-shelling, while A9 provides the workspace, the nuts and the few necessary tools.

Labor Relations

One of the most striking implications of offering temporary contracts is that it removes the ability of workers to bargain collectively, therefore prohibiting the use of strikes in wage negotiation. Statements made by union leaders at A6 and A7 indicate that employers have been purposely shifting the contracts of year-round production workers from permanent to temporary. Some permanent factory workers have been fired, only to be rehired with temporary contracts. The unions also stated that their greatest weakness was that their membership could easily be fired and replaced with temporary workers.[45]

With so few workers in agroindustry firms eligible to participate in collective bargaining negotiations, the ability of unions to negotiate wage increases has been severely hampered.[46] Yet union membership still serves an important purpose. In firms with little dialogue between management and staff, the union can serve as a vehicle for expressing worker grievances, particularly regarding their treatment by supervisors. Companies that have made efforts to increase dialogue with workers seem to have prevented unions from being formed. For example, at A3, discussion by workers in 1986 about forming a union motivated management to establish the Group of Eighty. Management felt that by organizing a monthly meeting group, information about the firm could be shared with more workers than just those who belonged to the union or were union leaders.

Of the nine firms participating in the study, three had unions: A5, A6 and A7.[47] Since A7's founding in 1978, there have been two unions in the company. The first union formed in 1988 but disbanded in 1996 when the company slashed employment from 1,200 to 300 workers. According to the president of the current union, the relationship between management and the first union had been marked by conflict, and the union was unsuccessful in gaining wage increases for its members. The union was relatively large by agroindustry standards, with about 150 members. More than 100 of the members were temporary workers, who by law cannot bargain collectively (though they can legally join the union). Frustrated by an inability to secure greater wage increases, and perhaps optimistic following the return to democracy in 1990, the union voted to go on strike during the collective bargaining negotiations of 1991. Management reacted by firing all of the temporary workers during the legally mandated three-day wait period that follows calling for a strike. This scared the forty permanent workers, who feared being fired as well. They called off the strike and accepted the collective bargaining contract offered by management.

After the job cuts of 1996, only 15 of the original 50 plant workers with permanent contracts remained. In 2000, these workers formed a union, signing a collective bargaining contract in July 2000 for the 2000–2002 period. The fifteen union members work in maintenance and low-level supervision. There are about ten temporary workers who have similar responsibilities as the union members and work throughout the year, yet the union has no plans to expand membership to include these workers, as the company will not extend the collective bargaining contract to them. Although the union members are not happy with their salaries, obtaining salary increases was not their primary purpose for forming the union.[48] Instead, the workers formed a union to have a voice in the company; a goal that they feel has been met. They now have monthly meetings with the general manager and the human resources manager where they discuss grievances, in particular, how factory management treats them. Through their dialogue with management, they were also able to negotiate three days off during summer, the peak season for production.[49]

A6, which has been in business since 1906, has had a union since 1939. During the military dictatorship, the union still existed but became very submissive to management. The three current union officers have headed the union since 1989, when they "lost their fear" and waged a successful challenge to the old union leadership. A6 employs 230 production workers year-round, of which 30 have permanent contracts. During the peak months, employment reaches 1,000 workers, with most workers on contracts of 3–4 months. Unlike at A7, the union of A6 includes long-term temporary workers. Of the 200 long-term temporary workers, 150 are union members; 21 of the 30 permanently employed production workers are members as well. Short-term temporary workers do not join. Like at A7, however, much of the motivation in belonging to a union is for the workers to have an outlet for voicing complaints regarding their treatment by supervisors. Also, although the temporary workers do not receive the full benefits negotiated in the collective bargaining contract, they do receive them in smaller proportion.[50] The union of A6 has been more successful in negotiating wage increases than A7, perhaps because of the company's better history of labor relations. According to the union leaders at both firms, output per worker has increased as workers have dedicated more effort to the job, and machinery has been upgraded. During the August 2001 collective bargaining negotiations, the union negotiated salary increases of 2 to 4 percent above inflation, with higher raises given to those earning less. The average salary earned by the semi-skilled union members is C$180,000 (about US$325 per month). Short-term temporary workers earn the minimum wage of C$105,000 (about US$190 per month).

CONCLUSION

Agroindustry is the "poster child" of a dynamic non-traditional export sector based on a developing country's abundant natural resources and low-skilled labor. Much of the industry's growth stems from the search by processed food manufacturers in the U.S. for lower-cost inputs. Through its position in the processed-foods commodity chain, agroindustry benefited from its clients who promoted machinery upgrading and strict quality control. The focus on quality control and the need to sell homogenous products meant that new machinery investments increased the number of line inspectors needed to sort the products. Thus the boom in exports was a boon for employment growth.

Because of the emergence of new suppliers for the processed-foods commodity chain, agroindustry sales have fallen since 1996. The limitations to selling commodities have become apparent, prompting firms to develop new products with lower price elasticities or find ways to successfully sell commodities. Developing new products typically means moving up the value chain to produce goods already packaged for retail sale. Since the challenge of entering the Northern market at this end of the value chain is formidable, firms that have developed higher value-added products are selling the products to the internal market or to nearby Latin American countries. In this way the firms earn rent from marketing and distributing, since in some cases, they are selling the products directly to retailers. The other approach is to improve productivity, either through mechanization or by investing in worker training. Both strategies have been successful but the industry faces a rocky future as the playing field expands.

Moving up the value chain, away from commodities, as well as investing in worker training both require a lengthening of the employment contract. The result is that employment stability has increased, boosting workers' overall earnings since they are employed longer. However, their average (hourly) pay has not increased beyond the minimum wage. Unlike semi-skilled workers, many of whom benefit by earning permanent contracts when the firms adopt strategies that extend job duration, low-skilled production workers still receive temporary contracts even when firms' extended operating season would allow them to make the workers permanent. Indeed, the main characteristic of the industry—regardless of the competitive strategy that firms pursue—has been its reliance on a temporary labor force, exemplified by the use of piece-work and homework.

As the workforce holds primarily temporary labor contracts, it is unable to bargain collectively to improve its wages. Agroindustry firms have taken advantage of this characteristic of its workforce to suppress wage growth. Low-skilled production workers earn the minimum wage plus incentive bonuses and overtime. During the 1980s, when the military government allowed the minimum wage to fall, there was no growth in the wages of low-skilled workers, though this trend reverted in the 1990s with the recovery of the minimum wage following the return to democracy.

The dynamism of the agroindustrial sector has not done much for low-skilled workers but provide unstable and poorly paid jobs. Even when firms move up the value chain—a goal to which they should aspire, according to the commodity-chain development literature—there is no apparent benefit to the low-skilled workers. Improvements in the working conditions of these workers will not occur through the market, but rather must be mandated through minimum wage and core labor standards, such as the freedom of association. Industrial upgrading alone will not suffice to improve the working conditions of low-skilled workers in agroindustry. With ample supplies of low-skilled labor and an increase in competition from low-wage countries such as China it is unlikely that Chilean agroindustry will move in the direction of better labor standards.

Chapter Six

Rent-Hoarding in an Open Economy: The Effects of Free Trade on Low-Skilled Chilean Workers

INTRODUCTION

The findings from the case studies illustrate the complexity of the wage determination process, in particular how wages depend on firm performance and the institutional environment—and not just supply and demand in the labor market. In this chapter, I argue that rising wage inequality in Chile is the outcome of shifts in the country's position in international trade, macroeconomic conditions as well institutional factors such as labor relations. All have affected the amount of rents a firm receives and how the rents are shared.

The amount of rents a firm receives is determined by the difference between mark-up over costs, meaning the profit that a firm receives from selling its output after paying production costs. Production costs are variable and include the wages of production workers plus raw material costs per unit of output. Prices of finished goods are set by producers who "mark-up" their costs to bring them profits, with the degree of mark-up depending on the market power of the firm.[1] Though wages are considered a cost, when profits increase, workers demand a share of the rents via wage increases, thus there is a give and take between employers and workers that is determined by the bargaining power of the two sides as well as the performance of the firm and the economy. This theory of the determination of profits and wages, based on Kalecki (1954), differs markedly from neoclassical economics, which assumes that "profits are the reward of capital and wages are the return to personal productivity, adjusted by the stock of available human capital" (Galbraith, 2001, p.7).

I argue that there has been a dividing of rents at three levels and that national and international conditions after 1973 turned the tide against low-skilled Chilean workers, limiting the rents they received. I identify the three levels of rent division and explain the different circumstances that caused a decline in low-skilled Chilean workers' earnings. Part of the purpose of the three-tier rent division is to emphasize that simply looking at skilled and low-skilled earnings based on supply and demand of labor is insufficient for an analysis of income distribution.

This chapter is organized around the discussion of the three levels of rent division. The first section considers the division of rents between Northern and Chilean capitalists. I argue that free trade has reduced the amount of rents that Chilean capitalists earn, while increasing rents going to the North. Free trade has reduced rents in both import-competing and exporting Chilean firms. Import-competing firms have been forced to lower their mark-ups as a result of increased imports, causing a decline in their rents. Exporting firms, on the other hand, have concentrated on selling natural-resource-based goods to Northern firms as part of a global value chain. They are unable to increase their selling price, as Northern firms have increased the pool of global suppliers, lowering goods' prices. Thus, any cost savings implemented by Chilean firms are eventually transferred to the Northern firms in the form of lower prices and greater Northern rents.

The second section concerns the division of rents between capitalists and workers in Chile. The wage bill accorded to Chilean workers, suffered with the macroeconomic slumps of the 1970s and 1980s and, unfortunately, did not recover as expected, because free trade allowed aggregate demand to leak from the economy as imports became more accessible. Facing more rigorous competition, Chilean-based capitalists were forced to invest earnings in technological improvements, though this eventually helped low-skilled workers as the technology increased employment. Yet the decline in rents encouraged Chilean-based capitalists to exploit the weak institutional environment that accompanied the labor repression policies of the military government. A new labor code, decreed in 1979, also provided more opportunities for Chilean-based capitalists to institute wage flexibility policies, decreasing workers' share of rents.

The third and final section of the chapter concerns the division of rents between skilled and low-skilled workers. In this section, I consider the explanations advanced by neoclassical economists for the declining wages of Chilean low-skilled workers. I show how labor supply actually worked in favor of low-skilled workers, as did technological change, which was low-skill biased as opposed to skill-biased. Thus, supply and demand cannot explain the increased relative wage gap between skilled and low-skilled workers. Instead, I argue that the weakness of the labor movement hurt low-skilled workers the most, as they are the ones who belong to unions and thus have been most affected by their troubles. Wage flexibility and wage discrimination policies have also been directed against low-skilled workers.

DIVISION OF RENTS BETWEEN NORTHERN AND CHILEAN CAPITALISTS

The first division of rents is at the international level and is determined by the trading relations of the country. Chile's integration into the world economy following liberalization in 1974 resulted in industrial restructuring towards production of natural-resource-based goods. Many of these goods are sold as intermediate inputs to Northern multinationals as part of the global value chain. Because of their position on the value chain, Chilean firms have limited prospects for increasing their share of rents. The shift towards production of natural-resource-based goods has resulted in a return to unequal trading relations that Chile sought to avoid when it adopted policies of import-substitution industrialization in the 1940s. Free trade has also brought about increased import competition. The renewed expansion of multinational investment in the 1990s, coupled with a shift in multinational production strategies towards regional factories, has allowed market-seeking, Northern multinational firms to capture market share in Chile. Chilean capitalists have been forced to drop their prices in response to the heightened competition, causing a decline in their rents.

Location on the Value Chain

Value chain (or commodity chain) analysis is a useful tool for analyzing how an industry's position in international production determines the amount of rents it receives. The analysis distinguishes between two types of commodity chains: buyer-driven and producer-driven commodity chains (Gereffi, 1999). Buyer-driven commodity chains are dominated by large retailers, branded marketers and branded manufacturers that coordinate decentralized and tiered production networks in a variety of exporting countries. In buyer-driven chains, rents accrue to those firms involved in marketing, retail and distribution, rather than in production. Production does not generate much rent because technology can be easily acquired, and because the coordinating firms at the end of the chain can pit suppliers against one another, lowering the price of the intermediate good. Marketing, distribution and retailing, however, does bring rents since by controlling these activities, firms are able to limit competition, allowing them to set prices above production costs. In producer-driven commodity chains, production brings rents, as a result of technological asymmetries. Because rents are associated with technological knowledge, large manufacturers in these chains play the central role in coordinating production networks, including backward and forward linkages.

Agroindustry is a prime example of a buyer-driven commodity chain. Chilean agroindustrial firms form part of the decentralized network of firms supplying Northern processed-food and beverage manufacturers. The cosmetics industry, on the other hand, has characteristics of both buyer-driven and producer-driven commodity chains. Though production may be decentralized across space, for the most part it is not externalized from the multinational firm, as in the agroindustry commodity chain. Yet the cosmetics multinationals' decision not to externalize is not due to technological asymmetries, since, as the case studies showed, technology could be easily acquired. Instead, the product itself represents a knowledge asset, where recipe mix, packaging and marketing are coveted firm secrets. It is this knowledge asset that spurs brand loyalty and generates rents. The importance of protecting its knowledge asset gives multinationals an incentive to internalize production and establish subsidiaries abroad (Dunning, 1993).

In agroindustry, rents accrue at the end of the chain from the ability of retailers, marketers, and manufacturers "to shape mass consumption via strong brand names and their reliance on global sourcing strategies to meet this demand" (Gereffi, 1999, p. 43). Marketing and management skills, export contacts, coordinated relationships with suppliers and customers, and reputation are non-tangible assets that yield rents for the Northern processed-food manufacturers. Moreover, as the producers of final goods, the Northern processed-food manufacturers determine the degree to which cost savings from competition among suppliers will translate into lower final goods prices or higher mark-up over costs.

Focusing solely on production, as many Chilean agroindustrial firms do, is less lucrative. As discussed in Chapter 5, Northern processed-food firms, sometimes operating via brokers, gain the upper hand in negotiating the price of goods by pitting suppliers against one another. With new and important suppliers emerging in Asia, particularly in China, the increased competition has contributed to lowering the world price of the intermediate goods.

This has not always been the case. During the 1970s and 1980s, when there were fewer suppliers selling to Northern processed food manufacturers, Chilean capitalists were able to obtain higher prices on natural-resource-based export goods such as fish, wood pulp, and agroindustry. Yet the emergence of new suppliers, both domestically and internationally, has dampened world commodity prices, lowering returns, while over-depletion has caused concern over the long-term viability of some of these sectors in Chile.[2] Alternative strategies, such as trying to control the upper end of the value chain, have only proved realistic at the domestic and regional level. Though promising, this also suggests that the benefits from global economic integration are less than anticipated since the greatest returns—those at the upper end of the value chain—are, for the most part, closed off to peripheral, supplying nations such as Chile.

Limits to Moving up the Value Chain

Because of the greater rents associated with the upper end of the buyer-driven commodity chain, one would expect that a worker would fare better in a firm that chooses to "move up the value chain" rather than concentrating solely on production. Moving up the value chain requires linking up with "lead firms," which results in an expansion of tasks. For example, in the apparel industry, if a firm links up with a lead firm, it can move away from assembly, into the more profitable activities of textile production, laundering, finishing, and distribution (Bair and Gereffi, 2001). By linking up with a lead firm, a firm benefits since lead firms "control access to major resources (such as product design, new technologies, brand names, or consumer demand) that generate the most profitable returns in the industry" (Bair and Gereffi, 2004, p.61). Thus, a major hypothesis of the value chain approach is that industrial upgrading will result in economic development.

Chile's agroindustrial sector has been limited in the extent that it can move up the value chain. American processed foods manufacturers are not interested in having Chileans produce final, full-packaged products and other even more modest forms of value added are discouraged. For example, although Chileans would like to, and are able to, process vitamin-enriched functional foods or pre-blended fruit juices, North American food manufacturers prefer to save these simple, yet profitable, tasks to themselves. Though they limit the amount of value added the Chileans can produce, they impose quality standards on the Chilean manufacturers that require investments in new machinery and training. At the same time, American processed food manufactures seek out new suppliers in Asia in an effort to lower the commodity's price, a process that has been particularly devastating for Chilean fruit juice producers.

In Chile's agroindustrial sector, firms have had difficulty achieving product differentiation in export markets and there is no evidence that pursuing product differentiation would accrue more rents. Indeed, in an analysis of the gains from differentiated coffee products, Fitter and Kaplinsky (2001) show that the introduction of higher-priced differentiated strains of coffee beans into the world coffee market did not benefit coffee farmers, despite an average world increase in coffee prices. Instead, the benefits accrued to economic agents in the importing countries.

If a Chilean agroindustrial firm wants to move up the value chain, it is limited to its own domestic market as well as other markets in Latin America. Some firms have opted for this approach, which appears to be a positive alternative. Producing for the Latin American market has the advantage of lower quality standards, which means firms can process the goods using reconditioned machinery, lowering their capital expenditures. In some cases, the firms can also shift production towards goods that are more easily mechanized, thus lowering the wage bill. More funds are then invested into distribution, marketing and retail, the most lucrative stages of the commodity chain.

Moving Down the Value Chain

In the cosmetics industry, the trend for domestic manufacturers has been to move "down" the value chain. Movement down the chain is based on domestic firms' new emphasis on third-party production. Though they have not abandoned full-package production—the distribution, marketing and retail activities at the upper end of the value chain (with the exception of C5)—they have increased sales from third-party subcontracting. Most multinational subsidiaries operating in Chile, on the other hand, are focusing only on the upper tail of the value chain, relocating lower-chain, production activities to regional centers outside the country.

Shifting Multinational Strategies

Another contributing factor to the more unequal division of rents between Northern and Chilean capitalists is shifting multinational strategies. In the 1990s, multinationals operating in Latin America regionalized production typically to larger domestic markets such as Brazil and Mexico, which took precedence over small countries such as Chile. In contrast, before 1990, and particularly during ISI, cosmetics multinationals established miniature replicas across Latin America that had their own (greenfield) factories as well as product line, marketing and advertising strategies that were specific to the country. The lowering of trade barriers throughout Latin America in the early 1990s led to an abandonment of the miniature replica strategy and a shift towards concentrating production in just a few countries acting as regional platforms.

Although under ISI, there was no guarantee (except where mandated by law) that firm profits be reinvested in the country, there were greater gains from multinational presence as multinationals established backward and forward linkages in the country with suppliers and distributors, generating rents for Chilean-owned firms. The new policy of regionalizing production has lessened linkages with Chilean firms, while increased import competition has taken away sales from domestically owned competitors. Both regionalization and increased import competition have decreased the rents of Chilean firms.

As shown in Chapter 4, Chilean-owned cosmetics firms have been forced to drop their prices in order to compete with the influx of multinational imports, many of which are mass-market products. Previously, cosmetics imports had been mostly limited to high-end niche products, yet the renewed aggression of multinationals seeking new markets, has meant that multinational cosmetics imports into Chile have been targeting the mass-market segment. Chilean firms have responded to the increased competition by lowering prices, causing a decline in their rents.

Trading Relations under Neoclassical Theory and In Practice

The Heckscher-Ohlin-Samuelson (HOS) theory assumes that the structure of demand is internationally identical, yet this is not always true. Different products have different elasticities of demand, depending on the structure of the market. The more inelastic that demand is for a product, the greater will be the rents that a firm receives from selling it, since oligopoly power allows the firm to set a higher mark-up over costs. The ability of firms to control part of the market and thus set prices above production in order to generate rents is not considered under HOS, which assumes perfect competition, specifically that the price of the commodity equals its production cost.[3] Yet imperfect competition is characteristic of international trading relations and important for the analysis of trading relations between Chile and the North.

While in theory, there is no reason why demand elasticities would be different for intermediate goods compared with final goods, in the case of Chile's traded goods, these elasticities are different. At the intermediate good stages, the elasticity of demand for the products is highly elastic, close to the conditions of perfect competition. On the other hand, at the final good stages, the products sold by the Northern manufacturers operate under oligopolistic conditions. Thus, elasticity of demand and location on the value chain are closely parallel, with a firm's position on the value chain affecting the amount of rents it receives. Unfortunately for Chile, their successful, new exporting industries face high demand elasticities as suppliers of intermediate goods. This has limited the rents they receive, while increasing the rents accrued to Northern firms.

Firms higher on the value chain face less elastic product demand for two principal reasons: first, the firms differentiate their products via brand loyalty, and second, the firms control distribution through their network of distributors and retailers.[4] Both competitive strategies decrease demand elasticity, allowing the firms to fix prices above production costs according to aggregate demand, thereby attaining higher rents. With their suppliers, firms at the upper end of the value chain have done precisely the opposite, increasing the demand elasticity of intermediate goods. The firms have created a decentralized network of suppliers, which they use to pit intermediate good suppliers against one another. By increasing the products' demand elasticity, intermediate-good-supplying firms are unable to set the price themselves, but rather are forced to participate in a flex-price market whereby price is determined by the strength of buyer's demands. The selling price is lowered as are the rents that intermediate-good-supplying firms receive.

By increasing the elasticity of demand of intermediate goods yet decreasing the elasticity of the final goods, the final goods producer can choose whether to pass on the savings to consumers or increase their mark-up, since the amount of pass-through depends on product demand elasticity (Milberg, 2004). In a perfectly competitive market, the elasticity of demand is infinite, thus a reduction in marginal costs will equal the reduction in price. On the other hand, in imperfectly competitive markets an oligopolistic firm can use the reduction in marginal costs to increase the mark-up. Thus the cost savings are less than fully passed through to consumers. The higher mark-up increases rents, making more funds available to potentially distribute with workers.

This implies that any savings in production costs that intermediate-good-selling firms attain, either through technological upgrading or wage flexibility policies, flow to the final goods producer rather than the intermediate manufacturer. Put simply, a firm can continue to exist via wage suppression policies, but it won't get any richer. The price of the intermediate good continues to fall because of its high demand elasticity resulting from increased suppliers. Buying firms at the upper end of the value chain use these savings to increase the mark-up, with none or some of the savings passed through to consumers. Even when a product is differentiated at the intermediate stage, the rents from product differentiation typically go to the upper end of the chain.

The monopoly power of firms at the upper end of the value chain gives these firms greater ability to pay higher wages than firms facing conditions of perfect competition (Galbraith, 2001).[5] Evidence from the case studies supports this argument. The cosmetics industry, an import-competing industry, has had greater ability to generate rent because of product differentiation and brand loyalty. The rent differential between the two industries has allowed cosmetics firms to pay their workers higher wages compared with similar workers in agroindustry, thus explaining the case study finding of inter-industry wage differentials. *Envasadoras* in cosmetics firms work on the line, filling and putting tops on cosmetics products; *temporeras* in agroindustry work on the line, sorting the processed, or soon to be processed, fruits and vegetables. Their tasks are similar, yet *envasadoras* make fifty percent above the minimum wage, while *temporeras* make five to ten percent above. Although some of the difference may be due to urban-rural wage differentials, many of the agroindustrial firms are located in the agricultural valley just outside of Santiago and rely on commuting Santiago residents for their work force.

An important policy implication from this analysis is that a country's overall welfare may improve if it develops policies that support the growth of higher-rent industries (Katz and Lawrence, 1989). The irony of this is that Chile did precisely the opposite. Abandoning ISI led to the demise of previously protected, high-rent, import-competing sectors, while the government program of export subsidies boosted the development of low-rent, natural-resource-based exporting sectors. Although this sector experienced an export boom in the 1970s and 1980s, by the 1990s, overinvestment, falling prices and poor competitive prospects signaled the boom's end. It is thus worth asking whether Chile would have been better off if the government had instituted programs that favored development of high-rent industries, as was done in South Korea,[6] even if this meant some protectionism.

The research on industrial restructuring in Chile post-liberalization suggests a return to the international division of labor that characterized world trade prior to the Great Depression. Before the Great Depression, Chile was an open economy, with no trade prohibitions, very few quotas, and an external dependence on the export of nitrate to Northern markets. The collapse of the nitrate sector in the 1930s caused a dramatic fall in exports and a severe depression that eventually led to a reevaluation of existing economic policy.

Spurred by the work of Raúl Prebisch, then head of the Santiago-based UN Economic Commission for Latin America, Chile embraced a comprehensive policy of import-substitution industrialization following WWII. Describing Latin America's position in the global capitalist system, Prebisch (1950) explained how the terms of trade were against the commodity-exporting countries of Latin America (the periphery), since the relative prices for commodities would continue to fall vis-à-vis the manufacturing commodities of developed countries (the center), due to the more inelastic demand for manufactured goods. Moreover, the terms of trade implied that peripheral nations such as Chile would not benefit from cost savings incurred by lower wages or technological progress. Instead, the cost savings would pass-through to center countries. The solution was to become more self-sufficient. Chile and other Latin American countries opted for import-substitution industrialization, erecting trade barriers, the highest of which were placed on final consumer goods. With these policies, Chile created a manufacturing sector, though in some sectors, such as autos, self-sufficiency and efficiency were quite elusive.

When ISI gave way to free trade in 1974, Chile once again subjected itself to the unequal dynamics of the international trading system.[7] It developed industries that specialized in supplying commodity products to Northern multinationals. Prices for these products have fallen, leading to fewer rents for these industries. Yet moving up the value chain, to the production of higher-value added products with greater mark-ups has proved difficult. As a result, the division of activities between multinational and domestic firms under external liberalization has come to be increasingly associated with an international division of labor reminiscent of its past.

Summary

As in previous times, Chilean industries are specializing in the less profitable activities of international trade. They do not have the benefit of technological asymmetries that allow them to differentiate their products from competing nations, thus they cannot command higher prices and are limited in the amount of rents they receive. Once again, there is an unequal division of rents between the North and the South, as Northern capitalists are distributors of the products and can thus control the degree of price competition in input goods. As in the period before ISI, firm efforts to improve productivity through technological upgrading are insufficient to ensure an increase in the standard of living of Chilean workers, since savings from technological upgrading, or wage flexibility policies, will transfer from the periphery to the center because Northern buyers can use their tiered production networks to reduce the price. Import-competing Chilean firms have also suffered, as the resurgence of multinational activity in developing country markets has caused price competition and a decline in industry rents. Without government policies to promote high-rent industries, Chilean industries are vulnerable to the more powerful Northern capitalists that dominate international trade.

DIVISION OF RENTS BETWEEN CAPITALISTS AND WORKERS IN CHILE

The second division of rents is the division between capitalists and workers in Chile. This level of rent division is what is most commonly thought of as rent-sharing. It is the decision by Chilean-based capitalists, both domestic and foreign capitalists operating in Chile, concerning how much of firm rents to dedicate to the wage bill. Essentially, it considers how the wage bill is determined and its relation to the level of profits of the firm. Under what conditions are capitalists more likely to share their rents with their workers? Macroeconomic conditions, mesoeconomic conditions (industry-level) as well as microeconomic (firm-level) considerations determine the size of the wage bill. Collective bargaining plays a critical role in a firm's decisions concerning the wage bill; its influence may be solely at the firm level, but can also be at the aggregate level, depending on the institutional environment.

Distribution at the Macroeconomic Level

Macroeconomics plays an important role in determining wages since the national distribution of income, understood as the ratio between aggregate wages and gross profits in an economy, will vary with the business cycle. Boom times fueled by greater investment (whether private or public) lead to greater employment and consumption and a greater share of wages in the national income. During macroeconomic slumps, which plagued Chile in the mid-1970s and early 1980s, the opposite occurs. Consumption falls and since workers' incomes ultimately depend on the level of consumption, their share in the national distribution of income falls (Kregel, 1979). This analysis, however, is primarily for closed economies. If the consumption boom is an import boom, then domestic workers' share in the national income will not improve. The import boom of the late 1970s—the first of Chile's so-called miracles—thus diluted the positive effects of this macroeconomic boom period, as monies were spent on imported as opposed to domestic goods. Meanwhile, workers' share in national income suffered during the recessions of the mid-1970s and early 1980s. In the 1990s, however, workers benefited from the more favorable macroeconomic conditions. Nonetheless, their share of the national distribution of income since liberalization has been affected by the needed for capitalists to retain a greater share of profits for increased investments in capital machinery. This has lessened the amount of rents available for the wage bill.

Retained Profits for Capital Investment

Until the mid-1980s and even the 1990s, multinational cosmetics firms would import new equipment for their Chilean factories, and Chilean-owned firms would buy reconditioned machinery, usually from abroad. When the multinationals closed their factories as part of their regionalization strategy, Chilean cosmetics firms went on a shopping spree, purchasing the multinationals' more advanced machinery. Besides taking advantage of bargain prices, Chilean managers were also trying to improve productivity and quality in response to increased competition with multinational imports. Similarly, the Chilean firms funneled money into improving the "look" of their products in an effort to boost sales. Thus, more revenues were dedicated to these investments. The investments were largely successful in improving productivity. Data from the manufacturing census revealed an increase in productivity between 1980 and 1995 associated with increased investments in machinery.

Similarly, Chilean agroindustrial firms have invested in technological upgrading in order to retain their contracts as multinational suppliers. Agroindustrial buyers stated how their clients would visit factories in Chile to ensure that they met their standards; during these visits they would oftentimes suggest equipment to purchase that would increase output as well as improve quality. Although buying the equipment was not forced upon them, Chilean firms recognized that these investments would increase their ability to service the Northern firms, possibly giving them an edge over their competitors.[8]

Although Chilean firms have had to dedicate more revenues to upgrading technology, the technology adopted has led to job growth, not job loss—in both the cosmetics industry and agroindustry, despite their different production methods and the different goods they produce. In cosmetics, new equipment improved quality and reduced output time, but because the firms used a small-batch production method to produce a wide variety of goods, tasks at the end of the line, such as putting on bottle tops or boxing the products, were performed manually. Consequently, with an increase in output, the need for workers to perform these and other labor-intensive tasks actually increased. In agroindustry, which operates under a continuous flow production method, new drying and freezing tunnels as well as pitting machines increased the volume of produce that could be processed, requiring more workers at the front of the line to remove blemished produce that could affect the homogeneity of the product. In some cases (pitting, for example), more workers were needed at the end of the line to ensure that the product had properly passed through the line and did not have to be removed.

Technological upgrading increased employment, and at the same time, improved productivity. Nevertheless, the case studies found little association between wages and productivity, in cosmetics, and for the most part, in agroindustry.[9] Aggregate data for the cosmetics industry showed that wage growth for low-skilled workers did not match gains in productivity during the 1979–1995 period. In agroindustry, aggregate data reveal that the increase in wages in the 1990s matched the rise in productivity, but much of the wage increases probably stemmed from increases in the minimum wage, which guided the wage-setting policies of the agroindustrial firms. At the firm-level, the incorporation of new technology or innovative work practices to improve productivity has not been associated with rising wages.

Even though Chilean-based capitalists have invested in improving technology in order to be competitive, technological upgrading alone is insufficient to explain the decline in the wage bill. As explained, technology increased demand for workers, particularly low-skilled workers, and in the process, improved their labor productivity. However, the increase in labor productivity was not matched by an increase in wages, as would be expected according to neoclassical economic theory.

Labor Policies

One possibility for why wages did not rise, despite productivity gains, is that an increase in surplus labor drove down the price of labor. Although there is some validity to this argument, it is not the whole story. Instead, part of the decline in the wage bill stems from the decision by Chilean capitalists to exploit the weak institutional environment that existed in the country following the coup d'etat. Chilean-based capitalists used the repression of labor to their advantage in an effort to compensate for the decline in rents under free trade. The new labor code limited union power, severely curtailing the ability of workers to negotiate a greater share of the rents. The labor code also made it easier for firms to institute policies that increased the numerical and wage flexibility of their labor force. An important result of this analysis, which I take up in the discussion of rent division between skilled and low-skilled workers, is that many of the policies aimed at squeezing workers' wages were directed at low-skilled workers. Thus, the wage bill shrunk, but it affected some workers more than others.

Labor Surplus

Labor surplus does seem to have contributed to the declining wage bill. Data from the Central Bank of Chile indicates that the labor force in Greater Santiago[10] increased from 1.0 million workers in 1970 to 1.6 million in 1985, an average annual increase of 3.5 percent. This is slightly lower than the 3.8 percent annual rate of population growth for those over 14, but much higher than the rate of job growth, which was 2.5 percent annually for the period. The result was a high rate of unemployment. After the recession of 1975, unemployment in Greater Santiago reached 18 percent, only to fall and then rise again to 23 percent in 1982, at the height of the debt crisis. By the late 1980s, unemployment had fallen dramatically, reaching a low of 6 percent in 1992. Econometric analysis by Berg and Contreras (2004) indicates that unemployment had a dampening effect on wages. For the period during and after the military government (1973–1996), the authors find a coefficient on the unemployment rate of –0.08, meaning that a doubling of unemployment led to a drop in wages of 8 percent.

After the mid-1980s, labor supply had less of an effect on wages, as the economic recovery reduced the amount of surplus labor in the economy. Between 1985 and 1995, the labor force continued to grow at an annual rate of 3.9 percent, yet job growth was strong, averaging an annual rate of 5.6 percent during this ten-year period.

Part of the reason for the increase in labor supply has been the strong growth in women's labor force participation. Between 1976 and 1993, women's labor force participation increased from 25 percent to 35 percent, where it remained into the early 2000s (Mizala and Romaguera, 1996; ILO, 2003). The increase in women's labor force participation is partly explained by the increase in women's overall educational level, though the decline in real wages and the high unemployment rate during the 1970s and 1980s also pushed many women into the labor market. Job loss in many households, where male heads were the sole breadwinner, forced many women into the labor market to compensate for their spouse's lost earnings. Many jobs in Chile are sex-segregated, so lost job opportunities for men did not necessarily translate into a lack of opportunities for women. Indeed, between 1981 and 1984, the years surrounding the debt crisis, women's labor force participation increased from 26.8 percent to 28.7 percent.

Collective Bargaining

Collective bargaining plays a critical role in rent-sharing between profits and wages. Blecker (1999) extends Kalecki's (1977) "Class Struggle and the National Distribution of Income" to an open economy, an analysis which is useful for understanding what occurred in Chile. He argues that, when an economy opens, mark-up pricing can be affected if a firm fears losing market share, which had otherwise been secure under a closed economy.

> If nominal wages increase proportionally in all firms in all industries in a closed economy, the higher costs will simply be passed on in the form of higher prices and (ceteris paribus) mark-ups will remain constant. However, if wages rise more in a particular industry, due to relatively stronger bargaining power of the unions in that industry, then the firms in that industry are also likely to raise prices but in a smaller proportion

than the wage increase in order to avoid loss of market share. (Blecker, 1999, p.125).

Under the scenario that Blecker lays out, firms will reduce their rents in order to not lose market share if unions have the power to force a wage increase. Fortunately for Chilean capitalists, the opposite occurred. In Chile, union power was drastically reduced at the same time that the economy opened. Facing reduced mark-ups, Chilean capitalists choose to compensate for the reduction in rents by squeezing wages, thereby protecting their rents—precisely what Kalecki would have predicted.

The military government's repressive policies towards labor unions and labor leaders coupled with new laws that limit collective bargaining have been effective in severely curtailing workers' ability to negotiate a greater wage share. Since the 1920s, when the country's first labor code was passed, until today, relations between managers and workers have been highly conflictive, with the size of the wage bill largely determined by the political power of the two sides. With the labor reforms instituted in Chile in the 1970s, Chilean workers lost the ability to bargain at the industry level; meanwhile, at the firm level, their union rights were greatly restricted. For example, until the early 1990s, strikes were limited to sixty days. The union movement did not recover in the 1990s, and by 2000, only 10 percent of salaried, non-governmental workers belonged to a union. Union affiliation remains weak even within firms that have a union. As a result of the weakened institutional environment, most collective bargaining agreements include adjustments for inflation and little else.

Numerical and Wage Flexibility Policies

Numerical flexibility leads to increased wage flexibility since it allows managers to introduce greater competition between individual workers. The numerical flexibility policies that the firms pursued included subcontracting, replacing permanent workers with temporary workers, and limiting new hires to temporary contracts. The new labor code introduced in 1979 made it easier for firms to subcontract work. Previously, if the work was related to the firm's core business, then the labor code prohibited it from being subcontracted. Increased outsourcing is apparent in the cosmetics subsidiaries of multinational corporations. In the 1990s, these subsidiaries have followed the trend of their headquarter offices in outsourcing non-core service workers, such as cleaning, maintenance and other non-essential staff. The effect has been a decline in earnings for these workers, as they earn less as outsourced workers than as employees of the multinational subsidiary.[11] The 1979 labor code also prohibited temporary workers from collective bargaining, giving firms an incentive to hire workers on temporary contracts. The case study of agroindustry showed that firms have been replacing permanent workers with temporary workers, reducing the number of workers eligible to bargain collectively. Moreover, temporary workers do not receive other benefits, such as severance and vacation pay.

Minimum Wage

Minimum wage laws are a form of collective bargaining in that the government, influenced by both business and labor, sets the minimum amount that a firm can pay its workers. The exclusion of labor from the political debate of the country during the military government allowed the minimum wage (and wage indexation) to fall, contributing to a lowering of workers' share of national rents. When the Concertación government was democratically elected in 1990 under the banner of "growth with equity," a tri-partite committee of government, business and labor was formed to increase the minimum wage among other reforms. These increases were instrumental in helping labor re-gain some of the wage share that it had lost during the 1970s and 1980s.

Wage growth in both industries has mirrored changes in the minimum wage since the 1970s.[12] Essentially, there was stagnant wage growth among low-skilled workers in both industries in the late 1970s and 1980s, and strong wage growth in the 1990s. Although regression analysis is necessary to quantify the influence of minimum wages on the median wage, case study evidence indicates that wage increases were highly influenced by changes in the minimum wage. In agroindustry, wages for low-skilled workers (*temporeras*) were either set at the minimum or five to ten percent above. In cosmetics, the low-skilled workers (*envasadoras*) were paid fifty percent above the minimum wage. Managers and union leaders said that increases in the minimum wage influenced their wage adjustments for these workers. Increases in the real value of the minimum wage in the 1990s played an important role in improving the distribution of rents towards Chilean workers.

Summary

Workers' share of rents was reduced during the economic recessions of the mid-1970s and early 1980s. The recessions also caused the amount of labor surplus to increase, driving down the price of labor. However, during the recovery periods, workers' share of rents did not increase, as would have been expected, since consumption was directed at purchasing imported rather than domestic goods. Liberalization added two other important twists: (1) it forced capitalists to make greater investments in technology to stay competitive, and (2) it reduced mark-ups in previously protected industries.

Although the finding of increased technological investments is important for our analysis of industrial restructuring under free trade, it does not seem to play an important role in explaining the declining wage bill, as the technology increased employment. Furthermore, earnings for low-skilled workers did not rise with the increase in productivity, casting doubt on neoclassical economic theory. An alternative explanation is that Chilean-based capitalists, seeking to recoup rents lost with the opening of the economy, used the decline in union power and more flexible labor laws to compensate for falling mark-ups. It was not until the 1990s, under the return to democracy, that Chilean workers were able to gain a greater share of the rents as a result of the increases in the minimum wage.

DIVISION OF RENTS BETWEEN SKILLED AND LOW-SKILLED WORKERS

This final level of rent division concerns the decision by capitalists of how to divide the rents within its workforce, essentially, how much of the wage bill should go to skilled as opposed to low-skilled workers? It is at this level of analysis—earnings of skilled versus low-skilled workers—that the debate on rising wage inequality in the North and the South, reviewed in Chapter 2, has been centered.

The decision regarding how much to pay skilled and low-skilled workers is linked to the division between profits and wages (division two), since many of the policies to squeeze rents from workers have been limited to specific groups of workers. An important hypothesis of this study is that the policies identified in division two have been directed at low-skilled workers as opposed to skilled workers. In other words, the decision by Chilean capitalists to exploit the weak institutional environment by squeezing workers' pay has affected low-skilled workers, not skilled workers.

Increased Wage Inequality according to Neoclassical Theory

One of the predictions of the neoclassical theory of international trade, HOS, is that under free trade production shifts toward the relatively abundant factor, which in the case of Chile, a developing country, is low-skilled labor. The findings from the two case studies support this prediction: production has remained labor-intensive, especially with regard to low-skilled workers.

In the cosmetics industry, Chilean companies have invested in semi-automated equipment, that although more productive, has increased the number of low-skilled workers employed relative to skilled workers. Moreover, the decision to invest in more productive equipment was not made in order to substitute capital for labor, but rather to produce a wider variety of goods, all of which are of higher quality. Chilean cosmetics firms have also accepted contracts as third-party manufacturers for multinationals, letting foreign capital specialize in high-skill marketing and sales activities while the Chileans concentrate on production.

Similarly, in agroindustry, firms have updated technology in order to process as many goods as possible in the short seasonal time frame or to improve quality in order to sell to new, more lucrative markets. Most technological upgrading has been complementary to low-skilled labor, as more workers are needed for quality control inspections. Overall, there has been an increase in the relative employment of low-skilled workers in the two industries, consistent with this prediction of HOS.

However, the Stolper-Samuelson corollary that the returns to low-skilled labor, the abundant factor, should increase, did not hold true. In both industries, skilled workers' wages increased relative to low-skilled workers, despite the emphasis on low-skilled, labor-intensive activities. Labor economists offer several explanations for this apparent anomaly, though the case studies reveal inconsistencies with many of these alternative explanations.

Is it simply greater demand for skilled workers?

Figure 6.1 depicts a conventional supply and demand graph of a labor market composed of substitutable skilled and unskilled workers. Like all graphs of this type, it assumes full employment. In the graph, there is an outward shift in both the supply and demand of skilled workers causing their wages to increase from WS1 to WS2. The opposite has occurred for unskilled workers: their relative supply has been reduced, but so has their demand. As a result, their wages have fallen from WU1 to WU2. As mentioned earlier, the supply of skilled workers in Chile has expanded greatly over the past forty years. Between the early 1960s and the 1990s, there was more than a tripling of the percentage of labour force participants in the Greater Santiago area with more than 12 years of schooling, from 6 percent to 22 percent. At the same time, the number of workers with less than 12 years of schooling was cut in half, from 84 percent to 43 percent. Thus, the relative supply shifts, have behaved according to the depiction in the graph. But this means that for the analysis to hold, it would be necessary to show that the demand shifts have also moved according to the graph. In other words, it would be necessary to show that the demand for skilled labour has swamped the substantial increase in skilled labour supply, which coupled with a fall in demand for skilled workers, led to rising wage inequality.

Figure 6.1: Increased Wage Inequality under Conventional Supply and Demand Analysis

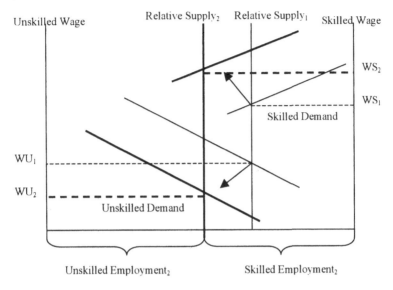

Source: Author's illustration based on Snower (1998).

Proponents of skill-biased technological change argue that, indeed, these demand shifts have occurred in Chile (Robbins, 1994; Beyer et al., 1999). As they explain, increased technological imports after liberalization were biased in favour of skilled workers, either through the replacement of tasks performed by low-skilled workers, or because the new technology demanded more skilled operators. In other words, technological imports should have decreased the demand for low-skilled workers, while increasing the demand for skilled workers, causing a greater wage gap. However, there is no evidence from the case study research—from either the interviews or the factory tours—that the new equipment is biased in favor of skilled workers. Indeed, the opposite has occurred, as the technology is complementary to low-skilled labor. The case studies also found that workers employed at firms that had upgraded their technology did not earn more than workers at firms with out-dated equipment.

The case study finding that technological upgrading did not cause rising wage inequality is also supported at the aggregate level. Figure 6.2, based on wage data collected by the National Statistical Institute, shows managerial earnings in Chile skyrocketing between 1982 and 1992, while non-managerial earnings fell dramatically following the 1982 crisis.[13]

Figure 6.2: Real Wages for Different Occupations, 1982–1992, Index 1982=100.

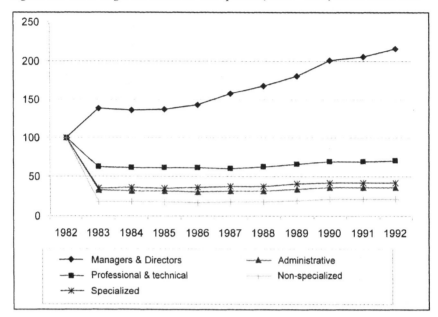

Source: INE, Encuesta de Remuneraciones.

Skilled professional and technical workers did see the greatest increase compared with other workers during the recovery period, but still their growth was at a much smaller rate that that of managers and directors. If the rise in wage inequality were driven by skill-biased technological change, then technical and professional earnings should have showed the greatest divergence compared with the other occupations. This suggests that the econometric finding of Robbins (1996), correlating rising wage inequality with increased machinery imports in Chile, is spurious. Skill-biased techno-logical change is insufficient for explaining rising wage inequality in Chile.

Labor Market Rigidity

Another explanation often given is that labour market rigidities have hurt low-skilled workers by impairing the labour market from properly adjust-ing to the new competitive environment. According to this argument, rigidi-ties, such as minimum wages and severance pay, have encouraged firms to favor capital over labour and are also responsible for insufficient job growth, in Chile as well as other countries.[14] In interviews, firm managers did not indicate any obstacles to their efforts to employ (or dismiss) workers because of rigid labor laws. Indeed, the case study narratives provide ample evidence of firm flexibility in employment practices, particularly in agroindustry where most low-skilled workers are hired on seasonal contracts that can end at a moment's notice. The finding supports empirical evidence of labor market flexibility in Chile (Berg and Contreras, 2004; Levinsohn, 1999).

Efficiency Wages

The theory of efficiency wages is also given as an explanation for rising wage inequality. According to the theory, the increased wage gap, post-liberalization stems from a decision by managers to raise the compensation of those workers using the newly imported technology in an attempt to prevent carelessness or sabotage by workers, or to reduce turnover.

Chilean cosmetics and agroindustrial managers stated that they paid higher wages to workers who knew how to repair equipment, or in the case of the cosmetics industry, to workers who were responsible for mixing large batches of expensive raw materials. Thus, the compensation strategy of the managers suggested a tendency towards efficiency wages for these semi-skilled workers. However, it is not clear that that this policy changed as a result of trade liberalization. Raw materials have always been imported and it has always been in the best interest of the firms to keep trained mixers on board. Regarding equipment repair workers, new equipment is more likely to make these workers' skills obsolete, since the new equipment is unfamiliar to them. In both industries, firms that bought new equipment received regular on-site training from the equipment manufacturers, thus limiting the ability of the machinery repair workers to force their employers to pay them higher wages because of their coveted knowledge. It therefore seems that although efficiency wages most likely play an important role in a firm's wage policies, efficiency wages are not more important now than when the economy was less open to trade.

Squeezing the Wages of the Low-Skilled: An Alternative Explanation

Marginal productivity theory cannot explain rising wage inequality in Chile following trade liberalization. Increased demand for skilled workers because of technological imports cannot explain increased wage inequality, nor can efficiency wages, or labor market rigidity. Instead, we must return to the analysis introduced in the previous division of rents, between capitalists and workers, to understand why low-skilled earnings fell relative to skilled workers under free trade.

Collective Bargaining

Labor unions in Chile are divided along class lines, with low-skilled and semi-skilled production workers belonging to a union, and skilled production workers, administrative staff and managerial personnel, generally not unionized.[15] Thus, collective bargaining negotiations affect just one class of workers. The decline in union power, as a result of repression and the introduction of neo-liberal labor laws, affected low-skilled workers as opposed to skilled workers. Indeed, skilled workers most likely benefited from the drop in low-skilled workers' wages, as this increased the amount of revenue available for their wages.[16]

Numerical and Wage Flexibility Policies

Subcontracting of non-core service personnel and the use of temporary contracts has affected low-skilled workers, not skilled workers. Outsourcing non-core tasks at cosmetics firms affected those employed in maintenance and other relatively unskilled positions. In agroindustrial firms, administrative staff would be hired on indefinite contracts, as would some skilled production staff, whereas low-skilled workers held temporary contracts. If the factory were closed during the winter months, then the skilled production staff would have an extended holiday, whereas low-skilled staff would have their contracts terminated. Thus the ability of firms to use numerical flexibility policies to lower the wage bill was only applied to low-skilled workers, lowering their yearly earnings.

Gender and Pay

Another important dimension of the case study analysis is the role of gender in suppressing wage growth. In both industries, women dominate the low-skilled jobs. They also dominate unstable jobs, supporting the finding that women's gross job reallocation rates in Chile are twice as high as the rates of men (Levinsohn, 1999). Moreover, the flexibility of women's wages is much higher than men's. A doubling of the unemployment rate reduces women's wages by 14 percent compared with 8 percent for the wages of workers as a whole (Berg and Contreras, 2004). Also, for the whole economy, women's earnings were 28 percent less than men's, after controlling for worker characteristics and industry. It is therefore likely that industry managers have been able to lower their wage bill as a result of the socially institutionalized system of female wage discrimination.

Summary

The evidence for Chile, at the case study as well as the aggregate level, supports a division of wages between Chilean skilled and low-skilled workers that is driven by institutional considerations, as opposed to the marginal productivity of the workers. Although managers' efficiency wage policies towards skilled and semi-skilled workers did not change as a result of trade liberalization, managers' wage policies towards low-skilled workers did change: they were no longer compelled to share rents with low-skilled workers. Thus, the issue is not that efficiency wages post-liberalization became important—they remained important—but rather that it was not necessary to compensate the low-skilled as they no longer had the political power to negotiate higher wages, either at the firm-level, or at the national level.

CONCLUSION

The analysis by the economics profession of increased wage inequality in Chile under free trade has been focused around the demand, or lack of demand, for skilled and low-skilled workers. Excess supply, coupled with skill-biased technological change, has been offered as an explanation for rising relative wage inequality between skilled and low-skilled workers. The analysis of rent division, undertaken in this chapter, sought to emphasize the complexity of wage determination, moving the discussion away from a simple supply and demand analysis based of the underlying price of labor and diminishing marginal returns. Instead, the rent division analysis stresses the need to consider other changes in the economy besides just the price and use of certain labor.

Low-skilled Chilean workers earnings have been affected at three different levels: (1) by the decrease in rents for Chilean capitalists compared with Northern capitalists, (2) by the decline in rents dedicated to the wage bill, and (3) by the squeezing of low-skilled workers' wages, as compared with skilled workers. To begin with, free trade has reduced the rent of Chilean firms, affecting the amount that can be shared with workers. Chilean import-competing firms have faced increased import competition, forcing them to lower their prices and reducing their rents. Chilean exporting firms have become intermediate good suppliers of a global value chain that is controlled by Northern capitalists. The Northern firms have succeeded in reducing the price of intermediate goods by increasing the number of suppliers. The result is that the savings that Chilean firms achieve, such as from increased productivity, end up being transferred to the North, rather than staying in Chile.

Chilean workers were also hurt by the macroeconomic volatility associated with trade liberalization in the 1970s and 1980s as well as by misguided macroeconomic policies. Workers earnings were reduced during the recessions, and during recovery, they did not benefit much as aggregate demand leaked out of the economy with the purchase of foreign goods. Facing declining rents, Chilean-based firms have taken advantage of labor's collective weakness by reducing labor's share of the rents. Collective bargaining negotiations have been prevented through anti-union practices and labor laws that prohibit temporary workers from joining unions. Furthermore, Chilean-based capitalists have achieved greater wage flexibility by outsourcing and replacing permanent with temporary workers. However, workers have regained some of their wage share in the 1990s with the national increases in the minimum wage, which took effect under the Concertación governments.

The policies to squeeze workers' earnings have been directed at low-skilled workers. The union movement is divided along class lines. Less-educated, low-skilled workers encompass the movement, and its weakness has affected their earnings. Chilean capitalists have continued to protect skilled and semi-skilled workers for efficiency wage considerations, as was done during ISI. This has made easily replaceable, low-skilled, and oftentimes female, workers an easy target for wage-squeezing policies.

Chapter Seven
Conclusion

The military coup of September 11, 1973 set Chile down a radically differ-ent political and economic course, with implications that linger well into the 21st century. Though Chile seemed a maverick in the region when it opted to dismantle its trade protections and open its economy to financial and goods competition, privatize its state-owned industries and pension system, as well as liberalize its labor market, thirty years later much of Latin America and the developing world had undertaken many of the same reforms. Still, the effects of these reforms, in Chile and elsewhere, are little understood.

The purpose of this study was to elucidate how the demand for skilled and low-skilled workers changed in Chile after the economy opened to free trade in 1974. How did industrial restructuring as a result of free trade affect firms' competitive strategies and in the process, their use of labor? Field research was useful in assessing the effects of liberalization, because it allowed consideration of possible causes of rising wage inequality that can-not be proxied for in econometric work. By "going to the field," I was able to consider the changing strategies of multinational firms, increased compe-tition, and a changed labor relations environment, on the employment and pay of skilled and low-skilled workers. A more dynamic picture emerged than under econometric work, which simply asks "how much" as opposed to "why" and "how."

The findings from the case study of the Chilean cosmetics industry provide insight into the causes of widening wage dispersion in Chile under free trade. My analysis of the production process reveals that widening wage dispersion is not simply the result of skill-biased technological change. Although multinational investment in the 1990s has been associ-ated with rising relative demand for skilled workers, it is because the deci-sion to regionalize operations has caused a gutting of production.

Outsourcing of non-core service workers has also contributed to the relative shift in demand. Within domestic firms, there have been investments in machinery with accompanying increases in productivity. These could be considered "technology spillovers" since most of the machinery purchases are of second-hand multinational firm equipment. Yet the technological investments led to an increase in the absolute and relative employment of low-skilled workers, as the production model still depends on workers to perform labor-intensive tasks.

Greater competition has brought lower prices and better quality cosmetics products to Chilean consumers. Yet because of the more competitive environment, domestic firms have been forced to lower prices to retain market share, while at the same time cutting costs to maintain rents. As domestic employers reward skilled workers for efficiency wage considerations, they have forced these cost savings onto low-skilled workers, who are easily replaceable and poorly organized.

Although agroindustry is an exporting industry and therefore, has a vastly different productive structure from the cosmetics industry, the two face many similar challenges. International competition in agroindustry heightened in the 1990s with the emergence of new competitors, particularly from China. Chilean agroindustrial firms sell many of their products as intermediate goods to Northern processed-food manufacturers, forming part of a global value chain. Because the Northern multinationals rely on a decentralized network of producers, the emergence of new suppliers has lowered the price of the intermediate goods, and subsequently, the profits of Chilean firms. Attempts by Chilean agroindustrial firms to move up the value chain to higher rent activities, such as selling and distributing final products, have only been successful in the Latin American market. Northern markets have proved to be beyond their reach. Chilean firms have also invested funds to upgrade technology, in an attempt to improve productivity, thereby lowering unit costs.

Despite investments in better technologies, the focus on quality control and the need to sell homogenous products have increased low-skilled employment, as more line inspectors are needed to sort the increased amount of goods passing through the line. The expansion in employment has been matched by an increase in the length of the employment contract, as some competitive strategies, such as product diversification and worker training, require workers year-round. However, declining profits and flexible labor laws have encouraged Chilean agroindustrial firms to shift the burden of cost minimization onto workers, as in the cosmetics industry. Workers on temporary contracts are prohibited by law from bargaining collectively, which coupled with other benefits to permanent contract workers, such as severance and vacation pay, has given agroindustrial managers an incentive to use temporary contracts. Without the right to bargain collectively, and facing dismissal at a moment's notice, low-skilled workers in the industry have had to rely on minimum wage increases to increase their earnings. Even though the industry faces uncertain times at present, its success since the early 1980s has done little to improve the financial standing of Chilean workers besides providing poorly paid and unstable jobs.

The case studies provide great insight into the applicability of the traditional view of trade and wages (HOS), and alternative explanations such as skill-biased technological change (SBTC) and labor market rigidity. The studies reveal that increased trade did lead to technological upgrading, but that this upgrading was not skilled-biased. Whenever possible, production remained labor-intensive along HOS lines. Technology was thus not a threat to the labor force but a facilitator of its success, as it improved the competitive position of the firms, while at the same time expanding employment.

This finding differs from many common arguments previously posited to explain rising wage inequality in Chile. The perceived failure of Chile's productive model to conform to the predictions of neoclassical trade theory, especially HOS, has been attributed to skill-biased technological change. Proponents of this idea argue that increased machinery imports post-liberalization have led to an insatiable demand for skilled workers, and thus a sharp rise in their earnings, and greater wage inequality. This theory, aside from lack of evidence, also falsely implies that technological catch-up has gone awry. Developing countries seek to eliminate technological gaps between themselves and developed countries, yet if SBTC were true, the cost of catching-up could outweigh the benefits, particularly in a country like Chile with its history of conflict-ridden class relations, and resulting need for greater social stability.

Another implication of the SBTC viewpoint is that global economic integration is not to blame for inequality. Instead, the fault lies with a labor force that is unable to adapt to the demands of the global economy. Yet this limited picture based on competitive supply and demand analysis leaves many questions answered and little policy prescription besides greater investments in education and worker training. It also ignores the social reality of the country.

My case studies show that firms had more than ample opportunity to adjust their labor force to fluctuations in the market, and that labor market flexibility was a tool used by Chilean firms to increase their rents. Highly flexible labor laws have facilitated dismissal, particularly in agroindustry. The laws have also served to limit union power. When unions do have the legal ability to exist they are often weak, the result of anti-union practices on the part of management or internal problems arising from a lack of dedication of both leaders and the rank and file. The weakness of the union movement is a legacy of the military dictatorship that has yet to be resolved.

Although the labor-intensity of production confirms HOS predictions, the corollary that the relatively abundant factor, low-skilled labor, would fare relatively better, was not confirmed. Contrary to the predictions of Stolper-Samuelson, earnings of low-skilled workers declined relative to skilled workers. To understand this contradiction between labor-intensity of production and declining relative pay for low-skilled workers, I proposed a division of rents at three levels, each of which has negatively affected the distribution of income for low-skilled Chilean workers. One of the benefits of analyzing earnings according to three levels of rent division is that it emphasizes the complexity in setting wages: other considerations besides labor supply and worker productivity affect how much a person earns.

The first level of rent division concerns international trading relations. Chilean firms have restructured toward the production of intermediate goods that yield comparatively fewer rents on the global value chain. The ability of foreign firms at the upper end of the value chain to lower prices by increasing the number of suppliers has left little opportunity for Chilean firms to increase their profits. Increased import competition, stemming from more aggressive multinational activity, has also lowered rents for Chilean firms selling to the domestic market, as these firms have had to lower their prices in order to retain and fight for market share.

The second level of rents concerns the division of profits among capitalists and workers. The recessions of the 1970s and 1980s reduced the wage share for Chilean workers. During boom times, the share did not entirely recover, as low trade barriers meant that domestic demand was used for purchasing imports rather than the goods of domestic industries. This meant that import competition not only reduced rents of Chilean import-competing firms, but also decreased the wage share in national income. Chilean capitalists have responded to import competition by cutting costs, through technological upgrading that increases productivity as well as wage squeezing. Although technological upgrading has resulted in increased employment, the weakness of labor market institutions in the country has made it easy for Chilean capitalists to introduce policies that enhance wage flexibility, such as subcontracting and replacing permanent workers with temporary ones. Chilean workers have had difficulty in countering these trends, as the labor movement was weakened by the repressive policies of the military government and a revised labor code that curtailed the power of unions. However, the recovery of the minimum wage following the return to democracy in the 1990s has helped to increase workers' share of the rents.

Finally, I argue that the division of the wage bill has favored skilled over low-skilled workers, as it is the low-skilled workers that have been most affected by the decline in unions and policies to increase labor flexibility. Chilean capitalists prefer to push cost-savings strategies onto their easily replaceable, low-skilled workers, rather than onto their trained skilled and semi-skilled workers.

An important implication of this study concerns the use of labor relations as a competitive strategy for Chilean firms. As a result of the country's flexible labor laws, Chilean firms have adopted low-road approaches to labor management. Although these policies have helped Chilean firms increase their rents in the face of international competition, the long-term viability of this strategy is cause for concern. With developing countries such as China emerging as powerful competitors in external markets, it will become more and more difficult for Chilean firms to squeeze Chilean workers' pay in order to compete with the Chinese, and other, lower-paid developing country workers. It thus remains clear that a competitive strategy based on cheap labor is not sustainable for a middle-income developing country like Chile.

Recognizing this, some Chilean capitalists have come to see their workforce as an advantage, rather than a liability, assuming the workers can be well-trained and committed to the firm. Yet, successfully developing a committed and trained workforce that can enhance a firm's competitiveness requires better dialogue between management and labor and better pay for its workers. Although some firms have begun to move in this direction, a shift in thinking about labor not as enemy but as partner, will take time, particularly in the presence of laws that do not encourage, and in the short-run penalize, such an approach. Yet an institutional environment, both legal and in practice, that recognizes the benefit of management-labor dialogue and works to develop human resource practices that increase worker dedication to the firm, while at the same time paying a living wage, are necessary for developing a more sustainable competitive advantage for the country under globalization. It would also help to ensure that the Chilean miracle is for the benefit of all.

Notes

NOTES TO CHAPTER TWO

1. See Howell (2002) for a detailed review of this debate.
2. One caveat to this point of view, however, is the level of disaggregation of the industry data, since industries can have different sub-industries that place different emphasis on low-skill and high-skill workers.
3. The study was later followed by Robbins (1996) and Gindling and Robbins (2001). Riveros (1990) was the first study to document the rising relative return to schooling. However, his analysis puts emphasis on changes in education policy, rather than trade, macroeconomic and labor reforms.
4. Both studies rely on data from the University of Chile household employment survey, which is limited to the Greater Santiago area and thus excludes mining, agriculture and fishing.
5. There has been less work in this area, mainly because none of Chile's three employment surveys includes variables that can proxy for labor market institutions. For example, neither the Greater Santiago employment survey, the annual manufacturing survey, nor the more recently instituted CASEN survey, has a question pertaining to unionization. The only survey to consider labor relations is the recently employed ENCLA survey undertaken by the Labor Inspectorate (Dirección del Trabajo). Unfortunately, it dates from 1999 and is limited to labor relations and general firm features (size, sector); it does not consider other firm attributes such as investment and output.

NOTES TO CHAPTER THREE

1. Edwards and Lederman (1998) argue that an economic philosophy did not fully emerge in the government until the April 1975 appointments of ardent free-market supporters, Jorge Cauas as Minister of Finance, and Sergio de Castro as Minister of Economics. However, these men held non-official advisory positions prior to their appointments, while 200 copies of the much touted "ladrillo" document, summarizing the free-market strategies

of the Chicago Boys, were distributed to government officials just one week after the coup.

2. The number of annual bankruptcies in manufacturing increased from 19 during 1965–1970 to 76 during 1975–1982 (Gatica Barros, 1989).

3. Unemployment figures are based on the University of Chile Employment Survey, a quarterly survey started in 1957. Like most household employment surveys, it follows the resolution adopted by the 13th International Conference of Labour Statisticians, which considers a person employed if they worked more than one hour the previous week, regardless of whether or not the work was informal. Approximately one-fourth of the employed labor force in Chile is working in the informal sector.

4. The tariff would later be reduced to 20 percent in June 1985 as the economy started to recover, and then to 15 percent in 1988.

5. Unlike the public enterprises sold during the first round of privatizations in the mid-1970s, these were operating better than the private sector. Another objective of privatization of state enterprises was to provide investment opportunities for the newly privatized pension funds. Because of this, the most common method of sale was through the purchase of minority ownership blocks on the stock exchange, which had the added benefit of reducing the concentration of ownership (Muñoz, 1992).

6. To qualify as a non-traditional export, the total value of exports of that product had to be below a certain threshold. For example, at three percent, the lowest refund rate, a maximum of US$20.9 million of exports of that product was allowed.

7. 1970 is often used as a benchmark, as it marks the end of the period before the run up in real wages during Allende's term. Real wages jumped from 108.9 in 1970 to 133.6 in 1971, based on an index that sets 1989 at 100. Real wages did not recover their 1971 level until 1997.

8. Based on findings from the CASEN national survey, 1987 and 1996.

9. Based on 1972 CUT election data given in Stallings (1978).

10. The increase in real wages between 1975 and 1982 as a result of the wage indexation policy has been blamed for the high unemployment rate of this period. Yet real wages were cut in half following the coup, which meant that despite the wage increases after 1975, wages in the 1975–1982 period had still not recovered their 1970 level. Meller (1984) defends the position that wage indexation did not cause unemployment during this period.

11. See Bergquist (1986) for a history of the Chilean labor movement beginning with the organization of the nitrate sector in the early 1900s, the formation of the first important workers' central in 1911, and the increased participation of the labor movement in the political process until the coup in 1973.

12. Despite the ability to bargain at the supra-firm level prior to 1973, most collective bargaining in Chile took place at the firm level (Cortázar, 1997).

13. The military forced the dissolution of the CUT (Central Única de Trabajadores) following the coup. In 1974, a new group emerged known as the CUT Coordinadora. It was replaced in 1976 by the Coordinadora Nacional Sindical (Frank, 1995).

14. Meller (1992) based on Campero and Cortázar (1988).
15. It also granted permanent workers the option of forming "negotiation groups" rather than unions to bargain collectively. A negotiation group is a group of workers elected democratically to negotiate a collective bargaining agreement. Once the negotiations are over, the group dissolves and must be formed again at the end of the agreement, usually in two years. Nevertheless, the group has the same rights as a union during the collective bargaining process, for example, it can call a strike.
16. Calculated from data given in Table A.4 of Stallings (1978) and Table 3.16 of Romaguera et al. (1995).
17. Between 1973–1976, the government deliberately indexed wages below the rate of inflation as part of its attempt to lower the rate of inflation in the economy. After 1976, the government committed itself to full indexation, though the CPI was underestimated in the 1976–1978 period (Cortázar, 1997).
18. Based on data given in Table 8–1 of Cortázar (1997).
19. Renamed the Central Unitaria de Trabajadores, the new CUT was formed in 1988 in preparation for the plebiscite against continuation of the military government. The labor movement believed it was more strategic to have a national union federation then several industry federations (Frank, 1995).
20. These included inappropriate behavior, unjustified absence from work, refusal to perform the work specified in the employment contract, actions that deliberately affect the safety and health of others, and deliberate material damage. An employment contract could be terminated for just cause and with severance pay for the following reasons: reorganization or modernization of the company, decrease in the worker's productivity, change in market conditions or the state of the economy, or lack of occupational or technical training.
21. The decrease in firm size has also caused the size of unions to shrink. In 1990, the average union had 68 members, falling to 50 members by 1995 and 40 members by 2000 (Data provided by Dirección del Trabajo).
22. Data from Dirección del Trabajo website (dt.gob.cl) and INE (at Banco Central website www.bcentral.cl).
23. Based on interview with the three officers of the Servipag union and their advisor in January 2001. I am grateful to Marcos Canales of the CUT for referring me to them.
24. Interview with Servipag union officers, January 2001.
25. If no contract currently exists, union demands may be presented at any time.
26. Based on interview with Guillermo Campero in June 2001.
27. Interview with Guillermo Campero, June 2001.
28. Based on interviews on May 23 and May 30, 2001.
29. July 2001 interview.
30. July 2001 interview. Espinosa (1996) gives a similar account of the labor-political party relationship prior to 1973.

31. Both Frias and Acevedo identified unions in the copper industry as those with the most "modern" labor relations.
32. Author's calculations based on data from the University of Chile Employment Survey.
33. Minimum wage in Chile for the second half of 2001.
34. The International Institute for Management Development conducts an annual survey of hours worked and publishes the results in its *World Competitiveness Report*. Information reported by Cindy Rivera, "Trabajólico," *El Mercurio*, May 2, 2001. Information on legislative changes for 2005 reported in "A partir del 2005 jornada laboral se reduce en 3 horas semanales," *El Mercurio*, June 14, 2001.
35. All permanent employees with more than one year of service receive 15 days vacation by law. After 10 years of service, employees receive an additional day for every three years worked.
36. Mainly bonuses for Christmas and Independence Day celebrations, but can also include benefit for death of a family member as well as help with children's school uniform expenses at the start of the academic year. These benefits are not mandated by law but it is common for firms to offer them. Depending on the firm they may be extended to temporary workers.
37. As mentioned earlier, permanent workers are entitled to severance of one year's pay for every year of service, up to a maximum of 11 years.
38. This section draws from an interview with Magdalena Echevarría, Research Division, Dirección del Trabajo, July 2001.
39. The first temporary agency to begin working in Chile was Manpower, opening its doors in 1963. In 1984, there were three temporary agencies operating in the country, increasing to 79 by 1986 and 150 by 1997. It is estimated that 30,000 individuals are employed through temporary agencies (Echeverría et al., 1998).
40. Temporary agencies often pay their workers on honorarium (Echeverría et al., 1998).

NOTES TO CHAPTER FOUR

1. Based on lists of cosmetics manufacturers and distributors maintained by the Cosmetics Industry Chamber of Commerce and the U.S. Embassy, the companies are all located in the Greater Santiago area. Though 50 may seem like a large number, this also includes small import businesses that import high-end niche goods for sale at department stores and do not manufacture. According to the manufacturing industry survey, there were 39 "soap and cleaning detergent" plants in 1995, though a company can have more than one plant.
2. This estimate is based on market size data from the Cosmetics Industry Chamber of Commerce, sales data, and ACNielsen marketing studies, and on the importance attributed to these firms from industry experts.

3. Classification and explanation of continuous versus discontinuous flow activities based on J. Katz, an expert on technological development in Latin America (Conversation with J. Katz, 2001 and Katz, 1986).

4. ASACH, Asociación Gremial de Supermercados de Chile. Information based on an interview with the general manager, Jonathan Powditch, in March, 2001 and data supplied by the association.

5. This section is based on interviews with the Human Resource Department and the Controller of the multinational subsidiary conducted in November and December of 2000, as well as information from the company's 1999 annual report.

6. "The basis for centralization is the harmonization of the product range across national borders. This year [1999] we started the standardization of recipes and packages for the entire region" (1999 annual report).

7. Information based on an interview with the general manager of the Chilean subsidiary in January 2001, articles in international and local business press, the company's annual report, and press releases.

8. *Business Week,* June 28, 1999.

9. According to an AC Nielson market study from January-February 2000, the company's line of cosmetics accounted for 16 percent of the number of units sold in the metropolitan region, second after the 33 percent unit share of a domestic makeup line. Because M2's prices are higher, it led the market in 2000 in terms of value of sales.

10. *Business Week,* June 28, 1999.

11. Interview with public relations manager, February 2001. Additional information was gleaned from the company's annual report.

12. M3's strategy to consolidate factories within Latin America for distribution within the region mirrors its European strategy. In the early 1990s, the European division of M3 standardized products to "consolidate their European production and distribution systems in order to reduce costs through greater plant specialization." Seven plants were involved in the restructuring, which led to the closing of one factory and the transferring of production of four different product lines. The measures favored "those plants located close to the European core to the detriment of peripheral sites" (Bailey et al., 1993, p.86).

13. As my research focused on the Chilean cosmetics industry, my interview with the general manager concerned only the cosmetics portion of the business.

14. The contract signed with subcontractor C5 stipulates that M4 must give a year's notice if it decides to cease using C5 as subcontractor.

15. *El Mercurio,* May 25, 2000.

16. Conversation with Howard Baker, Technical Consultant to the U.S. cosmetics industry, December 2001.

17. Interview with company president, February 2001.

18. *El Mercurio,* March 25,1997.

19. Cosmetics companies must provide their own reshelvers at the supermarkets. Local firms have banded together to hire reshelvers at large supermarkets, a

more effective strategy than having one reshelver running around all day to different stores.

20. Information based on interview with founder/owner/president of the firm in November 2000. He, along with his daughter, run the company.

21. Interviews with owner/general manager in November 2000 and July 2001. Between 1985 and 1995, C2 was owned by M1. In 1995, M1 made a company-wide decision to focus exclusively on hair products, leading it to sell this subsidiary, along with other international ventures in both cosmetics-related products, as well as furniture. Because of C2's committed consumer base and the present owner's familiarity with it—as a former employee of M1—the present owner purchased the company.

22. Interview with founder/owner/general manager in February 2001.

23. Interview with Sales Manager, February 2001, Production Manager, March 2001, and Chief of Production, July 2001.

24. C4's organizational structure lends itself to subcontracted manufacturing jobs, making it somewhat surprising that the firm does not accept such jobs. C4 is organized as part of a small holding company. It takes sales orders from the "commercial company" of the holding, manufactures the products, and then sells the goods to the commercial company. There are tax benefits to organizing as a holding. Also, it limits unionization since the unions can only form within the holding's smaller companies. This is discussed briefly in Chapter 3.

25. Interview with general manager in February 2001.

26. See Harrison (1997) for an in-depth discussion of this topic.

27. Between 1987 and 1999, output per worker (measured in hours worked rather than by employee) in the U.S. cosmetics industry grew 2.5 percent annually. Yet despite the higher rate of productivity growth in Chile, the industry still lags behind the U.S., which by 1980 had reached value added per employee of $100,000 (Wilder, 1982).

28. Updating product look is difficult and costly to do, since apart from the investments in redesigning and reconfiguring the machines for the new bottles or jars, the company must ensure that its loyal customers continue to purchase the product with the new look. Also, the firm must buy back the inventory of old products available at the stores when the new product is introduced since it is not a good idea to have old and new products selling simultaneously.

29. This discussion is based on an interview with two managers in the human resources department of the firm, both of whom had worked for the company prior to the reorganization. I also interviewed the firm's controller, a business-school trained American, who joined the company in 1998. He argued that the environment prior to the reorganization stifled creativity. As an example, he mentioned the practice on the part of upper management to have their lunch served by waiters while the rest of the staff went through the cafeteria line.

30. In February 2001, at the time of the interview, the minimum wage was C$100,000 pesos per month. It was raised to C$105,000 per month on July 1, 2001.

31. Conversation with German Acevedo, Ministry of Labor, May 2001.
32. As explained in Chapter 3, a *convenio colectivo* is a form of a collective negotiation whereby the workers elect three representatives to meet with management and negotiate wages for a two-year period. Workers do not have the right to strike under the rules of this agreement and wage increases are not binding.
33. Federación Nacional de Trabajadores Laboratorios Químicos Farmaceuticos y Cosméticos. Founded in the early 1940s, the Federation was outlawed during 1973–1990, though it operated in secret, mostly as a political organization in the fight for democracy (Conversation with Saul Troncoso, President of the Federation, June 2001). With the return to democracy in 1990, federations regained legal status, though industry-level collective bargaining is still prohibited, unless agreed to by the management of the firms.
34. Management of this firm denied my request for an interview, though I did get a tour of the facility and copies of the collective bargaining agreements during my meetings with the company's union leader. The company's union leader is the current president of the National Federation of Cosmetics and Pharmaceutical Laboratory Workers. The union is well organized, with ninety percent of blue-collar workers belonging to the union.
35. Union leaders are legally protected from being fired under the "fuero laboral."
36. Union dues were modest and in some cases, were returned to the members at the end of the year in a lump-sum check to help with holiday expenses.
37. Free-riding was partially offset by the 1990 change in the labor law which required employers to deduct the equivalent of 75 percent of union dues from the wages of non-union workers who received the benefits under the collective bargaining contract (Cortázar, 1997).

NOTES TO CHAPTER FIVE

1. Specifically juicing, dehydrating, canning or freezing fruits and vegetables. The term agroindustry is sometimes understood to include all processed agricultural products including dairy, fishing and livestock industries. The definition has been limited for purposes of this study.
2. Phone interview with David Olsen, U.S. sales representative for firm 3 and international fruit buyer (February 2002).
3. The interviews were conducted in 2001. Of the twelve firms that were asked to participate in the study, nine accepted, of which eight are agroindustrial manufacturers. Besides interviews with firm management and factory visits, I also interviewed industry experts and union leaders, when a union did exist. My analysis also relied on secondary information, including annual reports of two publicly traded companies, data from the manufacturing census, as well as the wide body of literature on the employment conditions of temporary workers in the fresh fruit industry. This literature is relevant for agroindustry, as the industry draws from and competes for the same labor pool.

4. Although exchange rate fluctuations can affect sales, it cannot explain the increase in sales until 1996 and the subsequent fall. Despite a steady appreciation of the real exchange rate between 1990 and 1996, there was strong growth in sales during those years. After 1996, the real exchange rate depreciated slightly from 84.7 in 1996 to 86.0 in 2000, based on an index of the Central Bank of Chile that sets the real exchange rate of 1986=100. The Chilean Central Bank reports exports in US$.

5. Chinese low-grade tomato paste sells at CIF prices that are US$120 below Chilean cost (Peppelenbos, 2000).

6. Interview with Gonzalo Jordán, Head of Agroindustry Department, Fundación Chile, May 2001 and former general manager of one of Chile's leading agroindustrial firms.

7. Between 1980 and 1990, annual productivity was –0.3 percent, between 1990 and 1995, it averaged 6 percent annual growth. Employment, on the other hand, grew at an annual rate of 9.9 percent between 1980 and 1990; between 1990 and 1995 employment growth slowed to a 3.2 percent annual increase.

8. Interview with Operations Manager, July 2001.

9. Laboratory workers ensure that the chemical balance of the products meets customer demands. They continuously run quality control tests on the goods being processed. The laboratory must operate when the line is moving, thus laboratory workers are staffed for three shifts per day.

10. Phone conversation with Dr. John Reid, Manager of the Technology Department, John Deere Technical Center, February 2002. See also Reid (2001).

11. Besides the optical sorting machine, most investments are in processing equipment. Improvements in this area cause a negligible reduction in labor intensity.

12. Conversation with Sandra Johnson, Sales Department, Key Technology, February 2002.

13. Interview with Training Manager, August 2001.

14. Although the firm emphasizes training more than equipment purchases, it nonetheless has updated some technology. Besides the continuous dryer, which was purchased in 1999, the company bought a drum drier in 2000 that uses dehydrates discards to produce fruit and vegetable flakes and powders.

15. To be ISO-certified means that a company's products or services have been carefully monitored for quality according to standards set by the International Standards Organization. Thus, by obtaining this certification, firms can sell to more exclusive clients, at higher prices.

16. Interview with Owner/General Manager, May 2001.

17. The company also got approval from the Dirección del Trabajo to reorganize the work shifts. Instead of working three shifts a day, six days per week, with one day off, which was leading to scheduling difficulties, the operators work four days consecutively, twelve hours per day, followed by two days off.

18. The owner considered including the workers in the company's profit-sharing plan to which management belongs. He decided, however, that the workers were not ready for this system. An employee has to be able to understand fluctuations in commodity prices and recognize that fluctuations in the market are real and that the company is not just tricking workers out of their fair share. For this reason, he decided that pay-for-productivity would be a more appropriate system.

19. Interview with General Manager and the Operations and Finance Manager, May 2001.

20. Measured in US$ FOB, exports have increased, in real terms, at 19 percent annually, despite greater production of higher-value added (pitted) prunes. Data are from FEPACH, based on the Central Bank of Chile; 1981 is the first available year given.

21. Hazard Analysis Critical Control Point. It is a system that guarantees quality at all stages of production.

22. Interview with one of the founding partners and managers of the firm, June 2001.

23. Interview with Owner/General Manager, May 2001.

24. Interview with Operations Manager, August 2001.

25. The war in Bosnia prompted the U.S. and Europe, in the early 1990s, to give preferential tariffs to countries of that region, an important berry-growing center. This hurt Chilean berry exports and prompted concern, among A8's management, about the future of this sector. (Follow-up conversation with Operations Manager, A8, February 2002).

26. Another area for growth, for both A7 and A8, is in importing and reselling prepackaged foods, using the companies' established distribution networks. A7 imports frozen deserts, fries and hamburgers from Argentina, the U.S. and Canada, for sale at supermarkets. A8's line of imported foods has grown to fifteen percent of their sales.

27. According to the operations manager, the central-valley factory is the most mechanized in South America, far ahead of its Chilean competition. Still, it trails behind the U.S., where frozen food factories produce far more products at much greater output levels. Nevertheless, the company does not believe that it needs to improve its machinery in order to compete and gain domestic market share. They see themselves as being at the optimum technological level and further technological investments are not central to their competitive strategy. (Interview with Operations Manager, A8, August 2001).

28. Interview with General Manager, June 2001.

29. Interview with Owner/General Manager, July 2001.

30. See "El Trabajo Agrícola de Temporada" under the Guías Laborales of the Dirección del Trabajo's website, www.dt.gob.cl.

31. Estimate based on factory visits and interviews with management. The manufacturing census reports that 50% of the unskilled jobs and 30% of the skilled jobs were filled by women. It is likely that these figures grossly underestimate female employment as women's more erratic employment contracts make them more difficult to account for. Moreover, the seasonal

workers in the industry are referred to as *temporeras* instead of *temporeros*, which includes both genders, and would be the noun of choice if indeed there were equitable distribution of seasonal jobs.

32. Based on interview with former laboratory head of A6, May 2001. The exception is A5, which keeps its four laboratory workers during the winter months to work on product development.

33. Factory visits confirmed the reports of secondary sources.

34. The irony, however, is that by returning to their full-time duties as homemakers during the winter months, the women are less able to renegotiate household duties so that their husbands take on greater responsibility in the home. Most women carry the double burden of paid work and housework during their employment in agroindustry. Yet despite the substantial increase in workload, most women prefer to work than not (Barrientos et al., 1999). Newman (1994) in her study of female grape packers found that most women would like to be able to work throughout the year, but that there were no such opportunities.

35. The company has maintained a consistent policy of offering ten percent above the minimum wage, despite the increases in the minimum wage during the 1990s. In June 2001, the salary worked out to about US$192 per month plus a 5% bonus for working the night shift. A worker with no absences received an attendance bonus worth US$12. The end-of-season bonus is US$80; in general, most workers who lasted through the season received the bonus.

36. "The issue of salary has fallen behind . . . [the return for their contribution] is more about status." Nevertheless, status—or the respect accorded to workers—is a recurring theme that I came across in both my primary and secondary research. See discussion of labor relations later in this chapter. Also, in a survey of workers in the fish-processing sector in Chile that asked what workers would most want to change about their jobs, the number two answer given was being treated with more respect (17%). Salary was the number one answer with 25% of responses (Schurman, 1993).

37. Part of the decline is also due to a loss in canned peach exports, which have suffered from a loss of business to subsidized Greek peaches. Canned peaches make up almost half of A6's sales.

38. Instead of working three shifts a day, six days per week, with one day off, which was leading to scheduling difficulties, the operators work four days consecutively, twelve hours per day, followed by two days off. The alternative work schedule was approved by the Dirección del Trabajo.

39. During the three months that the factory sits still, the workers take vacation (one month), perform maintenance (one month) and do small jobs around the factory such as painting during the third month. The four laboratory workers use the time for product development.

40. Data on temporary employment at Jucosa and Patagonia from annual reports. Data from A5 from interview with General Manager, 2001.

41. Employment data for A4 is not comparable with A5 because it also includes workers in the dehydration facility.

42. When the prune is dried it has a humidity level of 16%. Processing the prune involves first sterilizing it, then cleaning, and finally adding water to raise the humidity level to 25–28 percent. The pit is then removed, followed by quality control inspection, the adding of preservatives, and lastly, packaging (Factory Visit, A1).

43. Interview with the president of union, A8, July 2001. The 15 permanent non-managerial factory workers belong to the small, one-officer union.

44. Legally, an "honorarium" is a civil contract between two equal parties, differing from labor law, which recognizes the imbalance of power between employer and worker, and attempts to address this inequality. Although it is illegal to hire a worker on honorarium for the purpose of circumventing an employment contract, use of honoraria has become more widespread (Dirección del Trabajo, 2000; conversation with M.Echeverría, 2001).

45. Union officers are protected from being fired under the *fuero laboral*.

46. With the return to democracy in 1990, the labor code was reformed to allow temporary workers the right to form and join unions, yet they still do not earn the right to collective negotiation or to the right to strike, since strikes are only permissible during specific collective bargaining periods.

47. Since I met with the union officers of A6 and A7, I report their and management's accounts of labor relations in this section. I did not meet with the union head of A5. That union formed in 1999 in response to a difficult period in the company that led to lay-offs.

48. Nor were they able to obtain wage increases. In the collective bargaining contract signed in 2000, the union negotiated cost-of-living adjustments for their wages and bonuses, but was unable to secure a real wage increase. The bonuses the union members receive are standard in most union contracts. They include a back-to-school bonus that enables parents to buy new school uniforms, bonuses for Christmas and Independence Day holidays, and reimbursement for taking the bus to and from work.

49. Having several days to spend with their families during the summer vacation months was important to the workers. The union president, for example, had not had a day off during the summer in his fourteen years of working for the company.

50. The benefits include Christmas and Independence Day holiday bonuses, access to canned products that the firm produces, and a benefit in the case of death of a family member.

NOTES TO CHAPTER SIX

1. The elasticity of demand of the product is an indicator of the market power of the firm.

2. In a comprehensive study of the fishing industry in Chile between 1973 and 1990, Schurman (1993) shows how the high profits available in these industries in the late 1970s and 1980s gave way to overinvestment and resource depletion, so that by 1990 there were few rents left.

3. Models of imperfect competition (see Krugman, 1980, 1991) are useful for explaining intra-industry trade, but cannot explain unequal trading relations stemming from different degrees of monopoly power. Many of the assumptions of HOS are maintained, including identical structures of demand between the two trading nations.

4. These are the main sources of monopoly power for controlling firms of buyer-driven commodity chains. In producer-driven commodity chains another source of monopoly power is technological asymmetries.

5. The association between higher rent industries and higher wages is both an empirical finding and a theoretical proposition. See Galbraith (2001) for an explanation of the theoretical proposition; Katz and Summers (1989) provide empirical evidence for the United States.

6. See Amsden (1989) for an account of the development policies of the South Korean government following the Korean War.

7. This does not imply that Chile and other Latin American countries did not suffer from adverse terms of trade under ISI, but by closing itself off it was more insulated. See Prebisch (1981) for a discussion of the troubles Latin American countries faced during ISI.

8. An important implication of this finding is that technological spillovers are not simply the result of direct foreign investment, but rather the result of international competition. This competition occurs both externally as well as internally. Externally, Chilean firms must make technological investments to help their exports compete with the goods of other countries; similarly, firms competing with imports for the domestic market make investments to secure market share.

9. The exception is A5, which tied pay to productivity, and a productivity bonus negotiated for one cosmetics firm, whose management did not participate in the study.

10. The data are restricted to Greater Santiago because there does not exist a sufficiently long time series for the whole country. Approximately one-third of Chileans live and work in Santiago, which is also the country's manufacturing center.

11. The case study of the cosmetics industry confirmed the well-known finding that multinationals pay more than domestic firms—in cosmetics, almost double the domestic firms' unskilled wage rate of roughly US$275 per month. Unfortunately, managers could not convincingly explain why. In Chapter 4, I propose some explanations of this finding.

12. Between 1974 and 1989, the minimum wage fell drastically. By 1989, its real value was nearly sixty percent less than its value in 1970. However, it climbed again in the 1990s and by 2000, the minimum wage was 90 percent above its 1989 level.

13. Unfortunately, Chile's National Statistical Institute (INE) changed the questionnaire in 1992 making it incompatible with the previous series. In 2000, they once again changed the methodology.

14. See for example, Cox Edwards and Edwards, 1997; Márquez and Pagés, 1997; Heckman and Pagés, 2001.

15. In C4, the administrative staff has a union, though it is separate from the union of the production staff. The unions do not consult each other, either prior to or during contract negotiations.
16. Bacha and Taylor (1978) propose a similar explanation for rising wage inequality in Brazil in the 1960s. In their view, hierarchy in firm, rather than marginal productivity, determines a worker's earnings. As managers share in the residual income after workers are paid, they attempt to squeeze laborers' pay.

Bibliography

Abraham, Katherine and Susan Taylor (1993) "Firms' Use of Outside Contractors: Theory and Evidence," NBER Working Paper No. 4468.

Agosin, Manuel (1999) "Comercio y Crecimiento en Chile," *Revista de la Cepal 68*, August.

Alburquerque, Mario (1999) "Obstáculos a la modernización de las relaciones laborales en Chile. ¿Qué impide una extensión mayor de las experiencias de alianza estratégica en las empresas chilenas?" en C. Montero, M. Alburquerque y J. Ensignia (eds.), *Trabajo y Empresa: entre dos siglos*, Caracas: Editorial Nueva Sociedad.

Amadeo, Eduardo (1995) "International Trade, Outsourcing and Labor: A View from the Developing Countries," mimeo, PUC-Rio de Janeiro.

Amsden, Alice (2001) *The Rise of "The Rest": Challenges to the West from Late-Industrialization Economies*, New York: Oxford University Press.

Amsden, Alice (1989) *Asia's Next Giant: South Korea and Late Industrialization*, New York: Oxford University Press.

Asesorías Estratégicas (2000) *Tendencias Emergentes en la Negociación Colectiva: El Tránsito del Contrato al Convenio*, Cuaderno de Investigación 11, Santiago: Dirección del Trabajo.

Bacha, Edward and Lance Taylor (1978) "Brazilian Income Distribution in the 1960s: 'Facts,' Model Results and the Controversy," *Journal of Development Studies* 14 (3): 271–297.

Bailey, Paul, Aurelio Parisotto and Geoffrey Renshaw, eds. (1993) *Multinationals and Employment: The Global Economy of the 1990s*, Geneva: International Labour Office.

Bair, Jennifer and Gary Gereffi (2004) "Outsourcing and Changing Patterns of International Competitiveness in the Global Apparel Commodity Chain," in W. Milberg, ed., *Labor and the Globalization of Production*, Houndmills: Palgrave Macmillan.

Bair, Jennifer and Gary Gereffi (2001) "Local Clusters in Global Chains: The Causes and Consequences of Export Dynamism in Torreon's Blue Jean Industry," *World Development* 29 (11): 1885–1903.

Baker, Howard (2001) "It's a Small Run!" *Global Cosmetics Industry* 167 (5): 58–59.
Barrientos, Stephanie et. al. (1999*) Women and Agribusiness: Working Miracles in the Chilean Fruit Export Sector,* London: Macmillan Press.
Behrman, Jere, Nancy Birdsall and Miguel Székely (2000) "Economic Reforms and Wage Differentials in Latin America," Inter-American Development Bank, Working Paper #435, October.
Benería, Lourdes and Martha Roldán (1987) *The Crossroads of Class and Gender: Industrial Homework, Subcontracting and Household Dynamics in Mexico City,* Chicago: Univ. of Chicago Press.
Berg, Janine and Dante Contreras (2004) "Political-Economic Regime and the Wage Curve: Evidence from Chile, 1957–1996," *International Review of Applied Economics* 18, 2 (April): 151–165.
Bergquist, Charles (1986) *Labor in Latin America,* Stanford: Stanford University Press.
Berman, Eli, John Bound and Zvi Griliches (1994) "Changes in the Demand for Skilled Labor within U.S. Manufacturing: Evidence from the Annual Survey of Manufacturers," *Quarterly Journal of Economics* 109 (May): 367–397.
Berman, Eli and Stephen Machin (2000) "Skill Biased Technology Transfer: Evidence of Factor Biased Technological Change in Developing Countries," mimeo, January.
Beyer, Harald, Patricio Rojas and Rodrigo Vergara (1999) "Trade Liberalization and Wage Inequality," *Journal of Development Economics* 59: 103–123.
Blecker, Robert (1999) "Kaleckian models for open economies," in Johan Deprez and John Harvey, eds., *Foundations of International Economics: Post Keynesian Perspectives,* London: Routledge Press.
Bound, John and George Johnson (1992) "Changes in the Structure of Wages in the 1980s: An Evaluation of Alternative Perspectives," *American Economic Review* 82 (June): 201–232.
Bravo, David and Alejandra Marinovic (1997) "Wage Inequality in Chile: 40 Years of Evidence," mimeo, Universidad de Chile.
Bravo, David, et al. (1999) "Wage Inequality and the Labor Market in Chile, 1990–1996: A Non-Parametric Approach," mimeo, Universidad de Chile.
Brown, Clair and Benjamin Campbell (2001) "Technical Change, Wages and Employment in Semiconductor Manufacturing," *Industrial and Labor Relations Review* 54 (2A): 450–465.
Campero, Guillermo (2000) "Respuestas del sindicalismo ante la mundialización: El Caso de Chile" Instituto Nacional de Estudios Laborales, Ginebra, Documento de Trabajo 113.
Carr, Marilyn and Martha Chen (2004) "Globalization, social exclusion and gender," *International Labour Review* 143 (1–2): 129–160.
CASEN (1998) *Encuesta de Caracterización Socioeconómica Nacional,* Santiago: MIDEPLAN.
CEPAL (2002) *Panorama Social de América Latina 2001–2002,* Santiago : CEPAL.
CEPAL (1998) *Agroindustria y pequeña agricultura: vínculos, potencialidades y oportunidades comerciales,* Santiago: CEPAL.
CEPAL (1990) "La cadena de distribución y la competitividad de las exportaciones latinoamericanos: la fruta de Chile," LC/G.1639, Santiago: CEPAL.

Cline, William (1997) *Trade and Income Distribution,* Washington, D.C.: Institute for International Economics.

Corbo, Vittorio and Patricio Meller (1982) "Alternative Trade Strategies and Employment Implications: Chile," in A. Krueger, ed., *Trade and Employment in Developing Countries,* Cambridge: NBER.

Corbo, Vittorio and José Miguel Sánchez (1984) "Impact on Firms of the Liberalization and Stabilization Policies in Chile: Some Case Studies," PUC-Chile, Documento de Trabajo 91, May.

Cortázar, René (1997) "Chile: The Evolution and Reform of the Labor Market," in S. Edwards and N. Lustig, eds., *Labor Markets in Latin America,* Washington: Brookings Institution.

Cortázar, René (1993) *Política Laboral en el Chile Democrático,* Santiago: Dolmen Ediciones.

Cox Edwards, Alejandra (1993) "Labor Market Legislation in Latin America and the Caribbean," Education and Social Policy Report no. 31, Inter-American Development Bank.

Cox Edwards, Alejandra and Sebastian Edwards (1997) "Trade Liberalization and Unemployment: Policy Issues and Evidence from Chile," in J. Borkakoti and C. Milner, eds., *International Trade and Labor Markets,* London: Macmillan Press.

De Gregorio, José (1999) "Trade Liberalization, Macroeconomic Performance and Wage Inequality: The Chilean Experience," mimeo, Universidad de Chile.

Dirección del Trabajo (2000) *ENCLA Encuesta Laboral: Informe de Resultados,* Santiago.

Dirección del Trabajo (1997) *Sindicalismo en la empresa moderna: Ni ocaso, ni crisis terminal,* Cuaderno de Investigación 4, Santiago.

Dunning, John (1993) *Multinational Enterprises and the Global Economy,* Wokingham, England: Addison-Wesley.

Echeverría, Cristián (1997) "La institucionalidad laboral en Chile," mimeo, Ministerio del Trabajo.

Echeverría, Magdalena and Verónica Uribe (1998) "Condiciones de Trabajo en Sistema de Subcontratación," n. 81, OIT-ETM: Santiago.

Echeverría, Magdalena et al. (1998) *El Otro Trabajo: El suministro de personas de las empresas,* Cuaderno de Investigación 7, Santiago: Dirección del Trabajo.

Edwards, Sebastian and Alejandra Cox Edwards (1991) *Monetarism and Liberalization: The Chilean Experiment,* Chicago: University of Chicago Press.

Edwards, Sebastian and Daniel Lederman (1998) "The Political Economy of Unilateral Trade Liberalization: The Case of Chile," NBER Working paper 6510, April.

Espinosa, Malva (1996) *Tendencias Sindicales: Análisis de una Década,* Cuaderno de Investigación 2, Santiago: Dirección del Trabajo.

Feenstra, Robert C. (1998) "Integration of Trade and Disintegration of Production in the Global Economy," *Journal of Economic Perspectives* 12 (4): 31–50.

Feenstra, Robert C. and Gordon Hanson (1997) "Foreign direct investment and relative wages: Evidence from Mexico's Maquiladoras," *Journal of International Economics* 42: 371–393.

FEPACH (2001) *Exportaciones de Frutas y Hortalizas Procesadas, 1981–2000,* Santiago: FEPACH.

Ffrench-Davis, Ricardo (1999) *Entre el Neoliberalismo y el Crecimiento con Equidad: Tres Décadas de Política Económica en Chile,* Santiago: Dolmen Ediciones.

Fitter, Robert and Raphael Kaplinsky (2001) "Who Gains from Product Rents as the Coffee Market becomes more Differentiated?," *IDS Bulletin* 32 (3): 69–82.

Fortin, Nicole and Thomas Lemiux (1997) "Institutional Changes and Rising Wage Inequality: Is there a Linkage?" *Journal of Economic Perspectives* 11 (Spring): 75–96.

Frank, Volker Karl (1995) "Plant Level Leaders, the Union Movement, and the Return to Democracy in Chile," Ph.D. dissertation, University of Notre Dame.

Freeman, Richard B. (1995) "Are Your Wages Set in Beijing?," *Journal of Economic Perspectives* (Summer): 15–32.

Galbraith, James (2001) "The Distribution of Income," Richard Holt and Steven Pressman, eds., *The New Guide to Post Keynesian Economics,* London: Routledge Press.

Gatica Barros, Jaime (1989) *Deindustrialization in Chile,* Boulder: Westview Press.

Gerrefi, Gary (1999) "International trade and industrial upgrading in the apparel commodity chain, *Journal of International Economics* 48: 37–70

Gindling, Thomas and Donald Robbins (2001) "Patterns and Sources of Changing Wage Inequality in Chile and Costa Rica during Structural Adjustment," *World Development* 29 (4): 725–745.

Griliches, Zvi (1969) "Capital-Skill Complementarity," *Review of Economics and Statistics* 51: 465–468.

Hanson, Gordon and Ann Harrison (1995) "Trade, Technology and Wage Inequality," NBER Working Paper 5110, May.

Harrison, Bennett (1997) *Lean and Mean,* New York: Guilford Press.

Heckman, James and Carmen Pagés (2001) "Regulation and Deregulation: Lessons from Latin American Labor Markets," *Economía* 1(1):109–134.

Henríquez, Helia et al. (1994) "Temporeras del Sector Agrario: Sindicatos Débiles en Busqueda de Nuevas Perspectivas," Informe de Investigación 106, Santiago: PET.

Howell, David (2002) "Increasing Earnings Inequality and Unemployment in Developed Countries: Markets, Institutions and Unified Theory," CEPA Working Paper 2002–01, January.

Humphrey, John (2004) "Upgrading in Global Value Chains," Policy Integration Department Working Paper 28, Geneva: International Labour Office.

ILO (2003) *Key Indicators of the Labour Market, Third Edition,* Geneva: ILO.

INE (1979–1995) *Encuesta Nacional Industrial Annual* (ENIA), Santiago: Instituto Nacional de Estadística.

Infante, Ricardo and Emilio Klein (1992) "Chile: Transformaciones del mercado laboral y sus efectos sociales, 1965–1990," Documento de Trabajo, Ginebra: OIT/PREALC.

Kalecki, Michal (1954) "Theory of Economic Dynamics: An Essay on Cyclical and Long-run Changes in a Capitalist Economy," London.

Kaplinsky, Raphael (2000) "Globalisation and Unequalisation: What can be Learned from Value Chain Analysis?," *Journal of Development Studies* 37 (2, December): 117–146.

Katz, Harry and Owen Darbishire (2000) *Converging Divergences: Worldwide Changes in Employment Systems,* Cornell: Industrial and Labor Relations Press.

Katz, Jorge (1986) "La tecnología metalmecánica como factor determinante de la conducta técnica de la empresa y el sendero de expansión de la capacidad tecnológica doméstica," en Jorge Katz, ed., *Desarrollo y crisis de la capacidad tecnológica latinoamericana,* Buenos Aires: CEPAL.

Katz, Jorge and Hector Vera (1997) "The ongoing history of a Chilean metal products and machinery firm," *Cepal Review* 63, Santiago: ECLAC.

Katz, Lawrence and Lawrence Summers (1989) "Industry Rents: Evidence and Implications," *Brookings Papers on Economic Activity, Microeconomics* 1989: 209–275.

Koser, Glen (2001) "State of the Industry 2001," *Global Cosmetics Industry* 168 (6): 20–30.

Kregel, Jan (1979) "Income Distribution," in Alfred Eichner, ed., *A Guide to Post-Keynesian Economics,* New York: M. E. Sharpe.

Krugman, Paul (1991) "Increasing returns and economic geography," *Journal of Political Economy* 99: 183–199.

Krugman, Paul (1980) "Scale economies, product differentiation, and the pattern of trade," *American Economic Review* 70: 950–959.

Larrañaga, Osvaldo (1999) "Distribución de ingresos y crecimiento económico en Chile," Serie Reformas Económicas 35, Santiago: CEPAL.

Levinsohn, James (1999) "Employment responses to international liberalization in Chile," *Journal of International Economics* 47: 321–344.

Locke, Richard, Thomas Kochan and Michael Piore (1995) *Employment Relations in a Changing World Economy,* Cambridge: MIT Press.

Márquez, Gustavo and Carmen Pagés (1997) "Trade and Employment: Evidence from Latin America and the Caribbean," mimeo, Inter-American Development Bank, July.

Marshall, Adriana (1997) "State labour market intervention in Argentina, Chile and Uruguay: Common model, different versions," ILO Employment and Training Papers 10.

Martínez, María Laura (2000) "Detergentes: El año mas limpio del siglo." www.publicmark.cl/nanterior/n128/deter.html.

Meller, Patricio and Andrea Tokman (1998) "Chile: Apertura Comercial, Empleo y Salarios," Santiago: OIT/ETM.

Meller, Patricio (1992) "Labor Reforms,"in Oscar Muñoz, ed., *Economic Reforms in Chile,* Occasional Paper, Washington, D.C: Inter-American Development Bank.

Meller, Patricio (1984) "Análisis del problema de la elevada tasa de desocupación chilena," *Coleccion Estudios CIEPLAN,* 14 (septiembre): 9–41.

Milberg, William (2004) "Globalized Production: Structural Changes for Developing Country Workers," in W. Milberg, ed., *Labor and the Globalization of Production,* Houndmills: Palgrave MacMillan.

Milberg, William (1999) "Foreign Direct Investment and Development: Balancing Costs and Benefits," Paper prepared for the annual meeting of the Technical Group of the G-25, March.

Mizala, Alejandra (1992) "Las reformas económicas de los años setenta y la industria manufacturera chilena,"*Colección Estudios CIEPLAN* 35 (número especial):153–199.

Mizala, Alejandra and Pilar Romaguera (1996) "Flexibilidad del mercado del trabajo: El impacto del ajuste y los requisitos del crecimiento económico," *Colección Estudios CIEPLAN* 43: 15–48.

Morley, Samuel (1999) "The Impact of Reforms on Equity in Latin America," report submitted to the World Bank, July.

Muñoz, Oscar, ed. (1992) *Economic Reforms in Chile,* Occasional Paper, Washington, D.C: Inter-American Development Bank.

Newman, Constance (1994) "How are piece rates determined? A Micro-level analysis of piece rates in Chilean Table Grape Packing Sheds," Ph.D. Dissertation, Department of Agricultural Economics, UC-Davis.

OIT (1998) *Chile: Crecimiento, empleo y el desafío de la justicia social,* Santiago: OIT.

Pagés, Carmen and Claudio Montenegro (1997) "Job Security and the Age-Composition of Employment: Evidence from Chile," Working Paper 398, Washington: Inter-American Development Bank.

Pavcnik, Nina (2002) "What Explains Skill Upgrading in Developing Countries," NBER working paper, March.

Peppelenbos, Lucian (2000) "Hesitant Mechanization of Tomato Harvesting in Chile: An Inquiry into the Management of Agro-Industrialization," paper presented at the X World Congress of Rural Sociology, Rio de Janeiro, July 30–August 5.

Piore, Michael and Charles Sabel (1984) *The Second Industrial Divide,* New York: Basic Books.

Prebisch, Raúl (1950) "The Economic Development of Latin America and Its Principal Problems," Santiago: *ECLA Review.*

Prebisch, Raúl (1981) "The Latin American Periphery in the Global System of Capitalism," Santiago: *ECLA Review.*

Price Waterhouse (1997) "Outsourcing en Chile," Departamento de Servicios de Desarollo Empresarial, Abril.

Ravenga, Ana (1997) "Employment and Wage Effects of Trade Liberalization: The Case of Mexican Manufacturing, *Journal of Labor Economics* 15 (July): S20-S43.

Reid, John (2001) "An Overview of Machine Vision," *Food Product Design,* March.

Riveros, Luis (1990) "The Economic Return to Schooling in Chile. An Analysis of its Long-term Fluctuations," *Economics of Education Review* 9: 111–121.

Robbins, Donald (1996) "Evidence on Trade and Wages in Developing Countries," OECD Research Paper.

Robbins, Donald (1994) "Relative Wage Structure in Chile, 1957–1992: Changes in the Structure of Demand for Schooling," *Estudios de Economía,* University of Chile: Santiago, vol. 21.

Romaguera, Pilar (1991) "Wage Differentials and Efficiency Wage Models: Evidence from the Chilean Economy," Working Paper #153, Helen Kellog Institute for International Studies, Notre Dame University.

Romaguera, Pilar et al. (1995) "Chile," in Gustavo Márquez, ed., *Reforming the Labor Market in a Liberalized Economy,* Washington: Inter-American Development Bank.

Ruiz-Tagle, Jaime (1985) *El Sindicalismo Chileno después del Plan Laboral,* Santiago: PET.

Sachs, Jeffrey and Howard Shatz (1994) "Trade and Jobs in U.S. Manufacturing," *Brookings Paper on Economic Activity* 1: 1–84.

Saez, Raul (1993) "Las privatizaciones de empresas en Chile," in Oscar Muñoz, *Después de las Privatizaciones: Hacia el estado regulador,* Santiago: CIEPLAN.

Schurman, Rachel (2001) "Uncertain Gains: Labor in Chile's New Export Sectors," *Latin American Research Review* 36(2): 3–29.

Schurman, Rachel (1993) "Economic Development and Class Formation in an Extractive Economy: The Fragile Nature of the Chilean Fishing Industry, 1973–1990," Ph.D. dissertation, University of Wisconsin-Madison.

Silva Torrealba, Francisca (1999) "La Inversión en el Sector Agroindustrial Chileno," Serie Reformas Económicas 46, Santiago: CEPAL.

Singer, Paulo (1997) "Social Exclusion in Brazil," mimeo, International Institute for Labor Studies, Geneva: ILO.

Slaughter, Mathew (1997) "International Trade and Labor Demand Elasticities," NBER Working Paper 6262, November.

Snower, Dennis (1998) "Causes of Changing Earnings Inequality," paper presented at the Symposium on Income Inequality: Issues and Policy Options, Federal Reserve Bank of Kansas City, Jackson Hole, Wyoming, August 27–29.

Solow, Robert (1990) *The Labor Market as a Social Institution,* Cambridge: Basil Blackwell.

Stallings, Barbara (1978) *Class Conflict and Economic Development in Chile, 1958–1973,* Stanford: Stanford University Press.

U.S. Department of Commerce (2000) *Industry Sector Analysis Chile: Cosmetics,* Santiago: American Embassy.

U.S. Department of Commerce (1995) *Industry Sector Analysis Chile: Cosmetics,* Santiago: American Embassy.

Wilder, Patricia (1982) "Cosmetics Industry Achieves Long-Term Productivity Gains," *Monthly Labor Review,* December.

Wood, Adrian (1995) "How Trade Hurt Unskilled Workers," *Journal of Economic Perspectives,* Summer 9 (3): 57–80.

World Bank (1995) *World Development Report: Workers in an Integrating World,* New York: Oxford University Press.

Yañez, José (1992) "Tax Reforms,"in Oscar Muñoz, ed., *Economic Reforms in Chile,* Occasional Paper, Washington, D.C: Inter-American Development Bank.

Yin, Robert (1994) *Case Study Research: Design and Methods,* New York: Sage Publishers.

Index